Founders
of
Constructive Postmodern Philosophy

SUNY SERIES IN
CONSTRUCTIVE POSTMODERN THOUGHT
DAVID RAY GRIFFIN, EDITOR

FOUNDERS OF CONSTRUCTIVE POSTMODERN PHILOSOPHY

Peirce, James, Bergson, Whitehead, and Hartshorne

DAVID RAY GRIFFIN
JOHN B. COBB, JR.
MARCUS P. FORD
PETE A. Y. GUNTER
PETER OCHS

STATE UNIVERSITY OF NEW YORK PRESS

Published by
State University of New York Press, Albany

©*1993 State University of New York*

Printed in the United States of America

Production by Christine Lynch
Marketing by Dana E. Yanulavich

For information, address the State University of New York Press,
State University Plaza, Albany, NY 12246

Library of Congress Cataloging-in-Publication Data

Founders of constructive postmodern philosophy : Peirce, James, Bergson,
Whitehead, and Hartshorne / by David Ray Griffin et al.
    p.   cm. — (SUNY series in constructive postmodern thought)
    Includes bibliographical references and index.
    ISBN 0-7914-1333-0 (hard : alk. paper). — ISBN 0-7914-1334-9
(pbk. : alk. paper)
    1. Postmodernism. 2. Philosophy, Modern—20th century.
I. Griffin, David Ray, 1939-   . II. Series.
B831.2.F68 1993
190'.9'04—dc20   92-4274
                                                      CIP

10 9 8 7 6 5 4 3 2 1

CONTENTS

*We dedicate this book to
Ann, Jean, Sandra,
Elizabeth, and Vanessa*

Introduction to SUNY Series in Constructive Postmodern Thought

The rapid spread of the term *postmodern* in recent years witnesses to a growing dissatisfaction with modernity and to an increasing sense that the modern age not only had a beginning but can have an end as well. Whereas the word *modern* was almost always used until quite recently as a word of praise and as a synonym for *contemporary*, a growing sense is now evidenced that we can and should leave modernity behind—in fact, that we must if we are to avoid destroying ourselves and most of the life on our planet.

Modernity, rather than being regarded as the norm for human society toward which all history has been aiming and into which all societies should be ushered—forcibly if necessary—is instead increasingly seen as an aberration. A new respect for the wisdom of traditional societies is growing as we realize that they have endured for thousands of years and that, by contrast, the existence of modern society for even another century seems doubtful. Likewise, *modernism* as a worldview is less and less seen as The Final Truth, in comparison with which all divergent worldviews are automatically regarded as "superstitious." The modern worldview is increasingly relativized to the status of one among many, useful for some purposes, inadequate for others.

Although there have been antimodern movements before, beginning perhaps near the outset of the nineteenth century with the Romanticists and the Luddites, the rapidity with which the term *postmodern* has become widespread in our time suggests that the antimodern sentiment is more extensive and intense than before, and also that it includes the sense that modernity can be successfully overcome only by going beyond it, not by attempting to return to a premodern form of existence. Insofar as a common element is found in the various ways in which the term is used, *postmodernism* refers to a diffuse sentiment rather than to any common set of doctrines—the sentiment that humanity can and must go beyond the modern.

Beyond connoting this sentiment, the term *postmodern* is used in a confusing variety of ways, some of them contradictory to others. In artistic and literary circles, for example, postmodernism shares in this general sentiment but also involves a specific reaction against "modernism" in the narrow sense of a movement in artistic-literary circles in the late nineteenth and early twentieth centuries. Postmodern architecture is very different from postmodern literary criticism. In some circles, the term *postmodern* is used in reference to that potpourri of ideas and systems sometimes called *new age metaphysics*, although many of these ideas and systems are more premodern than postmodern. Even in philosophical and theological circles, the term *postmodern* refers to two quite different positions, one of which is reflected in this series. Each position seeks to transcend both *modernism* in the sense of the worldview that has developed out of the seventeenth-century Galilean-Cartesian-Baconian-Newtonian science, and *modernity* in the sense of the world order that both conditioned and was conditioned by this worldview. But the two positions seek to transcend the modern in different ways.

Closely related to literary-artistic postmodernism is a philosophical postmodernism inspired variously by pragmatism, physicalism, Ludwig Wittgenstein, Martin Heidegger, and Jacques Derrida and other recent French thinkers. By the use of terms that arise out of particular segments of this movement, it can be called *deconstructive* or *eliminative postmodernism*. It overcomes the modern worldview through an antiworldview: it deconstructs or eliminates the ingredients necessary for a worldview, such as God, self, purpose, meaning, a real world, and truth as correspondence. While motivated in some cases by the ethical concern to forestall totalitarian systems, this type of postmodern thought issues in relativism, even nihilism. It could also be called *ultramodernism*, in that its eliminations result from carrying modern premises to their logical conclusions.

The postmodernism of this series can, by contrast, be called *constructive* or *revisionary*. It seeks to overcome the modern worldview not by eliminating the possibility of worldviews as such, but by constructing a postmodern worldview through a revision of modern premises and traditional concepts. This constructive or revisionary postmodernism involves a new unity of scientific, ethical, aesthetic, and religious intuitions. It rejects not science as such but only that scientism in which the data of the modern natural sciences are alone allowed to contribute to the construction of our worldview.

The constructive activity of this type of postmodern thought is not limited to a revised worldview; it is equally concerned with a postmodern world that will support and be supported by the new worldview. A postmodern world will involve postmodern persons, with a postmodern spirituality, on the one hand, and a postmodern society, ultimately a postmodern global order, on the other. Going beyond the modern world will involve transcending its individualism, anthropocentrism, patriarchy, mechanization, economism, consumerism, nationalism, and militarism. Constructive postmodern thought provides support for the ecology, peace, feminist, and other emancipatory movements of our time, while stressing that the inclusive emancipation must be from modernity itself. The term *postmodern*, however, by contrast with *premodern*, emphasizes that the modern world has produced unparalleled advances that must not be lost in a general revulsion against its negative features.

From the point of view of deconstructive postmodernists, this constructive postmodernism is still hopelessly wedded to outdated concepts, because it wishes to salvage a positive meaning not only for the notions of the human self, historical meaning, and truth as correspondence, which were central to modernity, but also for premodern notions of a divine reality, cosmic meaning, and an enchanted nature. From the point of view of its advocates, however, this revisionary postmodernism is not only more adequate to our experience but also more genuinely postmodern. It does not simply carry the premises of modernity through to their logical conclusions, but criticizes and revises those premises. Through its return to organicism and its acceptance of nonsensory perception, it opens itself to the recovery of truths and values from various forms of premodern thought and practice that had been dogmatically rejected by modernity. This constructive, revisionary postmodernism involves a creative synthesis of modern and premodern truths and values.

This series does not seek to create a movement so much as to help shape and support an already existing movement convinced that modernity can and must be transcended. But those antimodern movements which arose in the past failed to deflect or even retard the onslaught of modernity. What reasons can we have to expect the current movement to be more successful? First, the previous antimodern movements were primarily calls to return to a premodern form of life and thought rather than calls to advance, and the human spirit does not rally to calls to turn back. Second, the previous antimodern movements either rejected modern science, reduced it to a description of mere appearances, or assumed its adequacy in principle; therefore, they could base their calls only on the negative social and spiritual effects of modernity. The current movement draws on natural science itself as a witness against the adequacy of the modern worldview. In the third place, the present movement has even more evidence than did previous movements of the ways in which modernity and its worldview *are* socially and spiritually destructive. The fourth and probably most decisive difference is that the present movement is based on the awareness that the *continuation of modernity threatens the very survival of life on our planet*. This awareness, combined with the growing knowledge of the interdependence of the modern worldview and the militarism, nuclearism, and ecological devastation of the modern world, is providing an unprecedented impetus for people to see the evidence for a postmodern worldview and to envisage postmodern ways of relating to each other, the rest of nature, and the cosmos as a whole. For these reasons, the failure of the previous antimodern movements says little about the possible success of the current movement.

Advocates of this movement do not hold the naively utopian belief that the success of this movement would bring about a global society of universal and lasting peace, harmony, and happiness, in which all spiritual problems, social conflicts, ecological destruction, and hard choices would vanish. There is, after all, surely a deep truth in the testimony of the world's religions to the presence of a transcultural proclivity to evil deep within the human heart, which no new paradigm, combined with a new economic order, new child-rearing practices, or any other social arrangements, will suddenly eliminate. Furthermore, it has correctly been said that "life is robbery": a strong element of competition is inherent within finite existence, which no social-political-economic-ecological order can overcome. These two truths, especially when contemplated together, should caution us against unrealistic hopes.

However, no such appeal to "universal constants" should reconcile us to the present order, as if this order were thereby uniquely legitimated. The human proclivity to evil in general, and to conflictual competition and ecological destruction in particular, can be greatly exacerbated or greatly mitigated by a world order and its worldview. Modernity exacerbates it about as much as imaginable. We can therefore envision, without being naively utopian, a far better world order, with a far less dangerous trajectory, than the one we now have.

This series, making no pretense of neutrality, is dedicated to the success of this movement toward a postmodern world.

David Ray Griffin
Series Editor

ACKNOWLEDGMENTS

Although all the chapters herein were written specifically for this volume, one was published previously: David Griffin's chapter appeared as "Charles Hartshorne's Postmodern Philosophy" in Robert Kane and Stephen Phillips, ed., *Hartshorne, Process Philosophy and Theology* (Albany: State University of New York Press, 1989); it is reprinted here with minor changes.

We want to express our thanks to William Eastman of SUNY Press for his continuing support of this series, and to Christine Lynch for efficiently guiding this volume through the production process.

Our dedication of this volume, finally, names those beloved individuals to whom each of us has the greatest gratitude and ongoing sense of indebtedness.

INTRODUCTION: CONSTRUCTIVE POSTMODERN PHILOSOPHY

David Ray Griffin

I. Postmodernism and Rationality

As mentioned in the foregoing introduction to the series, at least two very different types of philosophy are currently being called "postmodern." In the one type, the accent is on deconstruction; in the other type, considerable deconstruction is carried out, but the accent is on construction. This latter type of postmodernism perhaps should have been officially dubbed "*re*constructive" to indicate more clearly that a deconstructive moment is presupposed. In any case, the two types of postmodern philosophy differ not on the need to deconstruct various notions that were central to modern and in some cases premodern worldviews, but on the necessity and possibility of constructing a new cosmology that might become the worldview of future generations

Which of these two types of philosophy is more legitimately called "postmodern" is a point of contention. On the question of priority of usage, each side can make claims. On the one hand, in philosophical circles the term "postmodern" has thus far been most heavily associated with deconstruction, and this usage has been closely related to the use of "postmodern" in literary-artistic circles. But if the question is actual priority, rather than preponderance, of usage, the constructive type can probably claim priority, as the term "postmodern" was used in reference to Whitehead's philosophy as early as 1964.[1] But the question of priority is trivial. Much more important is the question of which movement is more truly postmodern.

1

On this issue, however, there is no neutral standpoint from which to make a judgment. Each side has its own view as to what *modernism*—or, more specifically, *modern philosophy*—is, and especially as to the objectionable aspect(s) of modernism that a properly *post*modern philosophy seeks to move beyond. To the extent that these judgments diverge, each type of postmodern philosophy will see the other as still modern, because still accepting notions regarded as belonging to the objectionable core of modernism. To the extent that one sees the other as not only accepting these notions but also carrying them to their logical conclusions, the former will judge the latter to be *ultra*-modern, *hyper*modern, *most*modern.

For example, John Cobb points out in his essay below that the ideal of rationality is such a contested notion. Deconstructive postmodernists typically regard it as part and parcel of the objectionable core of modernism. Such philosophers, accordingly, regard the philosophies of Whitehead and Hartshorne—insofar as they regard them at all—as quintessentially modern, because these philosophies seek to provide a metaphysical cosmology that meets the rational criteria of self-consistency and adequacy to all the facts of experience. But Whitehead, by contrast, regards modern philosophy, including modern science, as an essentially *anti*rational movement. From this perspective, accordingly, recovering the ideal of rationality can be viewed as postmodern, whereas those who urge us to become even more antirational than is modern thought can be viewed as hypermodern, as simply carrying a central tendency of modernism to extremes.

In this introductory essay, I write from the perspective of the constructive type of postmodern philosophy. More particularly, while seeing Peirce, James, Bergson, Whitehead, and Hartshorne as all having enough in common to be dubbed constructive postmodern philosophers, I primarily take Whitehead's position as the standpoint from which to characterize the commonalities. That is, although these five philosophers did indeed have much in common, they were all very different in temperament, they held differing views on a wide range of issues, and—most important—they each had different central intuitions and aims. So, whereas any of them looking at the other four would have seen that they all had much in common, each one of them would have identified the commonalities in more or less different ways. Whereas all of them might have agreed that the five of them could be grouped together as a distinct movement in philosophy, and might have even happily accepted "constructive postmodernism" as a name for this movement, they each would have described the nature and the most crucial aspects of this movement somewhat differently. My own characterization of this movement, in taking its primary orientation from Whitehead's philosophy, should be only slightly less adequate from a Hartshornean point of view because of the considerable overlap between these two philosophies (and also because my reading of Whitehead has been influenced by my reading of Hartshorne, as well as vice-versa). My characterization of constructive postmodern philosophy will be increasingly less representative, I suspect, of the Jamesian, the Bergsonian, and finally the Peircean perspective.

Having indicated the stance from which this introductory essay is written, I now continue the line of thought begun two paragraphs above. The next point is that the formal difference concerning rationality discussed there is related, in turn, to substantive differences concerning ontology and epistemology. From a (Whiteheadian) constructive postmodern perspective, the two fundamental flaws in modern philosophy have been an ontology based on a materialistic doctrine of nature and an epistemology based on a sensationist doctrine of perception. The sensationist doctrine of perception said not only that all knowledge is grounded on perception (with which constructive postmodernists agree), but also that perception is to be equated with sense-perception (with which they do not agree). The materialistic doctrine of nature—whether part of a materialistic ontology of reality in general or of a dualism between "mind" and "nature"— said that the ultimate units of nature are, in Whitehead's phrase, "vacuous actualities." That is, they are actualities (*contra* Bishop Berkeley), but they are completely devoid of experience. The materialistic ontology of nature also generally says that the ultimate units of nature are devoid of spontaneity or self-motion—the capacity to initiate movement of any sort. Most of the difficulties of modern philosophy are seen to result from its doctrine of perception, its ontology, or the combination of these two doctrines.

Indeed, one strand of modern philosophy gave up, at least in "theory," the materialistic doctrine of nature in favor of phenomenalism because of the tension between the ontological claim that the perceived world is comprised of vacuous actualities and the epistemological claim that that perception gives us nothing but sense-data. That is, the sensationist theory of perception entailed that we have no perceptual knowledge of the existence of actual things beyond ourselves, let alone any knowledge of their nature (such as whether they are vacuous or not). Given that view of perceptual experience, the desire to be rigorously empirical led Hume and others to reject ontological claims about what things are in themselves in favor of phenomenalism—the view that we cannot go beyond merely describing phenomena as they appear to us. (This shows that modernism's epistemology has been more fundamental than its ontology—that the sensationist theory of perception is even more basic to modern philosophy than the materialistic doctrine of nature.) A more accurate statement would, accordingly, have to characterize modern ontology not as an affirmation but as a rejection—namely, a rejection of the view that has generally been called "panpsychism" but is more helpfully called "panexperientialism." Panexperientialism is the view that nature is actual and that the ultimate units of nature are not vacuous but are something for themselves in the sense of having experience, however slight.

Thus modified, so as to combine a sensationist theory of perception with a rejection of panexperientialism (whether by affirming dualism, materialism, phenomenalism, or personal idealism), the characterization of modern philosophy given here applies equally well to Mersenne, Descartes, Malebranche, Geulincx, Locke, Berkeley, Hobbes, Newton, Hume, Reid, and Kant. Leibniz and Spinoza would be the two great exceptions in the early modern period—although even they were fully modern in their affirmation of the determinism that generally follows from the materialistic view of nature.

In any case, the difference between deconstructive and constructive (or reconstructive) postmodern philosophers can be stated in terms of the aspects of modern philosophy on which they set their deconstructive sights, and the assumptions they employ in carrying out their deconstructions. The differences here are closely correlated with the difference between recommending a new candidate for a worldview and recommending an antiworldview—an overcoming of all worldviews, all attempts to characterize the "totality." Deconstructive postmodernists deconstruct various notions—such as rationality, empirical givenness, and truth as correspondence—without which a worldview is impossible. And the assumptions used in the deconstruction of these and other notions—such as self, history, and the physical world—are such as to reinforce the impossibility of constructing, or even holding, a worldview. Constructive postmodernists, by contrast, take aim just at those notions—such as vacuous actuality and the equation of perception with sense-perception—that they see as making impossible the construction of a self-consistent, adequate cosmology, and that thereby have contributed to the antirationality of modernity, which finds its logical conclusion in deconstructive postmodernism.[2]

II. THE MODERN MIND-BODY PROBLEM
AND ANTIRATIONALITY

The connection between the substantive assumptions of modern philosophy and its antirationality can be illustrated in terms of the mind-body problem. Descartes' division of the world into completely different types of actualities—matter, which is extended but devoid of experience, and spirit, which experiences but is devoid of extension—made interaction between spiritual mind and material body, which he affirmed, seem impossible. Descartes attempted, feebly, to overcome the difficulty by reference to the pineal gland and "animal spirits," but eventually admitted that he could give no solution to the problem.[3] Malebranche, Geulincx, Berkeley, and Reid all appealed to God to solve the problem—the first three by denying that any real interaction occurs, and the latter by simply saying that God, being omnipotent and therefore deterred by none but logical impossibilities, could make unlikes interact. This latter solution was probably, in fact, the implicit solution of Descartes (who doubted whether even logical possibilities could constrain the divine omnipotence). Later philosophers, however, rightly resisted this appeal to, in Whitehead's words, "a *deus ex machina* who was capable of rising superior to the difficulties of metaphysics."[4] But, once this type of answer was forsworn, no answer could be given as to how experiencing and nonexperiencing things could interact. This led, on the one hand, to various phenomenalisms and idealisms, which denied the independent (from experience) existence of what we normally call the physical world, and, on the other hand, to various versions of materialism, which denied that what is normally called the "mind" is an actuality. While each of these moves involves inadequacy to obvious facts of experience, and thereby a contentment with an irrational position, I will focus first on the even more obvious irrationality accepted by modern dualists.

Karl Popper provides one example. In an early book, he assumed that a solution to the problem of dualistic interaction was both essential and possible, saying: "What we want is to understand how such nonphysical things as *purposes, deliberations, plans, decisions, theories, tensions,* and *values* can play a part in bringing about physical changes in the physical world." But by the time he and John Eccles wrote *The Self and its Brain,* he had evidently decided that a solution was not possible, and accordingly declared it not essential. He still affirmed ontological dualism, even accepting Gilbert Ryle's pejorative characterization of it as belief in the "ghost in the machine";[5] and he still affirmed interaction—the subtitle of the book, indeed, is *An Argument for Interaction.* But when he finally faced the question of how to understand interaction between ontologically different types of actualities, Popper dismissed the issue by saying: "Complete understanding, like complete knowledge, is unlikely to be achieved."[6] This contentment with mystery is an example of the antirationalism of the modern mind.

There is a type of mystery, to be sure, that we must accept, at least provisionally. This is the mystery that is made inevitable by the finitude of our knowledge. There are all sorts of things that we simply do not know, and there may be various things that no finite mind will ever know. Popper is correct to say of "complete knowledge" that it "is unlikely to be achieved."

But Popper's comment about "complete understanding" points to another type of mystery, the type that is exemplified by the problem of how mind and body, understood as entities of ontologically different kinds, can interact. This "mystery," unlike that of, say, how the universe originated, is not given to us by the universe, but is entirely of our own making. It is an artificial, not a natural, mystery. It is created by the decision to think of mind and body as ontologically different types of things. Contentment with artificial mystery represents an antirational frame of mind. The rational thing to do, when confronted by this "mystery," would be to ask if one had misunderstood the nature of mind, or of body, or perhaps of both.

If it be thought that Popper, being primarily a philosopher of science rather than a philosopher of nature, is not a good example, we can look at the position developed by Keith Campbell in *Body and Mind*. Campbell rehearses the well-known problems of dualism: How could spirit and matter interact? How could spirit emerge out of a wholly material universe? How could one specify a nonarbitrary time for this emergence?[7] But then he indicates that, although he once found central-state materialism adequate, he no longer does. In particular, he believes that phenomenal properties, such as the feeling of pain, cannot be properties a material object can have.[8] This leads him to affirm "a new epiphenomenalism." According to this doctrine, we do have a spiritual mind, which is produced by the body. But it does not act back upon the body: all human behavior is caused by the purely physical central nervous system, so a purely physicalist, deterministic account of human behavior is preserved.

Campbell realizes that this doctrine has all sorts of problems. It faces, for one thing, the same "equally embarrassing" questions as did dualism: "If, among the properties of the brain, are some which are not purely physico-chemical, at what point, and how, do such properties first make their appearance?"[9] With regard to the "how" question, Campbell says: "Epiphenomenalists must just accept . . . that the existence of nonmaterial properties is a fact for which they have no explanation."[10]

Campbell admits, furthermore, that epiphenomenalism's account of the causation of behavior is counterintuitive:

> To preserve the completeness of the physical accounts of human action, it must hold that, contrary to common belief, it is not the hurtfulness of pain which causes me to shun it. . . . Whether we suffer or enjoy can be a sign that a given state is aversive or attractive for us, but cannot be a cause of aversion or attraction.[11]

Besides being contrary to our experience, Campbell's doctrine is arbitrary: while denying "the action of spirit on matter," it affirms "the action of the material on the spiritual."[12] Recognizing the arbitrariness of the fact that the epiphenomenalist theory "rejects only one half of the interaction of matter and spirit," Campbell says that

> one who holds to the theory must just grit his teeth and assert that a fundamental, anomalous, causal connection relates some bodily processes to some nonmaterial processes. He must insist that this is a brute fact we must learn to live with, however inconvenient it might be for our tidy world-schemes.[13]

But "untidiness" is surely a mild term for this arbitrariness.

Finally, besides being counterintuitive and arbitrary, his theory is, Campbell admits, unintelligible. Having affirmed that "our awareness by phenomenal properties" is "caused by changes in sense organs and brain," he says:

> How this is done we do not know. . . . I suspect that we will never know how the trick is worked. This part of the Mind-Body problem seems insoluble. This aspect of humanity seems destined to remain forever beyond our understanding.[14]

Having found himself led to such a conclusion, he adds a Popper-like justification of contentment with mystery: "Philosophers ought to dislike skeptical conclusions, but . . . [w]e cannot guarantee in advance that the whole of human nature is open to human comprehension."[15] The same reply that was given to Popper applies: The issue is not whether the whole of human nature can be comprehended. The issue is whether, when we confront *artificial* mysteries—ones that were created solely by our own premises—we should rest content, declaring the problem permanently insoluble. Surely not. As Peirce said, we should not block the road of inquiry.[16] The rational response is to revise one or more of the premises that led to the cul-de-sac.

This is the approach taken by constructive postmodern philosophers. The idea of vacuous actuality is rejected; panexperientialism is affirmed. Both Popper and Campbell do consider this option; but it cannot be said that they consider it seriously. They deal only with its older and weaker forms, and then only in a cursory and, in Popper's case, a caricatured, fashion.[17]

III. MODERNITY'S ACCEPTANCE OF A MECHANISTIC NATURE

It is, of course, understandable that modern philosophers find it difficult to take panexperientialism seriously, because part of the defining essence of modern philosophy is the *rejection of* panexperientialism. This rejection is, one could say, part of the enculturation into modernity. The acceptance of a nonanimistic, mechanistic nature was, in fact, the central feature in the worldview with which what we call "modern science" came to be associated in the latter half of the seventeenth century.

Although this association has been so close that many have thought science and mechanism to be mutually implicated, so that the mechanistic view of nature was both presupposed by science and in turn scientifically verified, historians of science are now showing otherwise. Good science has not always presupposed a mechanistic worldview, which an examination of the thought of Copernicus, Kepler, Gilbert, and even Newton would show. As Jerome Ravetz says:

> The great historical myth of this [mechanistic] philosophy is that it was the necessary and sufficient cause of the great scientific progress of the seventeenth century. This was a central point in its propaganda, for itself at the time and in histories ever since. Yet the results of historical inquiry . . . contradict this claim.[18]

Rather than being the virtual beginning of real science, the so-called scientific revolution was, Ravetz says, "a campaign for a reform of ideas *about* science . . . injected into a continuous process of technical progress *within* science. . . . [The] scientific revolution was primarily and essentially about metaphysics."[19]

The new metaphysical idea was that the ultimate units of nature are completely devoid of both experience and self-motion. And this metaphysical idea, rather than being derived from empirical evidence, as propaganda would have it, was based primarily upon theological and sociological motives. It was used, for example, to support belief in God, miracles, and immortality, and to justify the exploitation of (nonhuman) nature. I will briefly describe the relation between the mechanistic idea of nature and the defense of each of these beliefs.

The mechanical philosophy supported belief in the existence of an external creator of the universe, over against pantheistic and atheistic philosophies, by pointing to the need for a first mover: if nature's basic units are *essentially* inert and yet are now *in fact* in motion, there must have been, argued Boyle and Newton among others, a supernatural being who put them in motion.[20] Newton also used another aspect of the mechanistic philosophy, the denial of an inherent capacity for action at a distance in nature's units, to prove the existence of God: the fact of universal gravitation shows that there must be something outside of nature that accounts for the apparent attraction between bits of matter.[21] This aspect of mechanism, its denial of an "occult" capacity for action at a distance, was also used by Mersenne to support the belief in genuine miracles. Some naturalists were arguing, on the basis of their animistic philosophies, that action at a distance is a purely natural, if extraordinary, capacity of minds and other things, and that, accordingly, the Christian "miracles" (which were used by Christian apologists to support the divine endorsement of Christianity as the one true religion) did not really require supernatural intervention. Boyle and Mersenne preferred the mechanistic philosophy of nature to all others, in part, because it said that all natural causal influence is exerted by contact; accordingly, the miraculous events in the New Testament and (for Mersenne) the later lives of the saints did betoken supernatural intervention.[22]

The mechanistic view of nature was also used to support belief in immortality against those who were arguing for "mortalism" on the basis of animistic philosophies according to which all things are self-moving. The body is made of self-moving things and yet it obviously decays, said these heretics, so the fact that the mind or soul is a self-moving thing provides no reason to believe that it will not decay too. One reason to recommend the mechanistic philosophy is that it defeats this argument, said Boyle among others: the fact that we are obviously self-moving things shows that there is something in us that is, by being self-moving, essentially different from our bodies, and that may be presumed, therefore, not to share the fate of our bodies.[23]

All of these theological beliefs were of extreme importance sociologically, of course, because the "stability" of society—which, translated, meant the maintenance of the monarchy and the hierarchical society—depended heavily upon the authority of the church; and the church's authority, in turn, depended upon the belief in God, in God's having authorized Christianity as the true religion, and in God's granting to the church the "keys to the kingdom," meaning the power to consign people to heaven or hell.

A final theological-sociological reason for favoring mechanism was the support it gave to the growing desire—which has been central to modernity from the outset—systematically to dominate nature for human benefit. Descartes' absolute dualism between spirit and matter, and his account of all (nonhuman) animals as insentient machines, was used, with Descartes' blessing, not only to justify believing that humans alone are immortal,[24] but also to justify practices such as hunting and vivisection.[25] Boyle argued that a proper respect for the "divine excellency" would prevent us from attributing any power of self-motion, which is a divine prerogative, to nature; but this theological nicety was not unrelated to a sociological concern. Boyle, who was for a time in charge of mining in the New World,[26] said, in criticizing the "vulgar" notion of nature, which sees it as having life and power: "The veneration, wherewith men are imbued for what they call nature, has been a discouraging impediment to the empire of man over the inferior creatures of God."[27]

The mechanistic view of nature, then, arose more out of motives of this type than out of empirical evidence. Some features of nature, to be sure, such as the locomotion of Galileo's steel balls, were completely explainable on the assumption that they were wholly devoid of all "final causation" in the sense of self-determination in terms of an end. But the supposition that the ultimate units comprising these steel balls are themselves analogous to the balls was pure supposition, based on wishful thinking rather than empirical evidence. Once this modern "paradigm" was established, the view that the ultimate units of nature are devoid of both experience and self-motion could be maintained apart from the motives on which it was originally based. The late modern worldview of atheistic materialism, accordingly, is simply a decapitated version of the early modern worldview. That is, God and the soul are lopped off, but the mechanistic view of nature is maintained.[28]

Given the fact that the mechanistic view of nature has been integral to the modern worldview from the outset (at least insofar as any realistic—as distinct from phenomenalistic or idealistic—view of nature has been affirmed), one should not be surprised—even if one cannot help being disappointed—to see how superficially, how unphilosophically, panexperientialism is treated in modern philosophy. Most philosophers do not even give it as much attention as do Popper and Campbell. When not simply ignored, it is usually dismissed as ridiculous, quaint, or sentimental. Philosophers who in one breath tell us that we cannot know what things are in themselves will, in the next, tell us that, of course, we do know that things in themselves are devoid of experience. Philosophers who debate endlessly about whether we can know for certain that the desks on which we are writing really exist seem to assume that, if they do exist, we can be certain that their constituents are devoid of experience.

IV. PANEXPERIENTIALISM AS POSTMODERN HYPOTHESIS

Constructive postmodern philosophers do not claim, to the contrary, that they *know* that all actualities do have experience. But they *offer panexperientialism as a hypothesis*, a hypothesis that will enable philosophers to overcome the inadequacies and apparently insoluble mysteries that seem otherwise inevitable. One of these apparently insoluble mysteries is how to do justice to the interaction between body and mind that we all inevitably presuppose in practice. Given the panexperientialist hypothesis, which is affirmed by all five of our authors, one can affirm both things needed to make interaction between mind and brain intelligible: mind and brain are (numerically) distinct; but mind and brain cells are not (ontologically) different types of entities.

Besides having trouble with the mind-body relation, modern philosophers have had an equally difficult problem with the closely related issue of freedom and determinism. It is closely related because, in Peirce's words, "the distinction between psychical and physical phenomena is the distinction between final and efficient causation."[29] Some dualistic interactionists have affirmed the freedom not only of the human mind but also, through the mind's influence on its body, of human behavior. But having the dualism between spirit and matter include the dualism between free and unfree only increases the unintelligibility of the interaction of mind and body. How can that which has freedom, by exercising final causation or self-determination, interact with that which is wholly unfree because completely determined by efficient causation from others? Central-state materialism, whether it takes an identist or more functionalist form, avoids this problem by denying human freedom—or, more characteristically, by redefining it so that it is compatible with complete determinism by physical causes. There can be no freedom in the sense of what Campbell calls "metaphysical choices," meaning choices that are not fully determined by prior physical causes and are thus partly *self*-determined. "If there is metaphysical choice," Campbell says, "Central-State Materialism is false."[30] And the same would be true of Campbell's epiphenomenalism; more precisely, he could allow metaphysical choice by the mind, but he could not allow this choice to influence bodily behavior. The problem with this solution, however, is that everyone, including the central-state materialist and the epiphenomenalist, presupposes in practice that we do exercise what Campbell calls (perhaps pejoratively) "metaphysical choices"—namely, choices in which an element of self-determination and hence genuine freedom is involved—and that these choices influence our bodily behavior. There is thus an inconsistency, in this case an inconsistency between the explicit doctrine of the philosophical theory and the implicit presupposition of the philosopher's practice.

Another way to avoid this problem of explaining the interaction of the experiencing and the nonexperiencing, the free and the determined—one of the currently most prevalent ways—is simply to deny that the mind has freedom and, in fact, that it even exists as an actuality. The mind is said to be identical with, that is, ontologically reducible to, the brain, and the activities of the brain are said to be as fully determined by efficient causes as any other activities of nature. The attempt to defend this position has led to "eliminative materialism," the doctrine that we can and should learn to describe human behavior exhaustively without using any subjective terms, such as "feeling," "pain," and "purpose." Other materialists, recognizing the identist program to be a failure, have endorsed functionalism, which involves the claim that what we call our mind is, while not strictly identical with the brain, entirely a function of it. Although this is a slightly weaker and thereby apparently less indefensible hypothesis, it still denies ideas that we all, including the philosopher in the very act of proposing the hypothesis, presuppose in practice—namely, that our experience (including the act of formulating and evaluating hypotheses) is partly self-determining in the moment, not wholly determined by antecedent events, that we make partly free choices in the light of ideal ends we want to bring about, and that our purposive, partly self-determining experiences influence our bodies and thereby the world beyond.

The materialistic approaches to the mind-body problem illustrate the other type of antirationalism Whitehead finds typical of modern philosophy (besides that of resting content with inconsistencies): "Failure to include some obvious elements of experience in the scope of the system is met by boldly denying the facts."[31] With regard to scientists whose system excludes anything not explainable in terms of physical and chemical laws, Whitehead comments: "Scientists animated by the purpose of proving that they are purposeless constitute an interesting subject for study."[32] That statement would apply equally well to many modern philosophers. "The rejection of any source of evidence," Whitehead says, "is always treason to that ultimate rationalism which urges forward science and philosophy alike."[33] This ultimate rationalism involves the drive to be adequate as well as consistent:

> A cosmology should above all things be adequate. It should not confine itself to the categoreal notions of one science, and explain away everything which will not fit in. Its business is not to refuse experience but to find the most general interpretative system.[34]

On this basis he lifts up for special praise a philosopher who was, he knew,[35] sometimes criticized for being anti-intellectual, William James: "His intellectual life was one protest against the dismissal of experience in the interest of system."[36]

It was because he saw that materialistic identism and functionalism could not do justice to human experience that Keith Campbell rejected materialism in favor of epiphenomenalism. But epiphenomenalism suffers from both inconsistency (like other forms of ontological dualism) and inadequacy, as we have seen.

The inconsistencies and inadequacies of dualism, epiphenomenalism, and materialism can be avoided by constructive postmodern philosophers on the basis of panexperientialism, which attributes to all individuals, including non-human individuals, some degree of real (self-determining) freedom, and says that different grades of individuals have different degrees of freedom. In Peirce's words, "all phenomena are of one character, though some are more mental and spontaneous, others more material and regular. Still all alike present [a] mixture of freedom and constraint."[37] The interaction of mind and brain cells is, accordingly, not that between the free and the unfree, but between the more and the less free. Further explanation is given in the chapters herein, especially those on Whitehead and Hartshorne.

Their positions, like that of James before them, built upon Bergson's insight that the reason modern science has seemed to make freedom impossible is that it has tried to reduce duration, which we experience, to the "spatialized" time of modern physics.[38] Bergson led the way in showing this "time" to be an abstraction. The way to reconcile duration, which we experience internally, with the time of physics is not to eliminate duration from our system of thought but to recognize the abstractness of the time of physical theory, and to say, accordingly, that the concrete actualities with which physics deals also, like us, enjoy duration.

This brings us to yet another difficulty for modern philosophy, that of making intelligible our presuppositions about time. On the one hand, most philosophers accept the evolutionary story of our universe, according to which billions of years passed before the rise of life. On the other hand, most philosophers who have thought about the nature of time—such as Adolf Grünbaum[39]—

say that time as we experience it, with a present "now," which separates past and future, and with an irreversible direction, cannot exist apart from experience. Philosophers who are willing to attribute experience only to human beings obviously have an enormous problem. But even those who, more reasonably, attribute experience to all forms of life have almost as great a problem insofar as they refuse to attribute experience to "inanimate nature." Assuming that life emerged about 4 billion years ago, and yet that the universe is about 15 billion years old, they must say that 11 billion years of evolution occurred *before* time existed!

An example is provided by J.T. Fraser. In a book entitled *The Genesis and Evolution of Time*, he suggests that there are six kinds of time: atemporality, prototemporality, eotemporality, biotemporality, nootemporality, and sociotemporality. These six kinds of time correspond with six periods of cosmic evolution. Although he refers to them all as kinds of time or temporality, it is hard to see how there is any real temporality in the first three levels. Even in the third level, the eotemporal, Fraser says that there is still no "now" and therefore no past and future. A "now" arises first in the biotemporal realm, meaning, of course, with the rise of life.[40] Fraser's assumption seems to be that experience, which is required for a "now" separating past and future, arises first with the emergence of life. And this leads to the problem I referred to above. "Creation was neither followed nor preceded by other instants, because the relationship future-past-present had no meaning in the atemporal, or even in the proto- or eotemporal worlds." Accordingly, because prior to life there could be no "relations among events corresponding to the notion of before and after," all those events we think of as occurring over 11 billion years must have all been "contiguous with the instant of Creation." Fraser adds that we are free to speak of that period *as if* it were a temporal process, provided that we realize this to be only a convenient way of speaking.[41]

There is even, Fraser recognizes, a self-contradiction built into the very title of his book, *The Genesis and Evolution of Time*. His thesis is that "time itself has developed along evolutionary steps," and yet he admits that "there is no noncontradictory way in which to state that time evolved in time."[42] He seeks to mitigate this difficulty by blaming the limitations of "prevailing linguistic customs." But the problem surely runs deeper (assuming, of course, as constructive postmodernists do, that there *is* something deeper than language).

The solution suggested by panexperientialists is that we need not speak of a "genesis" of time. If the ultimate units of the world are experiencing events, if some such experiencing events have always existed, and if each experience involves a reception of influences from past events, an element of spontaneity (so that the experience is not simply a product of prior events), and a contribution of influences to subsequent events, then time has always existed. This insistence on the fundamental reality of temporality is signalled by the fact that these constructive postmodern philosophies are generally called "process philosophies." Bergson's protest against the spatialization of time lies at the root of this aspect of the movement; closely related is Whitehead's idea that the denial of the ultimate reality of (asymmetrical, irreversible) time on the basis of physics results from the "fallacy of misplaced concreteness."[43]

Modern philosophers will, of course, consider outrageous the suggestion that to do justice to our presuppositions about time we must affirm panexperientialism. But if panexperientialism is the only intelligible way to avoid either denying the reality of prebiological evolution or resting content with self-contradiction, then we seem faced with the question: Which are we more willing to give up—the validity of the law of non-contradiction, the existence of evolution and thus of time prior to the existence of living things, or the belief that nonliving things are wholly devoid of experience? It is interesting, given the amount of attention showered by modern philosophers on the question of what we can know, how little attention is given to the assumption that they *know*, at least beyond reasonable doubt, that nonliving things are devoid of experience.

V. REJECTING THE SENSATIONIST VIEW OF PERCEPTION

I have thus far focused on panexperientialism as an ontological doctrine, showing how it can avoid several insoluble problems that have resulted from what Whitehead called "the disastrous metaphysical doctrine of physical matter . . . [as] devoid of self-enjoyment"[44]—the problems of mind-body interaction, of interaction between free and determined things, of the emergence of experience from nonexperiencing matter, and of the emergence of time in the evolutionary process. Each of these problems has resulted either in a contentment with an inconsistent position or in the denial of something that cannot be consistently denied, or, at the very least, something that we have more reason to have confidence in than the belief that nonliving things are wholly devoid of experience.

I turn now to the epistemological side of panexperientialism. This epistemological side involves the idea that sensory perception is not our only means of perceiving the world beyond our present experience. Even more, the claim is that sensory perception is not even our *primary* means of perception, that it is derivative from a nonsensory mode of perception. In Whitehead's words: "Sense-perception, despite its prominence in consciousness, belongs to the superficialities of experience."[45] This derivative nature of sensory perception is suggested by panexperientialism: If all individuals, not just those with sensory organs, experience, there must be a nonsensory mode of perception; and if sensory perception has evolved out of nonsensory perception, it is likely that creatures with this derivative form of perception still retain the more basic form as well. The relationship between panexperientialism and the reality of nonsensory perception goes the other way as well: evidence for nonsensory perception in ourselves, by showing that nonsensory perception is possible, provides some reason to think that individuals without sensory organs may have the capacity for perceptual experience.

In any case, from the point of view of constructive postmodern philosophers, this question should be given serious attention. As Whitehead says: "If we discover . . . instances of non-sensuous perception, then the tacit identification of perception with sense-perception must be a fatal error barring the advance of systematic metaphysics."[46] Of course, many modern philosophers are not interested in "systematic metaphysics" in general. But they *are* interested in that aspect of it called epistemology, which is what Whitehead here primarily has in mind. And the recent obituaries for epistemology written by deconstructive postmodernists,[47] it can be claimed, have resulted primarily from the "tacit identification of perception with sense-perception." That this identification is generally tacit is indeed the case. For example, in a recent anthology entitled *Perceptual Knowledge*, it is asserted unproblematically in the first paragraph of the editor's introduction that perceptual knowledge is the sort of knowledge we get by "using our senses,"[48] and I did not find a single place in the remainder of the anthology where this identification was questioned.

This identification has been questioned, however, by constructive postmodern philosophers, and not simply *a priori*, as above (as a deduction from panexperientialism), but also in terms of Whitehead's question of whether we can actually discover "instances of non-sensuous perception." Most intellectuals know William James' comment to the effect that it takes only one white crow to prove that not all crows are black. But few seem to know the issue James was discussing when he made this statement, which was just the issue at hand: "the orthodox belief that there can be nothing in any one's intellect that has not come in through ordinary experiences of sense."[49] To undermine this belief, James says, we need only one clear counterexample:

> If you will let me use the language of the professional logic-shop, a universal proposition can be made untrue by a particular instance. If you wish to upset the law that all crows are black, you mustn't seek to show that no crows are; it is enough if you prove one single crow to be white.

And then James announces that, for him, the counterexample has appeared: "My own white crow is Mrs. Piper. In the trances of this medium, I cannot resist the conviction that knowledge appears which she has never gained by the ordinary waking uses of her eyes and ears and wits."[50] James does not say, incidentally, that everything Mrs. Piper said was to be believed, or even that she was indeed serving as a "medium" between people in this world and the spirits of the dead. He remained, as Marcus Ford points out, agnostic to the end about life after death. His claim was only that Mrs. Piper seemed to know things that she could not have learned through ordinary sensory means.

One of the scandals of modern philosophy is the scant amount of attention given to psychical research or—to use the more recent term—parapsychology. James in his day cited with approval the moral philosopher Henry Sidgwick's statement that (in James' summary)

> the divided state of public opinion on all these matters was a scandal to science,—absolute disdain on *a priori* grounds characterizing what may be called professional opinion, while indiscriminate credulity was too often found among those who pretended to have a first-hand acquaintance with the facts.[51]

This same polarization of opinion obtains today, approximately 100 years later. Scientists and philosophers have not performed the public service that can rightly be expected of them. But even with respect to philosophy as a search for truth for its own sake, the failure to investigate parapsychological research is a serious failure. There is much talk these days about "paradigm changes" being brought about when the old paradigm is confronted with too many anomalies. James had made this point in his own day, beginning his article on "What Psychical Research Has Accomplished" with these words: "'The great field for new discoveries,' said a scientific friend to me the other day, 'is always the unclassified residuum.'"[52] And yet few philosophers or scientists have examined what is surely the greatest storehouse of ostensible anomalies, the records of psychical research. James continued: "No part of the unclassified residuum has usually been treated with a more contemptuous scientific disregard than the mass of phenomena generally called *Mystical*."[53] The situation is little changed today. True, a few well-respected philosophers besides James himself, such as C. D. Broad, H. H. Price, and C. J. Ducasse,[54] have given major attention to psychical research; but most other philosophers evidently do not even read these writings. Thousands of books and articles are written each year that presuppose the identification of perception with sense-perception, but hardly anyone takes up James' challenge to consider whether the evidence for extrasensory perception provides a reason to reject this identification.

This evidence is not examined, of course, in part precisely because of the power of the dogma that it would overthrow. One advantage of constructive postmodern philosophies is that they allow their adherents to consider this evidence more open-mindedly. Those who are strongly opposed to the existence of extrasensory perception, of course, will not consider it an "advantage" of a philosophical position that it allows this evidence to be examined open-mindedly.

This observation leads to the next point, which is that, if what is usually meant by extrasensory perception—namely, telepathy and clairvoyance—provided the only ostensible examples of nonsensory perception, there might seem to be little reason to reject the equation of perception with sensory perception. James would still be right *logically*: it takes only one counterexample to overturn a universal proposition. But *psychologically* it usually takes more. One could question the reliability of the report, or even the testimony of one's own senses. One could suspect that the bird in question was not really a crow, but perhaps a dove. In other words, one could simply say, especially from a comfortable distance, that the anomalous results were probably due to fraud, error, or some other "normal" explanation. And this is how, of course, the evidence for telepathy and clairvoyance, when it is considered at all, is usually treated. Keith Campbell, for instance (who is unusual in devoting even a little space to the subject), uses the standard Humean argument:

> The problem of fraud is that we know men can, and do, cheat and dissemble, but we do not know that they have paranormal capacities. On the contrary, the great weight of our fully attested knowledge of man's origin and constitution makes paranormal capacities extremely unlikely. So . . . the explanation by fraud is the more rational one.[55]

This type of *a priori* position, applied universally, would rule out any fundamental advance, and is thus an appeal to a dubious type of "rationality." Nevertheless, this position will generally continue to be taken with regard to psychical research as long as it is believed that "the great weight of our fully attested knowledge of [humanity's] origin and constitution makes paranormal capacities extremely unlikely."

Are there other types of what Whitehead calls "instances of non-sensuous perception?" In raising this issue, Whitehead, in fact, primarily had in mind not experiences such as telepathy, but issues that are more closely related to the concerns of most philosophers. In particular, he had in mind what is usually called the problem of our "knowledge of the external world." This is one of the other areas in which the premises of modern philosophy have led it to rest content with antirational positions.

The premises in question here are that our only possible source of information about the world beyond our own experience is sensory perception, and that sensory perception gives us nothing but sense-data. Given these premises, it is hard to see how we could escape solipsism, the doctrine that we have no knowledge that a world beyond our own experience exists. Descartes appealed to the goodness of God for the assurance that our sense-data really do represent a real world beyond themselves. Whitehead sums up the attitude of most subsequent philosophers in saying that this "pious dependence upon God . . . is a device very repugnant to a consistent rationality. The very possibility of knowledge should not be an accident of God's goodness. . . . After all, God's knowledge has equally to be explained."[56]

But without this irrational appeal to God, what is our escape from theoretical solipsism? Hume said that there was none, that we had to be content with a radical bifurcation between theory and practice. In practice, we assume that a real world exists, although in our philosophical theory we realize that there is no justification for this belief. This is a prime example of what Whitehead means by the antirationality of modern philosophy, its contentment with an admittedly inadequate theory. He argues, to the contrary:

> Whatever is found in 'practice' must lie within the scope of the metaphysical description. When the description fails to include the 'practice,' the metaphysics is inadequate and requires revision. There can be no appeal to practice to supplement metaphysics, so long as we remain contented with our metaphysical doctrines.[57]

Most modern philosophers, of course, have not remained contented with Hume's dichotomy between theory and practice, at least on this point. They have sought to find a way to justify the assumption—everybody's assumption in practice—of the existence of a real world, by showing how the inference from sense-data to a real world could be justified. But to show how this inference is justified has proved extremely difficult, to say the least.

At the root of these attempts has usually been the claim that sense-data are *given* to experience, or at least that there is a *given element* in sensory perception. This claim has been made, for example, by C. I. Lewis, H. H. Price, and Roderick Chisholm, three of the best-known defenders of what has come to be called "foundationalism." All of these philosophers make their claim about givenness in terms of the sense-data provided by sensory perception. For example, H. H. Price's chief example in his chapter entitled "The Given" is the visual perception of a tomato. What is said to be given, of course, is not the tomato in its actuality, but only certain sensory data, such as redness and roundness.[58] C. I. Lewis' position, which has been called "sensory foundationalism,"[59] is based on the idea that sensory perception includes a noninterpreted element in experience that is simply given. In articulating his foundationalism, Lewis says: "Our empirical knowledge rises as a structure of enormous complexity . . . all [parts] of which rest, at bottom, on direct findings of sense."[60] And Roderick Chisholm equates our apprehension of the "given" with our apprehension of "appearances," which he uses interchangeably with "sensations," "sense-impressions," "sensa," and "phenomena."[61] As examples of objects that are given in sensory perception, Chisholm mentions sensa such as blue, noise, hot, and bitter.[62] The case for givenness, then, by its most-discussed advocates, has been made in terms of sensory perception.

But, as is well known, Wilfrid Sellers has argued cogently that this idea of a given element in sensory data is a "myth," that sense-data are *constructed* by the perceiver, not passively received.[63] This claim has been a central plank in the extreme antifoundationalism that is central to deconstructive postmodern philosophy. The claim that nothing is given in sensory experience is taken—on the basis of the identification of perception with sensory perception—to mean that nothing is given to experience *as such*.

But if nothing is given, then all our beliefs about the world are arbitrary, and the very idea that there is a reality beyond ourselves to which our ideas could somehow correspond is groundless. As C. I. Lewis said in an oft-quoted statement: "If there be no datum given to the mind, then knowledge must be contentless and arbitrary; there would be nothing which it must be true to."[64] H.H. Price spoke similarly of the need to affirm "data *simpliciter* [in distinction from data *secundum quid*] which is not the result of any previous intellectual process."[65] But, although these statements by Lewis and Price make good sense, the acceptance of the sensationist view of perception vitiates their attempt to back them up. Besides the fact that their claim that sense-data are *simply given* to experience seems false, their endorsement of the sense-datum theory of givenness means that *actualities* beyond the present experience are not even *claimed* to be given.

Some defenders of a given element in sensory experience, however, reject the sense-datum theory of givenness, saying instead that the outer (extra-somatic) world is directly given in sensory perception. A particularly good statement of the case for this direct realism is provided by Peter Strawson. In a critique of A. J. Ayer, he says that it is inappropriate to speak of the realist com-monsense view of the world as (merely) "a theory with respect to the immedi-ate data of perception."[66] Rather, the immediate data *include* the reality of the world: "Mature sensible experience (in general) presents itself as . . . an imme-diate consciousness of the existence of things outside us." Accordingly, "the ordinary human commitment to a conceptual scheme of a realist character is . . . something given with the given."[67] Besides appealing to our own experi-ence, Strawson points out that no one can consistently reject a realist view. In speaking of "the grip that common-sense non-representative realism has on our ordinary thinking," he says:

> It is a view of the world which so thoroughly permeates our conscious-ness that even those who are intellectually convinced of its falsity remain subject to its power. [John] Mackie admits as much, saying that even when we are trying to entertain a Lockian or scientific realism, 'our lan-guage and our natural ways of thinking keep pulling us back' to a more primitive view.[68]

We seem to be at an impasse, as there seems to be important truth on both sides of the issue. On the one hand, there are good reasons to believe, from what we all presuppose in practice (that a real world exists, that its reality is given to us in perception, and that our ideas are true to the extent that they correspond to this world), that perception must include an element that is given. On the other hand, there are good reasons to believe that sense-data are constructed by the perceiver. Michael Williams provides a concise statement of this latter point and the skeptical conclusion: "Evidence from the psychology of perception all points to there being no such thing as a state of sensuous apprehension utterly unaffected by beliefs, desires, and expectations and consequently no experience of the given as such."[69] Is it possible to move beyond this impasse?

The way beyond, Whitehead suggests, is to see that sensory perception is not our primary mode of perceiving the world beyond ourselves. There is a more basic mode, a nonsensory mode, which he calls "perception in the mode of causal efficacy," through which we directly "prehend" other actual things as actual and causally efficacious for us. Sense-perception is based upon, or includes—one can put it either way[70]—this nonsensory mode of perception. On this basis, we can fully admit—indeed, insist upon—the constructed character of sense-data, without concluding that nothing is given to perceptual experience as such. The data of perception as such are not limited to sense-data, such as colors and shapes, but include actual entities and their causally efficacious power for our perception. On this basis, we can do justice to what Charles Peirce called "secondness," meaning actual existence with its forcibleness, and can thereby overcome what Whitehead called the greatest weakness of modern philosophy: its failure to do justice to what William James called "stubborn fact."[71] We can thereby explain what Strawson describes as our "assumption of a general causal dependence of our perceptual experiences on the independently existing things we take them to be of."[72] We can, that is, agree with the direct realists, who have insisted that in perception we *directly apprehend other actual things* beyond our own experience, while agreeing with phenomenalists that *sensory perception in providing us with sense-data does not give us this direct apprehension.* We can do this, again, either by saying that sensory perception is based upon a more primitive mode of perception in which that direct apprehension occurs, or by saying that sensory perception is a mixed mode of perception comprised of two pure modes, one of which provides (constructed) sense-data and the other of which provides (given) causally efficacious actualities. In either case, perception as such, in its wholeness, provides a direct apprehension of actualities beyond our present experience.

Constructive postmodern philosophy thus provides a version of givenness that has been widely ignored by advocates and critics of givenness alike. J. J. Ross pointed out in 1970, in *The Appeal to the Given*, that "contemporary discussions of 'the given' fail to take into consideration the fact that there are at least three different theories about the nature of 'the given'";[73] and this is generally true of the discussion since that time. Beyond the two views already discussed, the "sense-datum theory" and the "object theory" (according to which in sensory perception external [extrasomatic] objects are directly given [Strawson's view]), there is what Ross calls the "immediate experience theory" (IET), which he calls "an unusual [view] of whose existence many contemporary philosophers are hardly aware." He adds: "The IET view of the given is an important one. But . . . it has been . . . widely neglected."[74]

It is, in fact, still neglected, over twenty years after the publication of Ross's book. One reason may be that Ross tended to equate this alternative view with Bradley's version of it. Besides the fact that the theory was thereby associated with all the problems of Bradley's idealism, Bradley's view of the given was really very different from that of, say, James and Whitehead. Ross did recognize that the "view of the given . . . to be found in the works of William James and Alfred North Whitehead" is "by no means identical" with the view of Bradley.[75] But the respective views are, in fact, *very* different. For example, according to Bradley's position, as Ross explicates it, experience begins with a "sensuous whole"; experience as immediately given does not involve the relation of an object to a subject, the distinction between what is felt and what feels; what is given is not a Many but a One; and it is outside of time.[76] Whitehead's view agrees with none of this. With differences so great, it is hard to understand Ross's account of these views as "similar."[77] But it is not hard to see why Ross's book did not motivate philosophers to examine alternative versions of the given beyond the two oft-discussed ones. And indeed, Ross's purpose was not to encourage consideration of a view of givenness that he considered more adequate, but to take issue with "the American attempt" to defend the idea of the given as sound and basic to epistemology.[78] In spite of its weaknesses, however, Ross's book stands as a too-neglected reminder that philosophers should not call the idea that experience contains a given element a "myth" if they have examined only two of the possible (and even actual) attempts to explicate this idea. I will now continue with Whitehead's attempt.

Whitehead agrees with modern philosophy insofar as it accepts what he calls the "subjectivist bias" introduced into philosophy by Descartes, namely, that "subjects enjoying conscious experiences provide the primary data for philosophy, namely, themselves as in the enjoyment of such experience."[79] He agrees, in other words, that one should start with that of which one is most certain, and that this is one's own immediate experience. But he does not agree that this means that one is less certain of a world beyond one's present experience. This is because he rejects the idea that the datum of one's present experience is limited to sense-data and other universals. He speaks of a "reformed subjectivist principle," saying that "Descartes' discovery on the side of subjectivism requires balancing by an 'objectivist' principle as to the datum for experience."[80] The point is that the immediately given datum for experience includes the givenness of things that were external to this experience (prior to being internal to it). The reason that "common sense is inflexibly objectivist" is that "we perceive other things which are in the world of actualities in the same sense as we are."[81]

In Whitehead's analysis, we get this direct apprehension of an "external world" in three ways. First, we directly apprehend particular parts of our own bodies as causally efficacious for our sensory perceptions. As Whitehead points out, in response to Hume's rhetorical query as to how we perceive actual substances and causality as real influence—whether with our eyes, our ears, our palates, etc.—Hume thereby implicitly acknowledges that he knows that our various bodily organs are causally efficacious for our sensory perceptions.[82] Although, in asking about the existence of the "external world," we are generally asking about a world beyond our own bodies, the solipsistic question, strictly speaking, is whether we have direct knowledge of a world beyond our present moment of experience; to answer this question, the direct apprehension of our bodies serves as well as would a direct apprehension of any other part of nature. This direct knowledge *that* there are actualities beyond our present experience, and of *what* they are like, can then serve, by analogy, to ground our meaningful talk of other "physical things" beyond our bodies. This analogical basis was what was missing in attempts to infer the reality of this world from sense-data alone. As Whitehead points out, in response to Descartes' judgment that certain sense-data he is experiencing betoken the existence of actual things: "He arrives at the belief in the actual entity by 'the faculty of judgment.' But on this theory [that direct perception never contains anything other than sense-data] he has absolutely no analogy upon which to found any such inference with the faintest shred of probability."[83]

But Whitehead does not think that we know of the actuality of the world beyond our bodies solely by reasonable analogy with our direct apprehension of our bodies. He suggests, second, that, by prehending our bodies, we thereby indirectly apprehend the actualities beyond our bodies *insofar as those actualities beyond our bodies are present within actualities comprising our bodies.*[84] This point brings us to Whitehead's antifoundationalist belief that epistemology cannot be discussed in isolation from metaphysics.[85] The metaphysical point relevant here is his panexperientialist belief that each actual entity is an experience that prehends, thereby including into itself aspects of, prior actual entities. Because all the events (photonic and neuronic) connecting the tree I see and my brain are events of this type, aspects of the tree itself are present in my brain cells. In prehending my brain cells, accordingly, I prehend aspects of the external tree.

Yet a third way of directly apprehending the external world is a direct prehension of actualities beyond one's own body ("direct" means that it is not mediated through one's body). This type of direct prehension of remote actualities is negligible for conscious experience for most people most of the time. (It rises from an unconscious to a conscious perception only in those rare moments that lead us to speak of telepathy or clairvoyance.) But such a pervasive, unconscious apprehension of other actualities may help account for what Peirce calls our practically indubitable commonsense conviction of the reality of both "nature" and "other minds."

Although the question about the "external world" usually refers only to this issue of the reality of nature and other minds, the question as to whether we directly perceive *anything* beyond our present experience includes the question of whether we directly perceive the past. Santayana highlighted this aspect of the question by speaking of "solipsism of the present moment."[86] The experience we call "memory" is an answer to this aspect of the question. Due, at least in part, to the fact that we have generally thought of the "mind" as an enduring individual that is self-identical through time, we have not thought of memory as a form of perception.[87] But if we, with Bergson, James, Whitehead, and Hartshorne, think of the finally real things as momentary events, so that the enduring mind is in reality comprised of momentary "drops" (James) or "occasions" (Whitehead) of experience, then memory is to be regarded as a type of perception. It becomes yet another of those "instances of non-sensuous perception" that show the erroneous nature of "the tacit identification of perception with sense-perception."

VI. ANTIFOUNDATIONALISM WITHOUT EXTREME RELATIVISM

The prior discussion has broached the subject of foundationalism. I have indicated that constructive postmodern philosophy is neither foundationalist nor radically antifoundationalist. I will now explain the position between these two extremes that is held. This issue is complex because a number of issues are involved in the debate between those who affirm and those who reject foundationalism, and because, consequently, the terms "foundationalist" and "antifoundationalist" can be used to describe a wide range of positions.[88] I will here indicate only how constructive postmodern philosophers reject what is usually called "foundationalism" without accepting the irrationalism involved in what I am calling "extreme antifoundationalism."

Foundationalism is usually taken to involve the following ideas: Philosophy can and should begin with some "basic beliefs" whose truth is certain. These beliefs are justified in a context-independent way, without employing any dubious presuppositions, and without appealing to one's philosophical position as a whole or some aspects of it and thereby to nonbasic beliefs. The nonbasic beliefs in one's position are all to be justified by reference to the basic beliefs. Foundationalism, therefore, holds that philosophers can and should base their philosophical position as a whole on a foundation whose certain truth can be established prior to the construction of the rest of the edifice. Metaphysics thus presupposes epistemology, while epistemology does not presuppose metaphysics, and epistemology, at least in its basic propositions, can be presuppositionless.

Constructive postmodernists reject all of this. We begin philosophizing, as Peirce says, with a mind already chock full of beliefs of every type, and these cannot be laid aside when one becomes philosophical.

> There is but one state of mind from which you can 'set out,' namely, the very state of mind in which you actually find yourself at the time you do 'set out'—a state in which you are laden with an immense mass of cognition already formed, of which you cannot divest yourself if you would.[89]

And much of Whitehead's reflection on method is devoted to a critique of the way philosophy has been misled by mathematics to think that its method should be that of deduction from axiomatic certainties.[90] In a statement that could have been written today against foundationalism's one-way relation between basic and nonbasic propositions, about the role of "background beliefs," and about the indeterminate nature of language, Whitehead wrote:

> There are no precisely stated axiomatic certainties from which to start. There is not even the language in which to frame them. The only possible procedure is to start from verbal expressions which, when taken by themselves with the current meaning of their words, are ill-defined and ambiguous. These are not premises to be immediately reasoned from apart from elucidation by further discussion; they are endeavours to state general principles which will be exemplified in the subsequent description of the facts of experience. This subsequent elaboration should elucidate the meanings to be assigned to the words and phrases employed. Such meanings are incapable of accurate apprehension apart from a correspondingly accurate apprehension of the metaphysical background which the universe provides for them. But no language can be anything but elliptical, requiring a leap of the imagination to understand its meaning in its relevance to immediate experience.[91]

Elsewhere Whitehead refers, more briefly, to "the pathetic desire of mankind to find themselves starting from an intellectual basis which is clear, distinct, and certain," and he says that "the doctrine that science starts from clear and distinct elements in experience, and that it developed by a clear and distinct process of elaboration, dies hard."[92] Whitehead's contrasting view is that constructive philosophy should employ the method of the "working hypothesis," and in doing so must reject the "dogmatic method" with which philosophy has been afflicted, "which is the belief that the principles of its working hypotheses are clear, obvious, and irreformable."[93]

While this rejection of foundationalism, thus understood, is widespread, this rejection sometimes goes to extremes. Extreme antifoundationalism rejects not only foundationalism as characterized above, but also three other notions: a "given" element in perception, truth as correspondence of idea to referent, and any class of privileged, universal (to all cultures) beliefs that can serve as a criterion for evaluating less privileged beliefs. The issue of a given element in perception has been discussed above. What needs brief discussion here are the second and third issues: truth as correspondence, and a class of privileged beliefs that can serve as a criterion.

The idea of truth as correspondence is so embattled partly because its detractors generally take it to involve things that its defenders do not. For example, detractors often point to the impossibility of getting out of one's perspective to *show* that one's perspectival idea of something does indeed correspond to that thing; but the correspondence notion of truth is a notion about what "truth" *means*, not a theory about how our ideas as to what is true are to be verified.[94] These two issues should be kept distinct—at least by all philosophers who claim to have rejected the positivistic conflation of meaning and verification.

Upholding the correspondence notion of truth is sometimes taken to mean upholding naive realism, the belief that there is some kind of one-to-one correspondence between our sensory perceptions, the culturally conditioned "commonsense" beliefs of our time, and/or current scientific theories, on the one hand, and the world, or some aspect of it, as it really is, on the other hand. But there is no necessary connection between these two ideas; in fact, it is only by presupposing the notion of truth as correspondence that we can say that our sensory percepts, or the so-called commonsense beliefs of our time, or certain scientific constructs, *do not* give us the truth, at least not the whole truth, about things. Critics of the idea of correspondence are rightly bothered by presumptuous and imperialistic claims by some people, whether religious, moral, scientific, aesthetic, or political fundamentalists, to have *achieved* correspondence. But denying that truth *means* correspondence is not the way to undermine such claims. If we give up the notion that truth means correspondence, we give up the chief weapon of criticism.

The qualification "at least not the whole truth" a few sentences above points to yet another confusion. When a defender of truth as correspondence endorses some particular assertion as true, detractors of the idea of correspondence sometimes assume the defender to mean that the statement provides the whole truth about the thing in question. The detractors rightly point out that there is an indefinite number of finite perspectives from which a thing can be viewed (some of which might even not see the thing in question as a distinguishable "thing"), and that none of these perspectives is privileged. To take a particular assertion as *the* truth is said to rule out other equally valid perspectives. But to believe that a certain assertion about something is true does not entail that it is *the* truth (in the sense of the whole truth), or even the most important truth, about it. Every true assertion about something abstracts tremendously from the full truth about it. The full truth about something would consist of all the true propositions that apply to it; this full truth, even about something as simple as a molecule or an ant—let alone something as complex as a human being or a historical event—is only knowable to omniscience. Finite minds are capable of only an extremely remote approximation to this complete truth.

Finally, the notion that truth means correspondence between an idea and its referent is sometimes rejected on the grounds that it means the correspondence between a linguistic assertion (a sentence) and a nonlinguistic reality. The critic then points out that language can "correspond" only to language, not to a nonlinguistic entity. Such a critique is valid against positions that equate sentences with propositions, or meanings. But that equation need not be made, and is not made by constructive postmodern philosophy. Whitehead, who probably addressed this issue most directly, distinguished between a verbal statement and the proposition (or meaning) that it seeks to express or that it evokes in a reader or hearer. To say that verbal statements can correspond to (an extralinguistic) reality, then, means that language has the capacity to express and evoke modes of apprehending nonlinguistic reality that can more or less accurately correspond to particular features of that reality.

Some other reasons for the widespread suspicion about the propriety of speaking of truth as correspondence, reasons rooted in problematic features of modern philosophy itself, are addressed in the essays herein. I turn now to the third controversial affirmation by means of which constructive postmodern philosophy overcomes the complete relativism of extreme antifoundationalism: the idea of a class of privileged beliefs that can serve as a criterion for evaluating less privileged beliefs.

That any formulated beliefs cannot be privileged in the sense of being foundational (presuppositionless, absolutely certain, and the starting point from which other beliefs are to be derived deductively or inductively) has already been stated. But that is not the only sense in which beliefs can be privileged. Constructive postmodern philosophers hold that some beliefs are privileged in the sense that, once we become conscious of them (through whatever method), we should have more confidence in their truth than in the truth of any other beliefs from which their falsity could be deduced. The beliefs in question are *those that we inevitably presuppose in practice. even if we deny them verbally.* Whitehead formulates this principle as "the metaphysical rule of evidence: that we must bow to those presumptions, which, in despite of criticism, we still employ for the regulation of our lives."[95] Peirce speaks, as Ochs points out, of "common-sense beliefs" that are "functionally indubitable," which means that they are free from genuine doubt (as opposed to "make-believe doubt" or "paper doubt"). Although Peirce as a "fallibilist" did not claim that they were absolutely certain, it was central to his pragmaticism that we should not claim to doubt in our philosophies what we do not genuinely doubt in our minds.[96] It was central to the pragmatism of James, similarly, that beliefs that cannot be genuinely lived, such as absolute determinism, should not be espoused.[97] The idea that this set of beliefs that is inevitably presupposed in practice should serve as the ultimate criterion for a philosophical position is contained, as well, in what I call, in my essay below, Hartshorne's "deep empiricism." Hartshorne refers to this set of beliefs as constituting a bottom layer of experience that is common to all humanity.

Deconstructive postmodernists typically deny, whether explicitly or implicitly, that there is any such common layer of experience. Richard Rorty denies it explicitly. He does not deny that we have "deep intuitions," such as that truth means correspondence, that human responsibility presupposes genuine freedom, and that experience is not adequately describable without the use of subjective terms such as "pain." But he claims that we have such intuitions only because "we have been educated within an intellectual tradition built around such claims." Accordingly, in his version of what pragmatism is, he recommends "that we do our best to *stop having* such intuitions,"[98] as if they were culturally conditioned through and through.

Pragmatism as formulated by Peirce and James, and as adopted by the other constructive postmodern philosophers, says, by contrast, that we have intuitions that are not simply culturally produced. These thinkers can say this in part—to connect this point with the earlier discussion—because they hold that we have a presensory, prelinguistic, preconscious apprehension of reality. This preconscious apprehension of reality is necessarily *vague*. These beliefs are not clear and distinct; nor are they beliefs about clear and distinct elements of our experience. They are not, accordingly, what people usually mean by "beliefs," namely, consciously held, verbally formulated ideas. Rather, they are vague intuitions, usually located on the fringe of awareness. But they are, nevertheless, beliefs, because we are prepared to act upon them—in fact, we do act upon them all the time. And, although they are vague, permitting more than one formulation within a given linguistic system, they can serve as criteria, because they are insistent, and because the range of possible formulations is severely limited.

To refer to "privileged beliefs," accordingly, is not, in the first place, to refer to consciously held, verbally formulated statements. It is to refer to some vague intuitions of a certain class (namely, those that are inevitably presupposed in practice). But, of course, to play a role in a system of expressed beliefs they themselves must be given a verbal formulation. This formulation will always be fallible. It will be dependent upon a range of factors, such as the available linguistic tools, the insight and linguistic ability of the formulators, and the other beliefs of which they are strongly convinced. The words and phrases that attempt to express the intuition in question will always remain fallible symbols for the more-or-less vaguely grasped meaning. They are, in this respect, like all other verbally formulated words and phrases. But they, nevertheless, do have a privileged status, in a secondary sense, within the system precisely because they are explications of beliefs that are inevitably presupposed in practice. Accordingly, although they are not privileged in the sense of being infallible and thus beyond the possible need for reformulation, they are privileged within the entire set of fallible beliefs in the sense that they cannot be simply rejected.

Besides not holding that the verbal formulations of our "commonsense beliefs" are infallible, constructive postmodern philosophers also do not believe that our certitude about them is completely independent of metaphysical musings. They recognize, instead, that our confidence in the truth of these beliefs is increased by our ability to show how they are mutually consistent—for example, to show how the freedom that we presuppose in practice is compatible with the kind of determinism discovered in the world by science. Constructive postmodernists thereby affirm that relation of mutual support between the more and the less privileged beliefs that Susan Haack has dubbed "up-and-backism."[99]

These constructive postmodernists thus point a way between foundationalism, on the one hand, and, on the other hand, an extreme antifoundationalism that leads to relativism (with "relativism" here defined not in an extreme way [such as the view that every set of beliefs is as good as every other set] that would allow relativists to deny that they are such, but simply as the denial that there is *any basis* for holding that one system of beliefs corresponds to reality better than do any others).[100] It is partly because the premises of modern philosophy led to, in Whitehead's words, "negations of what in practice is presupposed"[101] that the constructive postmodern philosophers were led to reject those premises.

A final point: This talk of "privileged" notions, which are common to all people (in practice) and which prevent complete relativism, may seem, in spite of all the above qualifications, to be opposed to the pluralism, and respect for the "other," that is espoused by postmodernists of all stripes. But this is not the case (unless, of course, pluralism is thought to entail complete relativism, as characterized above). The notion that there is a set of presuppositions that, as

Hartshorne says, constitutes a bottom layer of experience that is common to all humanity does not, by any means, imply that any extant belief-system adequately reflects all of those universal presuppositions, or even comes anywhere close. The natural assumption, to the contrary, is that one tradition has done some justice to a limited set of these presuppositions, another tradition to another set, and so on. As Hartshorne suggests, the assumption that such a set of common presuppositions exists sets a *cooperative* task, for people from the various traditions, to try to discern just what this bottom layer of human thought and experience is. People from other traditions will be approached, accordingly, with the assumption that they know some things that we do not know. This assumption, accordingly, far from creating a sense of superiority and closedness to others, promotes a sense of humility, openness, and active interest.

VII. God, Truth, and Values

One of the differences between the constructive and deconstructive forms of postmodern philosophy with respect to relativism is that the former speaks of God. This speaking betokens no return, at least in most of our philosophers (Peirce's views are debated), to the traditional deity of premodern and early modern philosophy and theology. But God as something like a soul of the universe, as that which makes the universe an experiencing individual, is affirmed. Although this affirmation does not help us with the problem of discovering *what is true*, it does help with the problem of saying *what truth is* and *how it can exist*, so that we retain our confidence that there is something to discover. Deconstructive postmodernism has been heavily influenced by what Arthur Danto calls "Nietzsche's Perspectivism."[102] If God (in every sense) is dead, so that we believe that there is no all-inclusive perspective but only a multiplicity of finite perspectives, then it is difficult to see how *the* truth about anything could exist, because it could have no locus. Whitehead sums up the position of constructive postmodern philosophy in saying that "the truth itself is nothing else than how the [things] of the world obtain adequate representation in the divine nature."[103]

This postmodern belief in God grounds the truth not only of propositions about what *has happened* but also of propositions about *what should happen*—that is, moral propositions. Modern philosophy has, to be sure, sought valiantly to develop a moral philosophy that does not depend upon metaphysical beliefs in general, and upon theological beliefs in particular. But this attempt to develop a purely autonomous ethic has failed, resulting in the ethical relativism of deconstructive postmodernism. Just as belief in God as receptive soul of the universe provides a necessary condition for making sense of the belief, which we all presuppose in practice, that truth about facts exists, so belief in God as active (desiring, willing, appetitive) soul of the universe grounds the belief, which we all presuppose in practice, that some ways of being and acting are (morally) better than others.

For more on the meaning of "God" and the reasons for speaking of God, one should consult the various essays below. The present discussion is intended only to indicate how the belief or disbelief in an all-inclusive perspective is relevant to the issue of relativism. In any case, this difference leads in turn to a great difference with respect to the stance toward life that is deemed appropriate. Richard Rorty's "irony" is probably the best term for the stance toward life that follows from deconstructive postmodernism.[104] By contrast, the constructive postmodernist's belief in God and the objectivity of truth and values, including moral values, leads to what William James called "the strenuous mood," while the belief in God as the appreciative recipient of all values leads to what Hartshorne calls "contributionism." A rhetorical question: Deconstructive postmodernists generally say that we can refer to truth only in a pragmatic sense, according to which the true is defined as that which helps us reach our goals. Given a world with a growing ozone hole, imminent global warming, and an enormous stockpile of nuclear weapons, any of which could bring the human race and much of the rest of the life of the planet to a grossly premature end, and given a host of other interconnected problems of gargantuan proportions, should we not say, from this type of pragmatic point of view, that a philosophy that results in a strenuous contributionism is "truer" than one that promotes ironic detachment?[105]

In any case, these constructive postmodern philosophers, both by the content of their philosophies and by the example of their own practice, encourage the rest of us not to deal exclusively and endlessly with what Dewey called the "problems of philosophy" in distinction from the "problems of men"[106]—which we would today call the problems of human beings. And these practical problems must be enlarged to include the problems of all sentient creatures, insofar as these are caused by human activities. This is in no way to denigrate the importance of technical philosophical problems; as the essays herein demonstrate, all these philosophers thought long and hard about some of these issues. But it is to say that this type of reflection should not be disconnected from reflection about war, ecological devastation, economics, and other problems confronting the human race today. Both forms of postmodern philosophy claim roots in pragmatism. But it is difficult to see how any philosophy can merit the term "pragmatic" today if it fails to help us deal with these problems of life and death.

VIII. THE ESSAYS

I will conclude with a few comments about the essays that follow. First, with regard to stance and purpose: they are written primarily not for specialists in these particular thinkers (although it is hoped that even they can find points of interest in them), but for students of philosophy (and persons in other fields) who are interested in exploring alternatives to the type of philosophy that has been dominant in philosophy departments in recent decades. It is widely accepted that our culture is in the midst of a fundamental "paradigm shift," one that parallels in scope the change that occurred in the seventeenth and eighteenth centuries. This book contains essays *about* five philosophers who have already been influential in the present transformation. And these essays are *by* authors who believe that their respective philosophers can still be helpful in shaping the precise direction that this transformation will take. These essays, then, are advocacy pieces, in the sense that their authors believe that the philosophers they treat are eminently worth paying attention to. The purpose of the essays is to point, as briefly and clearly as possible, to some of the most important things these philosophers have said, especially those things that bring out constructive postmodern directions.

Because of this central purpose, fellow philosophers will not find some of the things to which they are accustomed. There is little attempt to argue for the truth of the positions explicated, and little reference to alternative interpretations on controversial points. Such things are to be expected in essays dealing with a single issue, or in book-length treatments of a philosopher's position as a whole. But the purpose of each of the present essays is to offer an interpretative overview of the thinker's philosophy, giving particular attention to aspects considered distinctively postmodern, with the aim of suggesting that there may be something there worthy of further exploration. The purpose is less to settle issues than to elicit interest.

With regard to the relation of the various essays to each other: there was no attempt, beyond the suggestion of a few possible topics, to have the essays be uniform, either in form or substance. Each author was encouraged to employ the approach that seemed best for his particular philosopher. Each was free to employ his own judgment as to what is "postmodern" in his philosopher. (Peter Ochs, for example, shares the doubts of deconstructive postmodernists about the correspondence view of truth.) Finally, because each of the essays is intended to be capable of standing alone, there has been no attempt to eliminate repetitions of points in the various essays. Although such repetitions can be annoying, they can also be valuable by emphasizing that these five philosophers share ideas that have been, to say the least, not widely shared by most recent philosophers.

Why "these five philosophers" and only them? After reading these essays, few readers will, I think, doubt that any of these five belong; they clearly have much in common that is distinctive. But many will wonder why certain others, such as Samuel Alexander, John Dewey, George Herbert Mead, Paul Weiss, or Justus Buchler, were not included. The answer with regard to each would be different, of course. But the general response is that a line had to be drawn somewhere, and these five seemed most clearly representative of what is intended by "constructive postmodern philosophy." Besides, the purpose of the book is not to discuss everyone who could with some justification be called a constructive postmodern philosopher, but to present this type of philosophy as worthy of consideration by thoughtful people today.

The most controversial aspect of the book among professional philosophers will probably be the very notion of "constructive postmodern philosophy." Many philosophers seem to think that the term "postmodern" definitely includes certain beliefs, attitudes, and stances, and definitely excludes others. Reviewers of previous books in this series have expressed surprise that certain ideas were included, because they considered them modern, while some other ideas, which they considered truly postmodern ones, were not included. These criticisms are based on two assumptions I have explicitly rejected.

One of these assumptions is that there is an "essence" to postmodernism that everything worthy of the name must embody, an essence consisting of various beliefs and attitudes. I hold, rather, that postmodernism (in general) is a sentiment—the sentiment that modernity is something we must get beyond. But beyond this sentiment, the more precise direction we should take is what is now at stake. There is more than one idea of what has been most problematic about modernism, and therefore of what should be affirmed and what denied by a helpful postmodernism.

The second assumption is that a position to be postmodern must reject *everything* modern. Of course, that assumption, baldly stated, would be endorsed by very few. And yet it seems operative when critics point out that certain features of so-called constructive postmodernism are fully modern. In any case, the postmodernism of this series is understood to be a creative synthesis of premodern *and* modern truths and values (along with some novel ideas). There is simply far too much truth and value in that which is distinctively modern to speak of rejecting modernism *in toto*. And few if any serious postmodern thinkers of any stripe really mean to do so. What is at issue is less what is modern and what is not than what aspects of modernism are especially problematic.

From the standpoint of constructive postmodernism, two of the most problematic doctrines of modern philosophy have been the sensationist doctrine of perception and the anti-animistic doctrine of nature. Those so-called postmodern philosophers who carry these doctrines to their logical conclusions are regarded as *mostmodern* rather than genuinely *postmodern*. But from the standpoint of a deconstructive postmodernism that sees the objectionable core of modernism as containing doctrines that are here affirmed, such as a correspondence view of truth or universally valid criteria of truth, the position taken here will seem still modern, or perhaps hypermodern. As I said at the outset, neither of these evaluations is made from a neutral position. Each reflects a particular assessment of what is especially objectionable in modern philosophy, and a corresponding advocacy of a particular direction the postmodern sentiment should take.

These essays are presented with the hope that they will contribute to a revitalization of philosophy in the coming decades and to a better fulfillment by philosophers of the cultural role they should play, and thereby, in some way, to a better world.

NOTES

1. John Cobb used the term "postmodern" in 1964 to refer to Whitehead's philosophy in "From Crisis Theology to the Post-Modern World," which was first published in the *Centennial Review* 8 (Spring 1964), 209-20. My own first use of the term was in "Post-Modern Theology for a New Christian Existence," which was written in 1972 and appeared in 1977 as the introduction to *John Cobb's Theology in Process*, ed. David Ray Griffin and Thomas J.J. Altizer (Philadelphia: Westminster Press). Frederick Ferré used the term in a constructive, Whiteheadian way in 1976 in *Shaping the Future: Resources for the Postmodern World* (San Francisco: Harper & Row), and again in 1982 in "Religious World Modeling and Postmodern Science" (*Journal of Religion* 62/3 [July] 261-70). Also in 1982, Stephen Toulmin, influenced by Ferré, used the term in *The Return to Cosmology: Postmodern Science and the Theology of Nature* (Berkeley: University of California Press). The term "postmodern science" was, incidentally, first used (to my knowledge) in 1964 by Floyd W. Matson, who drew heavily on Whitehead, in *The Broken Image: Man, Science and Society* (1964; Garden City: Doubleday & Co., 1966), vi, 139, 228. It was used a decade later by Harold K. Schilling, who had also been significantly influenced by Whitehead, in *The New Consciousness in Science and Religion* (Philadelphia: United Church Press, 1973), 17, 82, 175, 244-45.

2. I have discussed one version of deconstructive postmodernism, exploring both its similarities with and differences from a Whiteheadian constructive postmodernism, in "Postmodern Theology and A/theology: A Response to Mark C. Taylor," in David Ray Griffin, William A. Beardslee, and Joe Holland, *Varieties of Postmodern Theology* (Albany: State University of New York Press, 1989), 29-62.

3. *Descartes' Conversation with Burman*, trans. John Cottingham (Oxford: Oxford University Press, 1976), 28; Desmond Clarke, *Descartes' Philosophy of Science* (University Park: Pennsylvania State University Press, 1982), 27.

4. Alfred North Whitehead, *Science and the Modern World* (New York: Free Press, 1967), 156.

5. Karl R. Popper, *Of Clouds and Clocks* (St. Louis: Washington University Press, 1966), 15 (italics his). Karl R. Popper and John Eccles, *The Self and Its Brain: An Argument for Interaction* (Heidelberg: Springer-Verlag, 1977), 16, 37, 494-95.

6. *The Self and Its Brain*, 105. Popper's co-author, John Eccles, at least seeks an answer. But it can hardly be called a step forward. It is, in fact, a step backward, being, as C. Wade Savage has pointed out ("An Old Ghost in a New Body," in *Consciousness and the Brain: A Scientific and Philosophical Inquiry*, ed. Gordon G. Globus, Grover Maxwell, and Irwin Savodnik [New York: Plenum Press, 1976], 125-53, at 131), merely a new version of Descartes' appeal to a *tertium quid*. In Eccles' case, this *tertium quid* between the physical brain, which is devoid of sentience, and the mind, which is devoid of physical energy, is a set of "critically poised" neurons in the brain. Because they are so critically poised, it takes only a "vanishingly small" amount of energy to make them go this way or that (*The Self and Its Brain*, 514, 545; "Cerebral Activity and Consciousness," in *Studies in the Philosophy of Biology*, ed. Francisco J. Ayala and Theodosius Dobzhansky [Berkeley: University of California Press, 1974], 87-107, at 100). The problem, of course, is that something that is *wholly* devoid of physical energy cannot exert even a vanishingly small amount of it.

7. Keith Campbell, *Body and Mind*, 2nd ed. (Notre Dame: University of Notre Dame Press, 1984), 38, 48.

8. Ibid., 105-09.

9. Ibid., 135.

10. Ibid., 137. At a conference I attended in 1974, the great evolutionist Sewall Wright, who was a panpsychist, said: "Emergence of mind from no mind at all is sheer magic." Theodosius Dobzhansky, another great evolutionist, but not a panpsychist, replied: "Then I believe in magic!" For Wright's statement (Dobzhansky's oral comment did not make it into the volume), see John B. Cobb, Jr., and David Ray Griffin, eds., *Mind in Nature: Essays on the Interface of Science and Philosophy* (Washington, D.C. [later Lanham, Md.]: University Press of America, 1977), 82. While Dobzhansky's response was humorous, it perfectly illustrated the willingness of the modern mind to countenance unintelligibility more readily than to accept the idea that experience and spontaneity may be ultimate. (In an essay published the same year as the conference [1974], Dobzhansky repeated the general neo-Darwinian view that "chance" mutations do not arise from "some principle of spontaneity inherent in living nature" ["Chance and Creativity in Evolution," in *Studies in the Philosophy of Biology*, ed. Ayala and Dobzhansky, 307-38, at 313]).

11. Campbell, *Body and Mind*, 125.

12. Ibid., 131.

13. Ibid., 132.

14. Ibid., 131.

15. Ibid.

16. *Collected Papers of Charles Sanders Peirce*, ed. Charles Hartshorne and Paul Weiss (Cambridge: Harvard University Press, 1931-1958), 6.64, 6.171, 6.273.

17. For example, Popper assumes that a panpsychist necessarily holds that aggregates such as telephones experience (*The Self and Its Brain*, 55), whereas those in this volume follow Leibniz in distinguishing between individuals (both simple and compound), which experience, and aggregates, which do not. Also, Popper writes as if all panpsychists would necessarily follow Spinoza and Leibniz in affirming parallelism, whereas those in this volume affirm the interaction between mind and brain that Popper supports. (Incidentally, one reason the term "panexperientialism" is better for the positions of the philosophers in this book [with the exception of Peirce] is that "panpsychism" suggests that the ultimate units of the world are enduring psyches, and the difficulties in understanding how two enduring individuals could interact while maintaining their identities led Leibniz to parallelism. The view that the ultimate units are [momentary] experiences, which is part of what the term "panexperientialism" is meant to convey, avoids the Leibnizian problem.)

18. J. R. Ravetz, "The Varieties of Scientific Experience," in *The Sciences and Theology in the Twentieth Century*, ed. Arthur Peacocke (Notre Dame: Notre Dame University Press, 1982), 197-206, at 202.

19. Ibid., 200-01.

20. Eugene Klaaren, *Religious Origins of Modern Science: Belief in Creation in Seventeenth-Century Thought* (Grand Rapids, Mich.: William B. Eerdmans, 1977; Lanham, Md.: University Press of America, 1985), 98-99, 149, 173-77; Brian Easlea, *Witch Hunting, Magic and the New Philosophy: An Introduction to Debates of the Scientific Revolution 1450-1750* (Atlantic Highlands, N.J.: Humanities Press, 1980), 112, 138; Alexandre Koyré, *From the Closed World to the Infinite Universe* (Baltimore, Md.: Johns Hopkins University Press, 1968), 210-13.

21. Klaaren, *Religious Origins*, 173-74; Koyré, *From the Closed World*, 178-84, 210-13.

22. Easlea, *Witch Hunting*, 108-115, 138, 158, 210; James R. Jacob, *Robert Boyle and the English Revolution* (New York: Franklin, Burt Publishers, 1978), 161-76; Robert Lenoble, *Mersenne ou la naissance du mécanisme* (Paris: Libraire Philosophique J. Vrin, 1943), 133, 157-58, 210, 375, 381.

23. Easlea, *Witch Hunting*, 100-07, 113, 125, 130, 135, 137, 233-35; Jacob, *Robert Boyle*, 172.

24. Leonora Cohen Rosenfield, *From Beast-Machine to Man-Machine* (Oxford: Oxford University Press, 1940), 15-16, 22, 47-48.

25. Ibid., 54, 59, 212 n. 49; Easlea, *Witch Hunting*, 144.

26. Easlea, *Witch Hunting*, 139.

27. Robert Boyle, *The Notion of Nature*, vol. IV of *The Works of the Honorable Robert Boyle* (London: Miller, 1744), 363.

28. A few materialists, such as some of those in France in the latter part of the eighteenth century, and Karl Marx, whom they influenced, have attributed inherent motion to matter as part of their atheism. And some materialists in our century have made this affirmation under the impact of quantum physics. But very few thinkers have understood this inherent motion as self-motion, in the sense of a partially self-determining response in the moment that is not wholly determined by antecedent conditions. It is the rejection of inherent self-motion in this sense, along with experience, to matter that I am portraying as characteristic of modern thought.

29. Peirce, *Collected Papers* 7.366.

30. Keith Campbell, *Body and Mind*, 90.

31. Whitehead, *Process and Reality: An Essay in Cosmology*, corrected edition, ed. David Ray Griffin and Donald W. Sherburne (New York: Free Press, 1978), 6.

32. Whitehead, *The Function of Reason* (Boston: Beacon Press, 1958), 16.

33. Ibid., 61.

34. Ibid., 86.

35. *Process and Reality*, xii.

36. Whitehead, *Modes of Thought* (New York: Free Press, 1966), 3. To link James with what Whitehead means here by "rationalism" in a positive sense is not, of course, to deny that James rejected "rationalism" in some other sense(s) of the term. The same would be true of Bergson and Peirce and, indeed, Whitehead himself (and even Hartshorne).

37. Peirce, *Collected Papers* 7.570.

38. Henri Bergson, *Duration and Simultaneity*, trans. Leon Jacobson (Indianapolis: Bobbs-Merrill, 1965), 137, 146n. For a thorough and illuminating discussion of this aspect of Bergson's thought, see Milič Čapek, *The New Aspects of Time: Its Continuities and Novelties* (Dordrecht and Boston: Kluwer Academic Publishers, 1991).

39. Adolf Grünbaum, "The Anisotropy of Time," in *The Nature of Time*, ed. Thomas Gold (Ithaca, N.Y.: Cornell University Press, 1967), 149-86.

40. J. T. Fraser, *The Genesis and Evolution of Time: A Critique of Interpretation in Physics* (Amherst: University of Massachusetts Press, 1982), 34, 154.

41. Ibid., 132.

42. Ibid., 147.

43. See my "Introduction: Time and the Fallacy of Misplaced Concreteness," *Physics and the Ultimate Significance of Time: Bohm, Prigogine, and Process Philosophy* (Albany: State University of New York Press), 1-48.

44. Whitehead, *Adventures of Ideas* (New York: Free Press, 1967), 212.

45. Whitehead, *Adventures of Ideas*, 361.

46. Ibid., 231.

47. See Susan Haack, "Recent Obituaries of Epistemology," *American Philosophical Quarterly* 27/3 (July 1990), 199-212.

48. Jonathan Dancy, ed., *Perceptual Knowledge* (Oxford: Oxford University Press, 1988), 1.

49. William James, "What Psychical Research has Accomplished," *William James on Psychical Research*, ed. Gardner Murphy and Robert Ballou (Clifton, N.J.: Augustus M. Kelley, 1973), 25-47, at 40-41.

50. Ibid., 41.

51. Ibid., 39.

52. Ibid., 25.

53. Ibid., 26.

54. For C. D. Broad, see *Religion, Philosophy, and Psychical Research* (New York: Harcourt, Brace & World, 1953), and *Lectures on Psychical Research* (New York: Humanities Press, 1969). For C. J. Ducasse, see *A Critical Examination of the Belief in Life after Death* (Springfield, Ill.: Charles Thomas, 1961); "The Philosophical Importance of 'Psychic Phenomena,'" *Journal of Philosophy* 51 (1954), 810-23, repr. in *Philosophical Dimensions of Parapsychology*, ed. James M. O. Wheatley and Hoyt Edge (Springfield, Ill.: Charles Thomas, 1976); and "Broad on the Relevance of Psychical Research to Philosophy," in *The Philosophy of C. D. Broad*, ed. Paul A. Schilpp (New York: Tudor Publishing Co., 1959). For H. H. Price, see "Questions About Telepathy and Clairvoyance, " *Philosophy* 15 (1945), 363-85, repr. in *Philosophical Dimensions of Parapsychology*, ed. Wheatley and Edge; "Presidential Address," *Proceedings of the Society for Psychical Research* (London, 1948), 307-41; "Psychical Research and Human Personality," *Hibbert Journal* 47 (1948-49), 105-13, repr. in *Science and ESP*, ed. J. R. Smythies (London: Routledge & Kegan Paul, 1967); "Prof. C. D. Broad's *Religion, Philosophy, and Psychical Research*," *Journal of the American Society for Psychical Research* 48 (1954), 56-68; and "Parapsychology and Human Nature," *Journal of Parapsychology* 23 (1950), 178-95, repr. in *Philosophy and Parapsychology*, ed. Jan Ludwig (Buffalo: Prometheus Books, 1978).

55. Keith Campbell, *Body and Mind*, 95.

56. Whitehead, *Process and Reality*, 190. Whitehead, incidentally, does not mean by this statement that no reality that can be called "God" should be allowed to play an explanatory role in one's philosophy. Whitehead himself, in fact, explains various features of our experience and reality in general by appeal to an actuality he names "God." The kinds of appeals he considered acceptable and unacceptable are indicated in

his oft-quoted statement, "God is not to be treated as an exception to all metaphysical principles, invoked to save their collapse. He is their chief exemplification" (*Process and Reality*, 343).

57. Ibid., 13.

58. H. H. Price, *Perception* (London: Methuen, 1932), 4-6.

59. Timm Triplett, "Recent Work on Foundationalism," *American Philosophical Quarterly* 27/2 (April 1990), 93-116, at 99-100. Triplett points out specifically that Lewis developed the idea of the "sensory given" (95).

60. C. I. Lewis, *An Analysis of Knowledge and Valuation* (Lasalle, Ill.: Open Court, 1946), 171; quoted in Susan Haack, "C. I. Lewis," in *American Philosophy*, ed. Marcus G. Singer (Cambridge: Cambridge University Press, 1985), 215-38, at 219.

61. Roderick Chisholm, "Theory of Knowledge," Roderick Chisholm et al., *Philosophy* (Englewood Cliffs, N.J.: Prentice Hall, 1964), 235-344, at 261.

62. Roderick Chisholm, *Theory of Knowledge*, 2nd ed. (Englewood Cliffs, N.J.: Prentice-Hall, 1977), 28, 77.

63. Wilfrid Sellers, "Empiricism and the Philosophy of Mind," in *Foundations of Science and the Concepts of Psychology and Psychoanalysis*, ed. Herbert Feigl and Michael Scriven (Minneapolis: University of Minnesota Press, 1950), 253-329; repr. in Sellers, *Science, Perception and Reality* (New York: Humanities Press, 1963).

64. C. I. Lewis, *Mind and the World Order* (New York: Charles Scribner's Sons, 1929), 38-39.

65. H. H. Price, *Perception* (London: Methuen, 1964), 4.

66. Peter S. Strawson, "Perception and its Objects," in *Perceptual Knowledge*, ed. Jonathan Dancy, 92-112, at 88.

67. Ibid., 99.

68. Ibid., 106, citing John Mackie, *Problems from Locke* (Oxford: Oxford University Press, 1976), 68.

69. Michael Williams, *Groundless Belief: An Essay on the Possibility of Epistemology* (New Haven: Yale University Press, 1977), 45-57.

70. Whitehead sometimes treats sensory perception as a form of "perception in the mode of symbolic reference," which involves the interplay of two pure modes: perception in the mode of presentational immediacy, and perception in the mode of causal efficacy (e.g., *Process and Reality*, 121). John Cobb's essay herein follows this side of Whitehead. At other times, Whitehead equates sensory perception with perception in the mode of presentational immediacy (see *Process and Reality*, 36; *Symbolism: Its Meaning and Effect* [New York: Capricorn Books, 1959], 21; and *Modes of Thought*, 133, where he says: "Sense perception does not provide the data in terms of which we inter-

pret it"). In my essay on Hartshorne herein, I have followed this latter usage, saying that sensory perception is *based upon* the nonsensory mode of perception (whereas Cobb speaks of sensory perception as *including* the nonsensory mode).

71. *Process and Reality*, xiii, 129.

72. Strawson, "Perception and its Objects," 103.

73. Jacob Joshua Ross, *The Appeal to the Given: A Study in Epistemology* (London: George Allen & Unwin, 1970), 5.

74. Ibid., 24.

75. Ibid.

76. Ibid., 84-93.

77. Ibid., 24.

78. Ibid., 5.

79. Whitehead, *Process and Reality*, 159.

80. Ibid., 160.

81. Ibid., 158.

82. Ibid., 81, 117-18; *Symbolism*, 50-52.

83. *Process and Reality*, 49; cf. *The Function of Reason*, 68.

84. *Process and Reality*, 120, 180, 212, 237.

85. Ibid., 54.

86. George Santayana, *Scepticism and Animal Faith* (New York: Dover, 1955), 14-15.

87. Whitehead, *Adventures of Ideas*, 220-21.

88. See Susan Haack, "Recent Obituaries of Epistemology" (note 47, above), and Timm Triplett, "Recent Work on Foundationalism" (note 59, above).

89. Peirce, *Collected Papers* 5.416.

90. Whitehead, *Process and Reality*, 10.

91. Ibid., 13.

92. *The Function of Reason*, 51, 53.

93. *Adventures of Ideas*, 223.

94. This is not to deny that we need in some moments directly to experience correspondence; Cobb speaks to this issue on pp. 184-85.

95. *Process and Reality*, 151.

96. Peirce, *Collected Papers* 5.376n, 5.416.

97. Peirce and James were both influenced on this point by Alexander Bain, who had defined (genuine) belief as that upon which one is prepared to act (Vincent G. Potter, "Charles Sanders Peirce," in *American Philosophy*, ed. Marcus Singer, 21-41, at 32-33).

98. Richard Rorty, *Consequences of Pragmatism (Essays: 1972-1980)* (Minneapolis: University of Minnesota Press, 1982), xxix-xxx.

99. Susan Haack, "C.I. Lewis," in *American Philosophy*, ed. Marcus G. Singer, 218. Her "up-and-back-ism" is a rejection of the foundationalist claim that the process of lending credibility runs in only one direction, from "basic" to "nonbasic" beliefs. My account of constructive postmodern philosophy's middle position between foundationalism and extreme antifoundationalism is close to Haack's "foundherentism," which combines elements of foundationalism and coherentism. A crucial difference would exist, however, if she, as she sometimes seems to (e.g., 236), equates perceptual experience with *sensory* perception.

100. To reject complete relativism, and thereby to maintain that we have *some* basis for thinking one system of beliefs more accurate than another, is not necessarily to deny that there is always some circularity between the content of one's system and the norms one uses for evaluating systems. It is only to deny that this circularity is always so complete as to be vicious.

101. Whitehead, *Process and Reality*, 13.

102. Arthur Danto, "Nietzsche's Perspectivism," in *Nietzsche: A Collection of Critical Essays*, ed. Robert C. Solomon (1973; Notre Dame: University of Notre Dame Press, 1980), 29-57.

103. Whitehead, *Process and Reality*, 12.

104. See Richard Rorty, *Contingency, Irony, and Solidarity* (Cambridge: Cambridge University Press, 1989).

105. It may seem unfair to suggest that the "irony" Rorty advocates would result in detachment from the problems of the world, given the fact that the title of his book (see note 104) speaks also of "solidarity." However, besides the fact that the sense of solidarity of which he speaks is limited to members of his own species, rather than extending to all living beings, even this human solidarity is, by Rorty's own declaration, not promoted by his ironist philosophy: "ironist philosophy has not done, and will not do, much for freedom and equality" (94); "for us ironists, theory has become a means to private perfection rather than to human solidarity" (96). This solidarity is to be promoted by literature, not philosophy (xvi, 93-95).

For Rorty, it is enough to say that the ironist stance is not hostile to solidarity (xv). But even this modest claim is problematic. Ironists, for Rorty, are persons who realize that their way of understanding reality does not correspond more closely to reality than do other ways, that their central beliefs and desires are based on wholly contingent causal factors, that they do not correspond to any necessary, timeless principles (xv, 73-75). For example, liberal rejection of the racist belief that "Blacks have no rights which whites are bound to respect" is not based on any fact—such as the nature or will of God, or the intrinsic dignity of human beings *qua* human beings—in the nature of things (4-6, 77; "Postmodernist Bourgeois Liberalism," *Journal of Philosophy* 80 [1983], 583-89, esp. 588-89). Liberal ironists recognize, accordingly, that they can give no reason why human beings should care about other human beings, and not be cruel to them (*Contingency, Irony, and Solidarity*, 87, 94). Insofar as Rorty limits his claim to the extremely modest one that this ironism is *not incompatible* with a sense of human solidarity (87), he himself proves the point. But the claim that such ironism is *not hostile* to the sense of human solidarity is somewhat less modest, because this claim can be taken to mean "not hostile in the long run." If the ironist attitude became widespread, would it not have corrosive effects on liberal societies? Rorty admits that this is possible, but considers it unlikely (85). However, he admits that "The ironist theorist . . . is rarely a liberal" (102). And he concedes, furthermore, that ironists such as Nietzsche, Heidegger, and Derrida are, as public philosophers, "at best useless and at worst dangerous" (68). It is for this reason that Rorty seeks to privatize philosophy (meaning ironist philosophy), making it "irrelevant to politics" (197) in order to prevent it "from becoming a threat to political liberalism" (190). But is the complete separation Rorty wants between the public and the private possible?

Rorty in effect admits that this strategy will not work. Although he initially describes his liberal utopia as one in which ironism is universal (xv), he later qualifies this, saying that only the intellectuals would be ironists; "the nonintellectuals would not" (87). He even says: "I cannot . . . claim that there could or ought to be a culture whose public rhetoric is *ironist*. I cannot imagine a culture which socialized its youth in such a way as to make them continually dubious about their own process of socialization" (87). Rorty, in other words, seems to recognize that a society that sought to socialize its youth into wanting a cruelty-free world would undermine this effort if it simultaneously socialized them into ironism. The ironism of the elders—in fact, the intellectual elite among the elders—would have to be hidden from the youth until their consciences had been properly formed. The ironist stance *would* be hostile to solidarity, unless and until the solidarist stance had been so firmly inculcated that the ironist stance could remain, as Rorty wishes, "merely philosophical" ("Postmodernist Bourgeois Liberalism," 588-89). To make the point in another way: if the literature of the society were based on Rorty's ironism, this literature would *not* serve the "socially useful" function of promoting liberal solidarity that Rorty allocates to it (*Contingency*, xvi, 93-95)—his attempted readings of Nabokov and Orwell (chs. 7-8) notwithstanding.

This analysis fits with Rorty's own recognition that what he calls "democratic liberalism" and "solidarity" derived historically from the Christian tradition (55, 87n., 89). Rorty recognizes, furthermore, that he himself has been shaped by this tradition. He, for example, has said that "as a free-loading atheist" he gratefully invokes Judeo-Christian principles ("Postmodernist Bourgeois Liberalism," 588-89). So, the compatibility between ironism and solidarity that Rorty finds in himself is contingent (!) upon the fact that the sense of solidarity was formed in him long before his ironist stance developed. Rorty believes that "democracies are now in a position to throw away some of the ladders used in their own construction" (*Contingency,* 194). This may be possible; but that democracy can long survive if the thrown-away ladders (the "philosophical presuppositions" [192]) are not replaced by something equally sturdy is extremely unlikely. Even less likely, without a supporting worldview, than the retention of the fragile sense of human solidarity that we have had is—to return to the point alluded to at the outset of this note—the extension of the sense of solidarity to other species of living things.

106. John Dewey, *Problems of Men* (New York: Philosophical Library, 1946), 6-7.

—— My thanks to John Cobb, Marcus Ford, Pete Gunter, and Peter Ochs for helpful critiques of an earlier version of this introduction.

1

CHARLES SANDERS PEIRCE

Peter Ochs

By definition, a "logic of postmodernism" would appear to be a contradiction in terms: philosophic postmodernism emerged as a critique of attempts to found philosophy on some principle of reasoning and to found reasoning on some formal guidelines for how we ought to think. Nonetheless, there are two reasons why Charles Sanders Peirce (1839-1914) ought to be labelled the logician of postmodernism—the philosopher who, more than any other, etched out the normative guidelines for postmodern thinking. The first reason is that Peirce attempted to accomplish the impossible, or at least the contradictory. He launched his philosophic career with a logical critique of "Cartesianism"—his label for the modernist attempt to found philosophy on some formal principles of reasoning. He then attempted to replace the principles of Cartesian reasoning with a set of antimodernist principles that proved themselves to be as modernist as their contraries. The second reason for giving Peirce this label is that his failures to accomplish the impossible engendered in him something he was unable to achieve wilfully: a habit of self-critical yet self-affirming thinking that was neither modernist nor antimodernist but, rather, a disciplined variety of postmodern thinking. In his later years, Peirce began to sketch out the principles of philosophic postmodernism by describing features of his own emergent habit of thinking. The sketching comes close enough to what I would label a logic of postmodernism—where the method of logic is as postmodern as the thinking it describes.

As you may have surmised already, I do not believe Peirce's postmodernism is something one can study straight-on. His postmodernism was not a position or a place, but a process, of which his modernist struggles were an essential part. We must hence begin our study with Peirce's early modernism and then move forward, to see how his mature thought emerged as a way of completing and correcting his modernist project. After offering a few comments on Peirce's comparably complex life, I begin by reviewing Peirce's early critique of philosophic modernism. His own modernism is displayed in this technical critique—which means, I am afraid, that you will be confronted immediately with some rhetorical irony as well as with a strong dose of logical and epistemological argumentation. Relief will come slowly, as I then examine selected features of the habit of thinking that emerged from the contradictory tendencies in Peirce's early work. Making a postmodern move in my own method of analysis, I adopt Peirce's habit of thinking as a prototype for postmodern philosophy—suggesting that the norms of postmodern thinking must be embedded in the intellectual drama of certain ways of living. In conclusion, I reinterpret the claims of Peirce's mature philosophy as descriptions of selected features of his postmodern thinking. Among the topics considered are Peirce's claims about the self-correcting character of pragmatic reasoning; about the reality of chance, brute force and love as principles of cosmic evolution; and about the communal context of philosophic inquiry.

A few prefatory words, then, about some of the complexities of Peirce's life. First, the theological complexities. The dominant influence in Peirce's early life was his father, the eminent Harvard mathematician Benjamin Peirce. Benjamin was a devout Unitarian who, in the words of Peirce biographer Joseph Brent, "taught mathematics as a kind of religious worship."[1] Charles retained from his father's teaching a profound conviction that we live in God's creation and that, through this creation, we have immediate contact with God, or, as Peirce phrased it at age 24 to a philosophical audience, with reality itself:

When the conclusion of our age comes, and skepticism and materialism have done their perfect work, we shall have a far greater faith than ever before. For then man will see God's wisdom and mercy not only in every event of his own life, but in that of the gorilla, the lion, the fish, the polyp, the tree, the crystal, the grain of dust, the atom.[2]

On the other hand, Benjamin did not engender in Charles the need to participate, in a disciplined fashion, in any particular hermeneutical or ecclesiastical system. Thus Charles wrote, near the end of his life:

I abominate the unitarians myself, because all through my boyhood I heard in our unitarian family nothing but angry squabbles between

Calvinists and Unitarians, and though the latter were less absurd than the former, I thought their church was based on mere denial and when I grew up I joined the Episcopal church, without believing anything but the general essence and spirit of it. *That* I did and do profoundly believe.[3]

Peirce's love of irony and his tendency simultaneously to affirm and to deny, or at least to criticize, are displayed as well in these excerpts from his entry into the Harvard Class-Book of 1860:

1839 September 10. Tuesday. Born. . . .
1844 Fell Violently in love with Miss W. and commenced my education. . . .
1847 Began to be most seriously and hopelessly in love. Sought to drown my care by taking up the subject of Chemistry—an antidote which long experience enables me to recommend as sovereign. . . .
1850 Wrote a "History of Chemistry". . . .
1853 Set up for a fast man and became a bad schoolboy. . . .
1856 SOPHOMORE. Gave up the idea of being a fast man and undertook the pursuit of pleasure.
1857 JUNIOR. Gave up the pursuit of pleasure and undertook to enjoy life.
1858 SENIOR. Gave up enjoying life and exclaimed "Vanity of vanities! All is vanity!"
1859 Wondered what I would do in life.
Appointed Aid on the Coast Survey. Went to Maine and then to Louisiana.[4]

Peirce did not have the reputation of being disciplined in his personal life. In his wife's words, "All his life from boyhood it seems as though everything had conspired to spoil him with indulgence."[4a] One of the results was an uneven employment record.

Peirce's first expertise was in chemistry. In 1863 he graduated from the Lawrence Scientific School with a B.S. *summa cum laude* in Chemistry, and he continued throughout his life to call himself a chemist. Until the 1890s, however, his gainful employment was with the Coast and Geodetic Survey, for whom he served as administrator and conducted gravimetric and other basic research. At the same time, through all these years, Peirce's central intellectual foci were logic and philosophy, and his first interest was to teach these fields in the university. Peirce made major contributions to numerous subfields in the logic and philosophy of science, formal and mathematical logic, topology, semiotics, linguistics and epistemology; he was most widely recognized as the founder of pragmatism. Nevertheless, contentious and undisciplined as he was, he was unable to procure a permanent teaching position.[5]

Even William James, perhaps Peirce's truest friend and admirer, was unable to convince Harvard administrators that Peirce, one of the greatest American philosophers, merited a place on their faculty. James did succeed, however, in securing Peirce's scholarly reputation as the founder of pragmatism. In an 1898 address to the Philosophical Union at the University of California, James said,

> I will seek to define with you merely what seems to be the most likely direction in which to start upon the trail of truth. Years ago this direction was given to me by an American philosopher whose home is in the East, and whose published words, few as they are and scattered in periodicals, are not fit expression of his powers. I refer to Mr. Charles S. Peirce, with whose very existence as a philosopher I dare say many of you are unacquainted. He is one of the most original of contemporary thinkers; and the principle of practicalism—or pragmatism, as he called it, when I first heard him enunciate it at Cambridge in the early '70s—is the clue or compass by following which I find myself more and more confirmed in believing we may keep our feet upon the proper trail.[6]

In the early 1870s, Peirce and James discussed pragmatism in a Metaphysical Club that met in Cambridge, Massachusetts, for about a decade.[7] Peirce laid the foundations for his pragmatism several years earlier with his first published critique of modernism.

I. THE CRITIQUE OF MODERNISM:
PEIRCE'S ANTI-CARTESIANISM

In a series of papers published in the *Journal of Speculative Philosophy* in 1867-68,[8] Peirce sought to uncover the fundamental error that misled modern philosophers since Descartes into fearing they had to discover the foundation of all reasoning and then into believing they had found it. Peirce believed that this search for foundations reasserted platonic idealism in a new, subjective key, leading the philosophers of modernity into a war with the everyday. He believed that, from Descartes on, they rightfully objected to the ecclesiastic elitism of their scholastic progenitors, but then wrongfully replaced it with an elitism of their own—preferring genius over hoary learning, mathematical imagination over saintliness, the systematizing capacities of a few individual reasoners over the organic life of a community of inquirers. Peirce did not object to the need to refashion ecclesial authority, nor to the benefits of genius, imagination, and system. But he argued that these are gifts to be offered in the service of everyday life and everyday community, rather than as alternatives.

Without idealizing the everyday and without calling for any atavistic returns to "a time when," he was a critic of the modern intellectual rather than of ordinary life. He called for the most sophisticated development of intellectual life, but in the service of a master who valued such a life only for its contributions to our worldly existence, or at least for its potential contributions to how we will ultimately exist in this world. Later, we may name this master "God," but not in a way that is overly influenced by classical-modern spiritualism or spirit-body dualism. For now, it is best to keep this master unnamed and to take note only of the effect of Peirce's references to it. This effect is to correct what Peirce considered the hubris of modern conceptions of the self.

According to Peirce, modern philosophy tended to encourage the egoism he saw manifested in the idolatries of his age: individualism (displayed, for example, in his scholarly peers' vainglorious defense of unverified and even untestable pet theories), economic materialism (the adoration of Mammon), social Darwinism (the anti-gospel of a societal survival of the fittest), and—his most general term of opprobrium—"nominalism." In fact, he took nominalism to underlie all the other negative tendencies of modernism.

In the great medieval controversies, the realists (such as Duns Scotus) believed that our ideas of universals correspond to something real, while the nominalists (such as William of Ockham) did not, claiming, instead, that only individual entities are real and that universals are merely names *(nomen)* we use to talk about collections of individuals. For many modern philosophers, this controversy seemed an empty and interminable dispute. According to Peirce, however, modernists belittled the dispute only because they had long since opted for the nominalist position, which they treated as if it were self-evident. In other words, he treated the medieval debate as if it were still raging, albeit in different terms, and as if "nominalism" referred to the epistemological doctrine that underlay all the other tendencies of modernism ("the nominalistic *Weltanschauung* has become incorporated into what I will venture to call the very flesh and blood of the average modern mind"[9]). Labeling himself a "scholastic realist," Peirce then set out to resuscitate Scotus' doctrine as his weapon against modernism. Playing the game of philosophic debate, he confronted modern philosophy in its own terms, offering logical, epistemological and empirical arguments against the claims of modern nominalism. Peirce's most convincing arguments were pragmatic ones, however. Undercutting the terms of philosophic debate, these did not neatly fit into the theater of scholastic disputation, and Peirce did not offer them explicitly for another ten years.

In his 1867-68 papers, Peirce offered what I call his nonpragmatic argumentation. His argument was based on the premise that nominalists question the reality of universals because, assuming that we acquire our universal beliefs on the authority of parents, teachers, ecclesial leaders and so on, they question the validity of such authority. Rather than trust such authorities, nominalists rely on immediate human judgments—perceptions, sensations, intuitions—which, they believe, offer us knowledge of individual entities, but not of any universals. Trusting immediate over learned knowledge, nominalists therefore tend to favor individuality over sociality, insight and genius over wisdom, and autonomy over relationship. Peirce concluded that nominalist systems stand or fall on the strength of their explanations of how, in fact, we have immediate knowledge of the real world. He offered his nonpragmatic argumentation as a critique of such explanations.

According to Peirce, Descartes' intuitionism provided the prototype for modernist attempts to account for our capacity to know the world immediately. It was what Descartes considered the Archimedean point upon which to ground the modern project of philosophy.[10] Peirce defined intuitionism as the claim that we have cognitions of objects outside of consciousness and uninfluenced by previous cognitions, and that we know, intuitively, that we have such knowledge independently of the influence of any previous knowledge. Peirce argued that "there is no evidence that we have this faculty [of knowing that we have intuitions uninfluenced by previous cognitions], except that we seem to *feel* that we have it."[11] Were this feeling to serve as our Archimedean point, then it would itself have to deliver information about its authority as well as about whatever it is about. The very simplicity of feeling, however, precludes its fulfilling such a dual function. For Peirce, the claim *that* a feeling or an intuition is authoritative must therefore belong to subsequent interpretation, and not to the feeling or intuition itself.

Peirce argued that a more reasonable interpretation of the empirical evidence is that whatever *appears* to us to be an immediate intuition is itself the product of previous cognitions. He suggested we consider, for example,

> the perception of two dimensions of space. This appears to be an immediate intuition. But if we were to *see* immediately an extended surface, our retinas must be spread out in an extended surface. Instead of that, the retina consists of innumerable needles pointing toward the light, and whose distances from one another are decidedly greater than the *minimum visible*. Suppose each of those nerve-points conveys the sensation of a little colored surface. Still, what we immediately see must even then be, not a continuous surface, but a collection of spots. Who could discover this by mere intuition? But all the analogies of the nervous system are against the supposition that the excitation of a single nerve cell can produce an idea as complicated as that of space, however small. If the excitation of no one of these nerve points can immediately convey the impression of space, the excitation of all cannot do so. . . . [H]ence, the sum of these impressions is a necessary condition of any perception produced by the excitation of all.[12]

As additional examples, he suggested that we consider the way our visual field is uninterrupted by the blind spot that appears in the middle of the retina; the way we hear pitch independently of the aural impressions that contribute to it; or the way we perceive the duration of time: "That the course of time should be immediately felt is obviously impossible. For, in that case, there must be an element of this feeling at each instant. But in an instant there is no duration and hence no immediate feeling of duration."[13] (Peirce's later arguments were consistent with the claims of Bergson, James, Husserl, Whitehead, and Heidegger that the feeling of duration is itself a duration. At this point, however, Peirce's accomplishment was merely critical. Having displayed the inadequacies of intuitionism, he tended to replace it with a conversely dogmatic logicism: the claim that, if we are to have any certainty, then the way we interpret cognitions must be guided by indubitable modes of reasoning, rather than by infallible modes of intuition.) Peirce adduced comparable evidences against the various corollaries of intuitionism, such as the claims that we have intuitive self-consciousness (even Kant knew that children lacked this)[14] and a power of introspection (we lack an intuitive faculty of identifying elements of consciousness as "inner" or "outer") and, finally, a power to think without signs. Peirce concluded that "every thought is a sign," and, because signs are general, that "generals must therefore have a real existence."[15] At this stage in his thinking, in other words, Peirce linked his critique of intuitionism with a reassertion of realism. He believed that, if there are no primary intuitions, then there must, at least, be primary modes of interpreting intuitions—what he would later call indubitable habits of belief, whose generality he would later identify with the generality of real signs or symbols.[16]

In sum, Peirce believed he had offered a critique of, and an alternative to, the nominalist foundation of modern philosophy. Having argued that intuitionism is ungrounded, he believed he had both removed the intellectual supports of modern individualism and offered good reasons in support of its contrary: a kind of socialism and, underlying it, a kind of cognitivism. This latter is the claim that, if our knowledge is not about objects outside of consciousness, then it must be about previous knowledge.

In offering his cognitivist conclusions, however, Peirce reasserted a fundamental element of the nominalist argumentation he had sought to refute. In appearance, Peirce's cognitivism offered an alternative to the nominalists' subjectivism or self-reference. Having shown that intuitions are merely private, he concluded that non-private knowledge must be non-intuitional. Having defined intuitions as cognitions that refer directly to objects outside of consciousness, he concluded that non-intuitions are cognitions that refer only to other cognitions. But how, then, do cognitions refer to objects? Did Peirce not replace intuitionism with a vicious conceptualism[17]—a system of cognitions that refers only to itself the way each intuition refers only to itself? In the next stage of his work,

Peirce introduced a mode of inquiry in terms of which he could identify the logical assumptions he had shared, in 1867, with the nominalists. While they offered contrary arguments, both the nominalists and he made use of the same method of argumentation, and the fallacy of modernist thinking lay in this *method*, not merely in the claims to which the method was applied. As we will see, Peirce called this the *a priori* method of thinking. For now, we may note that one of its leading principles is the law of excluded middle ("a" or "not a"). Both Peirce and the nominalists argued as if epistemological inquiry could be divided between mutually exclusive alternatives, in this case between the logical contraries "intuitionism" or "non-intuitionism." Following this method of reasoning, if intuitionism is false then its contrary must be true; in Peirce's argument, if intuitionism is false, then cognitivism is true, defined as non-intuitionism. Such a contrary represents a mere logical possibility, however, established on merely *a priori* grounds. We would have reason to expect that cognitivism, so defined, has as little to do with actual experience as intuitionism, so defined. Peirce's task, in the next stage of his work, was to search for an epistemological option that was neither intuitionist nor non-intuitionist, but rather some third something: intuitionism's logical contradictory, rather than its contrary.

II. The Critique of Modernism: Peirce's Early Pragmatism

In what would become his most famous series of papers, the "Illustrations of the Logic of Science" of 1877-78,[18] Peirce developed a methodological critique of modernism. While Peirce's first arguments against intuitionism were epistemological and empirical, he now offered a critique of Descartes' method of argument itself: if Descartes' claim was not based on the facts of reason and experience, then it must have been based on something else. Rather than responding to nominalistic claims on their own terms, Peirce reduced them to their governing methods, or "guiding principles," and then evaluated them within a new taxonomy of what he called the "methods of fixing belief."[19] Laying the groundwork for his emergent pragmatism, he said: before worrying out the details of nominalistic claims, let us not suppose that every claim we hear is meaningful within the terms we bring to it or even within the terms it purports to bring to us. Let us first ask: out of what environment of inquiry does it come to us?

Peirce nurtured this question through several years of spirited discussions at the Cambridge Metaphysical Club in which James first heard his ideas about pragmatism. In the Club, an informal group of lawyers (Nicholas St. John Green and at times Oliver Wendell Holmes and Joseph Warner), scientists

(Chauncy Wright, Peirce himself), psychologists (James) and philosophers of religion and science (Francis Abbot and John Fiske) debated questions of morality, science, and religion after Darwin. Green introduced Peirce to the theories of Alexander Bain, the English psychologist, in particular the theory that "belief is 'that upon which a . . . [person] is prepared to act.'"[20] Peirce was struck by this notion and expanded it into the theory of doubt and belief on which he based his taxonomy of methods of fixing belief:

> Our beliefs guide our desires and shape our actions. . . . The feeling of believing is a more or less sure indication of there being established in our nature some habit which will determine our actions. . . . Doubt is an uneasy and dissatisfied state from which we struggle to free ourselves and pass into a state of belief, while the latter is a calm and satisfactory state which we do not wish to avoid, or to change to a belief in anything else. . . .
>
> The irritation of doubt causes a struggle to attain a state of belief. I shall term this struggle *Inquiry*, though it must be admitted that this is sometimes not a very apt designation. . . .
>
> The irritation of doubt is the only immediate motive for the struggle to attain belief. . . . With the doubt . . . the struggle begins, and with the cessation of doubt it ends. Hence the sole object of inquiry is the settlement of opinion.[21]

On the basis of this theory, Peirce identified four prototypical methods of fixing belief in response to doubt, of which the third one underlies Cartesian intuitionism. The first is the method of tenacity, which is simply "taking as an answer to a question any we may fancy, and constantly reiterating it to ourselves, dwelling on all which may conduce to that belief, and learning to turn with contempt and hatred from anything that might disturb it."[22] Of course, this approach cannot hold its ground for very long in social practice.

A primary method for fixing belief in the community is, instead, that of authority: to "let an institution be created which shall have for its object to keep correct doctrines before the attention of the people, to reiterate them perpetually, and to teach them to the young; having at the same time power to prevent contrary doctrines from being taught, advocated or expressed." Peirce explained that, while this method has underwritten the development of strong, "priest-ridden states," it fails wherever citizens "possess a wider sort of social feeling." Observing the relativity of their inherited doctrines among the community of nations, these citizens suffer doubts about what they have learned on the basis of authority alone. They "further perceive that such doubts as these must exist in their minds with reference to every belief which seems to be determined by the caprice either of themselves or of those who originated the popular opinions." To settle these doubts, they appeal to a method of authoritative tenacity that Peirce dubbed the *"a priori* method."

According to Peirce, this third method for fixing belief, the *a priori* method, has until now been the darling of modern western philosophic tradition: it was anticipated by Plato and favored by Ockham, Descartes, Leibniz, even Kant and Hegel.[23] Proponents of this method say: "let the action of natural preferences be unimpeded . . . and, under their influence let men, conversing together and regarding matters in different lights, gradually develop beliefs in harmony with natural causes." Let them, in other words, believe what appears to be consistent with what *they* take to be their natural dispositions. According to Peirce, Descartes' approach boils down to this method alone. Having, like the enlightened citizens, lost faith in the mere authority of scholastic tradition, Descartes turned, instead, to the authority of his own deepest inclinations, which seemed to lead him, irresistibly, to the beliefs (1) that he did not doubt that he doubted, (2) that he had an idea of a perfect Being who is perfect necessarily, and (3) that that Being could not be a deceiver. In other words, if Descartes maintained his intuitionism independently of the empirical evidence, it is because he replaced scholastic authority with a new form of dogmatism. As restated in Susan Haack's very helpful formulation, Peirce believed that Descartes quieted his overgeneralized doubts (his "unwarranted skepticism") with an overstated certainty (an "unwarranted dogmatism").[24] Peirce argued that this method fails the way the method of authority failed: those who do not happen to share a given dogma will discover that dogmas, in general, may be relative to particular dispositions. Relativism does not, however, quiet our doubts.

This brings us to the turning point in Peirce's early pragmatism. By identifying the fallacy of modernism with *a priorism* in general rather than only with the intuitionist variety of *a priorism*, Peirce opened himself to his own criticism. He could now disclaim the cognitivism of his 1867-68 papers as another variety of *a priorism*, and he could replace it with something else. But with what? I do not believe that, deep down, he was yet certain, because *a priorism* remained as close to his heart as it was to Descartes', and, however much he saw its errors, he did not yet see very clearly how to avoid them. Thus, as I will explain in a moment, he argued strongly on behalf of science, defined in a new way, as the fourth method of fixing belief. But his arguments for this new science tended to reinforce the dogmatic habits of modernism as much as they introduced postmodern paradigms. His pragmatism seemed to offer a method for undoing dogmatic habits, but, not yet fully realizing its force, he tended to promote pragmatism as if it were another, better way of completing the modernist quest for *a priori* certainty. What else could he do? I believe the solution lay in his looking more carefully within, to discern precisely which of his tendencies encouraged his *a priorism* and which of them encouraged his pragmatism. If the solution did indeed lay within, then it took Peirce some thirty years to develop the epistemological tools he needed to get to know himself. For it was not until 1905 that Peirce made a clear break with his philosophic modernism.

Rather than lead you through all the ins and outs of Peirce's years of precise and yet equivocal argumentation, allow me to substitute a tally sheet of where, in his early pragmatism, his thinking led back to elements of modernism and where it pointed forward. The distinction between the backward and forward elements of Peirce's thinking will introduce a distinction to be made later between his modernism and postmodernism.

(1) On the subject of science as a better method of fixing belief:

Peirce's thinking led *forward* toward the view that, within its historical context, modernism is a sign of the failures of scholastic science and of the need for a new paradigm for conducting empirical inquiry. This means that modernists doubted the capacity of the Aristotelean-Church system to account for new discoveries in the natural world. To overcome the *a priorism* that they have asserted in place of scholastic authority, these modernists need, instead, to locate a method "by which our beliefs may be determined by nothing human, but by some external permanency—by something upon which our thinking has no effect." They were searching, in other words, for a new paradigm of science, based on the realist hypothesis that "there are Real things, whose characters are entirely independent of our opinions about them; . . . [which] Reals affect our senses according to regular, [knowable] laws," the investigation of which would lead anyone with sufficient experience and reason to true conclusions. This science would not proceed from induction to theory building (the intuitionist model), nor from theory to inferences deduced from it (the authoritarian model), but from hypothesis-making to the inductions through which they would be tested. Induction would be a way of calculating the probability that inquirers would experience the world in ways their hypotheses would lead them to expect. Hypothesis-making would be a way of generating expectations about portions of experience that remain as yet incompletely considered in the traditions of science inherited by modernity. These expectations would remain, at the same time, consistent with those presuppositions of scientific tradition that remain unquestioned. The clearest prototype for this way of conducting science is to be found in the emergent practice of laboratory experimentalism. We have yet to identify the analogues of laboratory experimentalism within the verities of empirical inquiry.

Peirce's thinking led *backward* toward the dogmatic view that this theory of science does not merely correct modernism within the scholastic context of its complaints, but offers, rather, the best possible model of how to conduct the enterprise of knowing. In this view, experimentalism is the answer to a series of foundational questions, among them, "If we offer hypotheses to extend knowledge beyond its present limits, on what are our hypotheses fundamentally grounded? How do we delimit the range of possibilities we might imagine?" Among the foundational answers Peirce offered is this one: "we have the good fortune of guessing correctly more often than chance would allow, because the human mind 'is strongly adapted to the comprehension of the world.'" (Peirce's foundational question is based on the modernist's assumption that, whenever we doubt or extend ourselves beyond the limits of traditional knowledge, we find ourselves stripped of normal, linguistic resources and left to confront nature itself, in the raw. We must then identify our ultimate source of knowledge: either a plenum of pure possibility or else our own instincts and sensations in their prelinguistic purity. In his answer—in this case, that our minds are adapted to the world—Peirce transformed an intriguing theory of evolutionary adaptation into the unnecessarily foundational claim that, when all else fails, our own instincts will display to us the fundamental laws of nature.[25] From the perspective of Peirce's postmodernism, however, the question need not arise in the first place, since our doubts leave intact a host of epistemic supports for inquiry, whose ultimate sources we cannot clearly identify.)

(2) On the subject of how modernists should transform their dogmatisms into patterns of inquiry that may settle their doubts:

Peirce introduced his pragmatism, formally, as a maxim about how we can make our ideas clear: "Consider what effects, that might conceivably have practical bearings, we conceive the object of our conception to have. Then, our conception of these effects is the whole of our conception of the object."[26] This pragmatic maxim meant different things, however, in Peirce's forward and backward thinking.

Peirce's thinking led *forward* to the view that the pragmatic maxim was directed specifically to modernists, offering them advice we might paraphrase this way: "You present as dogmas certain clear and distinct ideas about the world. Instead, you ought to ask yourselves either of two questions, both of which will give you the same answer. Ask from what practice of inquiry you have abstracted the ideas through which you present your dogmas. Or ask from what complex of observable behaviors you have abstracted your description of the objects signified by your dogmas. You will find that the practice of inquiry and the complex of observable behaviors are inseparable one from the other and that your dogmas are merely shorthand ways of drawing our attention to both of these. To overcome your dogmatism, go out now and tell us how the dogmas relate back to the practices and the complexes, what you specifically want to tell us about them, and what we have left to learn." Consider, for example, the nominalist dogma that we know only particulars. Applying the pragmatic maxim, nominalists might say that, in response to doubts about their inherited traditions of knowledge, they identified "universals" with the unreliable claims of their forebears and "particulars" with whatever judgments of experience they could make themselves, without relying on such claims. In other words, offering the dogma was a way of expressing their disappointment with both their forebears' claims and their forebears' insistence that these claims be accepted on authority. We might imagine that, if pressed, erstwhile nominalists might agree to abandon their own universal claim about particulars, in exchange for a policy of testing and, if necessary, revising those traditional claims that they had specific reasons to doubt.

Peirce's thinking led *backwards* to the view that pragmatism provided an epistemological alternative to Cartesian intuitionism. In this view, modernist dogmatisms arose out of the errant assumption that knowing a thing clearly is simply a matter of getting our ideas about it in order, as if there corresponded to everything in the world some single set of ideas that represented truly what it really is. The way to correct this assumption is to replace it with the pragmatic assumption that knowing a thing means being able to anticipate how it would act or appear in given circumstances. When we claim to know something, we mean knowing in this second sense. The pragmatic maxim thus tells us what we do when we claim to know something. (The problem with this version of pragmatism is that it adopts what it calls the modernist assumption of knowledge in the very process of attempting to refute it. This version places pragmatic and modernist claims side by side, as if they were two competing views of the way humans actually know things, one view being true and the other false. This is, however, to adopt the modernist assumption that knowing something—in this case, human knowledge—clearly is to represent it as it really is. A corollary problem with this version of pragmatism is that it offers modernism a rebuttal rather than a remedy: rather than offer modernists a way of discovering the truths within or behind their claims, it suggests that they abandon these claims in favor of some others.)

(3) Finally, then, to return to the subject of Peirce's critique of modernist conceptions of the self:[27]

Peirce's pragmatism generated the metaphysical claim that the "soul" of anything, human or extrahuman, is its tendency to act in certain ways in certain circumstances. Peirce put this claim to the service of his different ways of thinking.

His thinking led *backwards* to the view that the modernist conception of the self was simply erroneous, built on a failed logic and an empty metaphysics and contributing to unethical conduct. This erroneous conception was that the human self is an incorporeal substance, ultimately unknowable, self-contained and ultimately self-referring; that it is the subject of all perceptions and cogitations; that it asserts itself, over against the material substance to which it is attached, over against the world, and over against other selves. According to this view of Peirce's, such a conception is false because it is incompatible with a pragmatic conception of the human soul. As a complex of tendencies to act, the soul must be corporeal (as well as incorporeal), knowable, relational, and other-referring; it must mediate between subjects and objects of knowing, among other selves and the world. The modernist self appears only as the negation of the actual life of such a soul. "The individual man, since his separate existence is manifested only by ignorance and error, so far as he is anything apart from his fellows, and from what he and they are to be, is only a negation."[28]

Peirce's thinking led *forward* to the view that the modernist conception of the self was an assertion of loneliness and distress, of complaint and the need for truth and love, of the plenitude of possibility as well as the fearsomeness of infinity. In this view of Peirce's, the modernist self is, indeed, an abstraction and thus an incomplete sign. But it is the sort of sign that calls for a redeeming love: the compassionate interpretation that would relink the sign to the community of interpretation in which it displayed its full meaning. Unlike Job's sorry comforters, the compassionate interpreter would not suppose that the process of relinking was an obvious affair. To relink the sign to its context of meaning would be to reintroduce the self to its community of practice, in which it would find its particular history and a more open future. Because, however, the self is a sign of inadequacies in that very community, such a reintroduction would come only through great effort, involving the reformation of community as well as the transformation of self. In the process, the community would itself appear as a self, or as an individuated part of a wider society, and its wider society would appear this way, as well. The emergent, postmodern understanding of the modern self would relink conceptions of self to conceptions of the human soul as a center of ways of acting. This relinking would not be merely a conceptual affair, but a matter of real work.

III. FROM MODERN PRAGMATISM
TO POSTMODERN PRAGMATICISM

In the 1877-78 "Illustrations of the Logic of Science," Peirce first offered his pragmatism to the world. In a series of articles published in *The Monist* in 1905, he threatened to take his pragmatism back. He claimed that, in the intervening years, the scholarly world had misrepresented what pragmatism really means, forcing him, at this time, to re-explain and, in fact, rename it. Speaking of himself, he wrote

His word "pragmatism" has gained general recognition in a generalized
sense that seems to argue power of growth and vitality. The famed psychologist, James, first took it up, seeing that his "radical empiricism"
substantially answered to the writer's definition of pragmatism, albeit
with a certain difference in the point of view. Next, the admirably clear
and brilliant thinker, Mr. Ferdinand C. S. Schiller, casting about for a
more attractive name for the "anthropomorphism" of his *Riddle of the
Sphinx*, lit . . . upon the same designation "pragmatism." . . . So far all
went happily. But at present, the word begins to be met with occasionally
in the literary journals, where it gets abused in the merciless way that
words have to expect when they fall into literary clutches. Sometimes the
manners of the British have effloresced in scolding at the word as ill-
chosen—ill-chosen, that is, to express some meaning that it was rather
designed to exclude. So then, the writer, finding his bantling "pragmatism" so promoted, feels that it is time to kiss his child good-by and
relinquish it to its higher destiny; while to serve the precise purpose of
expressing the original definition, he begs to announce the birth of the
word "*pragmaticism*," which is ugly enough to be safe from kidnap-
pers.[29]

We might take Peirce's protestations with a grain of salt. As Peirce averred in
a footnote, he had never previously made popular use of the term "pragmatism"
in writing. In his 1907 lecture "What Pragmatism Means," James recalled that
Peirce's principle of pragmatism

lay entirely unnoticed by any one for twenty years, until I, in an address
before Professor Howison's Philosophical Union at the University of
California,[30] brought it forward again and made a special application of it
to religion.[31] By that date the times seemed ripe for its reception. The
word "pragmatism" spread, and at present it fairly spots the pages of the
philosophic journals.[32]

While grateful for the publicity, and generally pleased by James' work,
Peirce found James' pragmatism itself too "nominalistic" for his purposes. As
John E. Smith writes, "James, with his incipient nominalism, was always hes-
itant about allowing concepts to have any other than a representational meaning
or a surrogate function."[33] Peirce's pragmaticism was thus a response to James
as well as to the "literary circles." But on what was this response based? Peirce
claimed that he was returning to his "original definition." However, as I have
suggested earlier, Peirce spent many years taking up his original definition in a
modernist, as well as a postmodernist, way. Peirce's misinterpreters were led by
the modernist (or "backward") tendency in Peirce's own writings. This all

means that pragmaticism was Peirce's way of kissing good-by to the child of his own modernism, of which the nominalisms of his interpreters were mere reflections.

I belabor these autobiographical points not as a matter of mere scholarly erudition, but, rather, to suggest that the principles of Peirce's postmodernism are principles of critical self-reflection, of which Peirce's own self-corrections are prototypical. We will take "pragmaticism" to be a general label for the way Peirce sought to recover what, in our terms, was postmodern in his earlier studies of pragmatism and to elide what was not. Returning to the distinctions I made between what was *forward*- and what was *backward*-looking in Peirce's pragmatism, we may then relabel pragmaticism a restatement of the principles displayed in his forward-looking thinking. I mentioned three areas of forward thinking on Peirce's part. These areas may be viewed as various expressions of a single tendency of thinking, of which we may discern the following aspects, or subtendencies. (The order of presentation here is arbitrary. On this occasion, I am portraying postmodern thinking as a reflection on the way modernist thinking responds to problems in premodern "practice," which means premodern patterns of thinking-and-acting. Each of the aspects I describe represents what I am picturing to be stages or moments in this process of reflection. I am obviously asking for a little trust at this point, because I have not yet displayed the criteria I used to distinguish forward from backward, or postmodern from modern, tendencies. I am trying to display the criteria in use, before labelling them abstractly. Once you get through this, you will see what I was doing and will then have the freedom to evaluate it.)

The first aspect is the *negative or critical character* of Peirce's forward thinking, which began with the discovery of a problem in modernist thinking. Peirce's postmodern thinking began as a way of responding to problems, rather than as a way of generating ideas for their own sake. Its occasion was not wonder or curiosity or assertion, but rather the intrusion of something insistent and unpleasant: a kind of suffering. It was therefore an activity whose subject matter lay behind it, as the still unknown source of the discomforts that moved it forward.

A second aspect is the *reflexive character* of Peirce's forward thinking, which was a way of recollecting the source of discomfort out of which it arose. The negativity of Peirce's postmodernism was thus merely a reflection of the negativity of modernity. Modernist thinking *expresses* this negativity, while postmodernist thinking identifies it *as* negative: identifying the discomforts of modernity as symptoms of disruptions in modernity's antecedent traditions of practice. From this perspective, postmodernist thinking is modernist thinking reflecting on itself, its origins and its future. Peirce's later writings on *self-control* and on *semiotics* displayed his attentiveness to the phenomenon of reflexivity.[34] Reflection is an activity of *self-control*, and *semiotics* displays its logic: interpreting negative thinking as the *sign* of some antecedent problem—as *object*—and of some consequent response—as what Peirce called the *interpretant* of a sign. (On self-control, Peirce wrote that "the term 'reasoning' ought to be confined to such fixation of one belief by another as is reasonable, deliberate, self-controlled";[35] and, "the pragmaticist does not make the *summum bonum* to consist in action, but makes it to consist in that process of evolution whereby the existent comes more and more to embody [real generals, which are general conditional propositions as to the future] . . . , which is what we strive to express in calling them *reasonable*. In its higher stages, evolution takes place more and more largely through self-control. . . . "[36])

A third aspect is the contribution Peirce's forward thinking made to *solving whatever problem* stimulated it. Peirce's postmodernist thinking was a *performative activity*, which embodied its purposes in the way it actually responded to the discomforts of modernity. Its reflexivity was thus not an end in itself, but a moment in an extended process of referring the complaints of modernity back to the antecedent practices to which they refer and then forward to the reformation of practice to which it contributes. While prompted by suffering, Peirce's postmodernism was thus animated by hope.

A fourth aspect is the *reaffirmation* implicit in Peirce's forward thinking. If his postmodernism reflected the negativity of modernity, it also exhibited the relationship of modernity to its antecedent practices, which Peirce identified with the practices of scholastic philosophy and science. Peirce considered these practices to be the sources of both the problems of modernity *and* the capacity of modernity to solve those problems. He said the best way to understand this duality is to conceive of there being two levels of regularity within the practices. On one level, the practices apply to context-specific ways of acting and are thus highly informative, but subject more readily to change, since they must be responsive to the variable character of their contexts. All practices of which we are conscious belong to this first level. The second level is inhabited by all those practices of which we are not ordinarily conscious: what he would later call the original, commonsense beliefs that we share with members of our species, or perhaps with culture-specific subgroups of the species. These practices are indubitable for all practical purposes and therefore appear to be neither context-specific nor informative. Nevertheless, we must conceive of these practices as providing the rules that inform our reflections on the first-level practices.

Note that Peirce conceived of these levels of practice in a relational way: the second level was indubitable only relative to our experiences of the world. He meant that, if modernists have doubts about antecedent practices, then these are, by definition, doubts about first-level practices,[37] offered with respect to the rules of judgment and doubt provided by second-level practices.[38] He believed that his pragmatism belonged to and exhibited the rules of modernity's second-level practices: for that reason, in fact, both he and James considered pragma-tism "a new name for an old way of thinking." Applying to scholastic thinking the same reflexivity he applied to modernist thinking, Peirce was prepared to identify this old way of thinking with the deeper level of the scholastics' own inherited practices. The ground of Peirce's hope lay therefore in his reaffirming the ancient or, ultimately, primeval roots of modern practices, as exhibited in chronologically successive contexts of critical thinking.[39]

A fifth aspect is the *fallibilistic character* of Peirce's forward thinking. Invoking the terminology of the Scotch commonsense realists,[40] Peirce called his reaffirmation of our indubitable beliefs his "commonsensism." He added, however, that the commonsense realists erred in imagining that the second-level practices were indubitable in any and all circumstances: "one thing the Scotch failed to recognize is that the original beliefs only remain indubitable in their application to affairs that resemble those of a primitive mode of life."[41] For example, he wrote that while we act on the belief that there are only three dimensions, "it is . . . quite open to reasonable doubt whether the motions of electrons are confined to three dimensions, although it is good methodeutic to presume that they are until some evidence to the contrary is forthcoming."[42] Peirce named his position *critical* commonsensism. All practices are poten-tially corrigible. "Not only is our knowledge thus limited in scope, but it is even more important that we should thoroughly realize that the very best of what we, humanly speaking, know [we know] only in an uncertain and inexact way."[43] The negativity of modernity was a sign of this uncertainty and, thus, of postmodernity's need to reform a first level of practices, as guided by a second level of practices. Peirce recognized that the second level was potentially cor-rigible. ("'Indubitability,' for Peirce, did not mean 'absolute certainty.' Rather, it meant 'freedom from genuine doubt.'"[44]) He also recognized that this poten-tiality did not preclude its functioning, now, as the condition of our knowing the real. As we will discuss later, he believed that the fallibility of human knowl-edge is, rather, a sign of the indefinite character of the real itself.

A sixth aspect is the role of *creativity and imagination* in Peirce's for-ward thinking. Peirce sought to reform first-level practices by reaffirming the reformatory guidance offered by second-level practices. To doubt the authority of one practice—for example, obedience to the church, or to the Aristotelean syllogistic—we rely on the authority of more fundamental standards of behav-ior or of reasoning. Peirce argued, however, that these deeper practices are not informative in themselves. They reveal themselves only *in actu* and, that means, only relative to the tasks we ask them to perform. On one level, this means that we would, following Kant, attempt to discover the fundamental practices by asking what all our other practices must presuppose. This also means, however, that our presuppositions would only be as revealing as our practices; our inquiry would be limited by the kinds of practice we know how to practice. We might expect the pragmatist to answer, "But the limit of knowledge is simply that: the limit of action!" Without officially departing from the disciplines of his pragmatism, Peirce stretched this answer to its limits by adding words that I will paraphrase, less formally, in this way: "Then again, the limit of action is the limit of *conceivable* action. In this sense, we know how to practice whatever we can conceive of practicing, and we discover more about our presuppositions the more we expand our capacities to conceive of what we *might* do on this earth, even if what we might do remains a way of reforming what we already do."

Peirce invented the term *abductive reasoning* to refer to the inquiry we undertake to generate hypotheses about how we might reform what we already do. He believed this mode of reasoning was a power as well as a skill that could be improved by practice and by discipline. And he believed that, by improving our capacity to imagine new possibilities, we deepened our capacity to display our fundamental beliefs. Of course, abductive reasoning generates mere hypotheses. Peirce argued that, to separate the fundamental from the fanciful, we had to test our hypotheses' usefulness in actually reforming our practices and, thus, resolving the real doubts and problems that stimulated our inquiry in the first place. To test them, he suggested we employ what he called the methods of deductive reasoning (to indicate precisely how, if successful, the hypotheses *would* contribute to the reform of antecedent practices) and inductive reasoning (to evaluate their success in actual practice).[45]

We have, then, a collection of six aspects of Peirce's actual practice of forward thinking, which was negative, reflexive, devoted to problem-solving, affirming of original beliefs, fallibilistic, and creative. What does this tell us? If we were modernists, we might ask, "What does philosophy have to learn from descriptions of a particular person's style of thinking? If this person were creator of our world, we might take these to be descriptions of our god's essential attributes and see in these attributes the limits toward which the activities of this world might tend. But Peirce is no god, and the most we can see in these descriptions are the attributes of his own creative activity, his own world. We learn very little about *our* various worlds, or about any world we might share." If we were the relativistic sort of postmodernists, we might admire the beauty, power, or curiosity of this person's style of thinking, all the while treating with some condescension his apparent belief that his critique of modernity told us something positive about a world we share. We would see in his style of thinking only a style of thinking, acceptable and even attractive as long as it abandoned its claim to be any more than that. In the context of this book, however, we bring to the study of Peirce's thinking the perspective of a nonrelativistic postmodernism. This means we are predisposed to accept his claim that, after the critique of modernist intuitionism and substantialism, philosophy may still have something to say about the world we share or, to reinvoke scholastic terminology, something to say about "the real." This critique means, however, that we do not expect philosophy to talk about the real the same way it did previously. In this essay, we consider the claim that Peirce displayed a new way of talking about the real. But, up to this point, all we have before us are descriptions of his postmodern manner of thinking. What do these descriptions tell us about the real?

I hesitate to trot out the "principles of Peirce's postmodernism" as an answer to this question, because I do not want to give the impression that these principles were the kinds of propositions dogmatic metaphysicians offered before Kant and, then again, among the romantic responses to Kant. Peirce's critique of Cartesianism meant that he could no longer portray himself as having arrived at certain propositions whose subjects designated reality and whose predicates designated reality's essential characters. He rejected the notion that we know reality by arriving at propositions that mirror it. His postmodern thinking implied, instead, that we know reality by imitating it in our own activity: the way a theologian would say we know God by imitating God, or the way Jesus said "Follow me and leave self behind." That is, "leave behind the *ego cogito*, whose abstractions do not imitate God or God's creation, and follow me, instead, with your *whole* being." Our descriptions of Peirce's forward thinking are not adequate representations of his whole being, but, within the limits of a philosophic study like this, they are meant at least to symbolize it. In Whitehead's terms, they represent *prehensions* of reality within the context of Peirce's work. In what we are about to learn are Peirce's terms, they represent the *interpretants* of reality within Peirce's work. This means that they belong "merely" to Peirce's life, but also that Peirce's life, like any life displayed in its wholeness, really tells us about the reality it interprets. Like all lives displayed in their wholeness, Peirce's life was more than Peirce's. If we take it up into our lives, in their wholeness, then it implicates our lives as well.

It takes an indefinitely long time to display the wholeness of a life, and, in philosophic conversation, we ask to get to the bottom of a life in a very short time. Even in its postmodern form, philosophic conversation is therefore somewhat abusive. Nevertheless, we know that, on pages like these, we are simply trying to offer brief glimpses of processes that continue to run deeply even as we describe them. We know that these glimpses do not display the realities of which they are glimpses until we have fleshed them out within our own lives. We know, then, that there is no single, privileged way in which they display their realities. Yet we also trust that, in bringing these glimpses into our various lives, as we do, we also share in some activity that is one despite the irreducible multiplicity of its appearances. The glimpses we presume to offer are offered, therefore, merely as attempts to share with one another our firm sense and our fallible understanding of the oneness that binds us together: the oneness of a process that is symbolized for us in the ways we find to identify what we share with another human life.

In the following section, I attempt to identify what we might share with Peirce's life by posing certain questions of his life that may be of interest to us in the context of this volume. Of course, Peirce is not here to answer, but our interest need not, at any rate, be merely in what Peirce would literally have said. What he literally wrote were answers to questions posed by his contemporaries, and these are not necessarily questions we are asking now. We may, instead, take the risk of imagining Peirce's responding to questions he may not have asked in the way we are asking them. We would thereby elicit answers that belong, at once, to our lives (for we posed the questions), to the life about which we are asking (displayed through Peirce's writing), and to the specific context we are considering. For the present discussion, I will define these triply limited and triply relational answers as *the principles of a life*. This will be my way of introducing *principles* into our discussion without fearing that I have led you to associate these principles with dogmatic propositions. I will, then, present the principles of Peirce's post-modernism *as the answers I imagine the forward-thinking Peirce would have offered to a series of questions of interest to us as nonrelativistic postmodernists.*

IV. THE PRINCIPLES OF PEIRCE'S POSTMODERNISM

We begin with three preliminary questions, the answers to which constitute a first principle of postmodernism, or a principle about principles. The first question is: if, in its wholeness, any human life tells us about the reality it interprets, why would we want to learn about other lives? The answer is that every life tells us about the real, but in a finite way, which means that learning about other lives is a way to expand the limits of our own finitude and learn about reality more fully. The second question is: why would we learn more from Peirce's life than from another life? The answer is that a reflective life is one that asks questions about itself and, therefore, generates answers. Living his life in a particularly reflective way, Peirce generated a particularly informative array of answers. These answers may function as *principles of life* for those who may ask similar questions. The third question is: why would these function as principles of postmodern living in particular? According to the perspective I have adopted in this essay, the answer is that the questions Peirce asked of himself were principally questions about the burdens of his own modernist thinking. The greatest of these burdens was the gulf he sensed between his modernist thinking and the needs of everyday life, including *his* everyday life. The principles of postmodern living are ways of living in response to, hopefully as a remedy to, one's own modernism.

The primary questions we will ask the postmodern Peirce to answer are:

what kind of activity is your postmodernist thinking? what does it tell us about? and, to whom does it tell this? His imagined answers will represent the principles of Peirce's postmodernism.

A. What Kind of Activity is Peirce's Postmodern Thinking?

Principle A1: It is a semiotic activity. I have structured this essay so far according to the most powerful principle I see embedded in Peirce's work: that postmodern thinking is a way of interpreting the meaning of modernist thinking. Peirce's most powerful instrument for articulating the process of interpretation was *semiotics*, or the science of signs he later came to identify with logic. He called the process of sign interpretation *semiosis*,[46] meaning "an action, or influence, which is, or involves, a cooperation of *three* subjects, such as a sign, its object and its interpretant, this tri-relative influence not being in any way resolvable into actions between pairs."[47] He would say that, in the process of interpretation, we interpret some entity as a *sign* that refers to its *object*, or meaning, with respect to some *interpretant*, or mode of interpretation for which the sign displays that meaning. Semiosis is thus always a relational activity involving three entities. Before considering how Peirce's postmodern thinking may appear as a process of sign interpretation, allow me to explain somewhat more technically how Peirce identified the three elements of semiosis in general.

Peirce said that his semiotics presupposed two formal sciences. The first was *mathematics*, by which he meant not merely various theories of quantity, but also what others may call formal logic: "the study of what is true of hypothetical states of things."[48] We might call this the disciplined study of creative imagination: a process of diagramming, or drawing pictures of, the elemental rules the imagination suggests to itself when left fully to its own devices. For example, a thinker may take a blank page, then draw a dot on it, then a line and a dot, then a line connecting two dots, and so on. What unseen rule guides the thinker's drawing? Peirce discovered that, giving his imagination a free voice, he was not satisfied to draw any single diagram, but was moved to construct another diagram and another: "Beginning with suitable examples and thence proceeding to others, one finds that the diagram itself, in its individuality, is not what the reasoning is concerned with. . . . In passing [rather] from one diagram to the other, the [reasoner] . . . will be supposed to *see* something, which will present this little difficulty for the theory of vision, that it is of a *general nature*."[49] This *seeing* is a way of conceiving the rule whose urgings led the reasoner to draw the individual diagrams. Of course, the seeing is itself a kind of diagramming, which means the process can continue on and on. Peirce found that the minimal elements of any such diagramming are three: the initial act of drawing something, the repetition or iteration of the act, and the activity of linking the repetitions together.[50] The simplest way to diagram the act of diagramming would, then, be to distinguish between what Peirce called the *monadic* character of a simple act, the *dyadic* character of a repetition (one act plus one act) and the *triadic* character of the act of linkage (one plus one plus the linkage or relation).

The second science presupposed by semiotics was *phenomenology*,[51] which "treats of the universal Qualities of Phenomena,"[52] or of "the collective total of all that is in any way or in any sense present to the mind."[53] Put crudely, the phenomenologists' job is to see how much sense they can make of our experiences by supposing that the elemental characters of mathematical reasoning, or of imagination, will appear again as the most general qualities of all phenomena. Peirce thus identified the three categories of experience as Firstness, Secondness, and Thirdness. He labelled "Firsts" all phenomena that display merely monadic or simple qualities, such as simple states of consciousness, like the feeling of redness. He labelled "Seconds" all phenomena that display dyadic qualities, such as divided states of consciousness, in which something inner is opposed to something outer. An example of the latter is the shock of surprise, which signals the interruption of one state by something other. He labelled "Thirds" all phenomena that display triadic qualities: these are all phenomena of mediation, relationality, or representation. Signs are paradigmatic Thirds.

Within his phenomenology, Peirce defined a sign as something that stands *for* something (its object) *to* the idea that it produces or modifies (its *interpretant*).[54] Once again, the key to Peirce's semiotic is his conception of the tri-relationality of the sign. A sign is obviously not a sign just by itself, but it is also not a sign if considered merely in relation to its object: as if a sign (*signe* for de Saussure) had a meaning *(signifié)* in general—some privileged partner out there in the universe to which it was connected independently of some third something, some mediator. For Peirce such a two-part relation would be an instance of mere Secondness, such as the rude shock of an unexpected encounter—a real event, but one as yet without any meaning. In fact, we may consider the reduction of signification to dyadic relations an emblem of modernist nominalism: an emblem of the belief that our concepts are records of merely chance or brute encounters. This belief implies that we can make whatever use we wish of such records, but that we cannot expect them to guide us. A genuine sign is, instead, a sign that has its meaning *with respect to* its interpretant. This means that meaning is not simply projected out into empty space, but is offered to some being for some reason. Meaning is an aspect of relationship. A sign relates beings together.

Technically speaking, Peirce classified phenomenology as the first subscience of philosophy. He said the business of philosophy "is to find out all that can be found out from those universal experiences which confront every [person] in every waking hour."[55] As pragmaticist, he added that we seek to find these things out in order to solve the problems that arise in everyday experience. Within this inquiry, phenomenology sketches out the elemental qualities of everyday experience. What he called the "normative sciences"—aesthetics, ethics and logic—identify the rules of reasoning and practice we adopt in making assertions about everyday experience and, thus, in solving the problems that confront us. Metaphysics, finally, articulates a vision of the entire universe of mind and matter that we would inhabit if those rules of reasoning and practice were rules of being itself. Within this scheme, Peirce came to employ semiotics as his language of logic.[56] It is a particularly integrative language, which enables us both to perceive the elements of experience that delimit the activity of reasoning and to imagine the rules of being that issue from it.

For the semiotician, reasoning is itself a process of semiosis, the elements of which are all the possible kinds of relationship that can connect sign to sign, sign to object, sign to interpretant, object to interpretant, sign to object to interpretant, and so on. For example, Peirce said a sign can refer to its object in any of three ways. An *icon* is a sign that refers to its object "by virtue of characters of its own, and which it possesses . . . whether any such object actually exists or not." An example is a painting, which depicts its object only by virtue of the oil, brush, canvas and imagination of the painter. An *index* is a sign that refers to its object "by virtue of really being affected by that object," as well as by sharing some quality in common with the object. An example is a weather vane, which is actually moved by the wind whose directionality it both shares and depicts. A *symbol* is a sign that refers to its object "by virtue of a law . . . which operates to cause the symbol to be interpreted as referring to that object. . . . " Not only is the symbol itself "a general type, or law . . . but the object to which it refers is [also] of a general nature."[57] Examples of symbols are linguistic terms or predicates, propositions and arguments, all of which are partial embodiments of genuine or triadic processes of semiosis.[58]

Terms, such as "scholastic thinking," or predicates, such as "_____ is an index of problems in scholastic thinking," symbolize the iconic or monadic character of a process of semiosis. Propositions, such as "Modernist thinking is an index of problems in scholastic thinking," symbolize the indexical or dyadic character of a process of semiosis. Such arguments as the following one symbolize the symbolic or triadic character of a process of semiosis:

> Modernist thinking is a way of criticizing the inadequacies of traditions of practice in general.
> Problems in scholastic thinking may give rise to criticisms of the inadequacies of traditions of practice in general.
> Modernist thinking may be an index of problems in scholastic thinking.

Such arguments, finally, presuppose the formal and material *leading principles* that enable us to reason from their premises to their conclusions. In this case, among the formal principles is the rule of abduction or hypothesis-making, which enables us to say "If A is B, and C can be signified by B, then maybe A is a sign of C." Among the material principles are theories of postmodern thinking—Peirce's theory, for example, which was a tendency of thinking that provided a context of interpretation, or interpretant, with respect to which modernist thinking appeared as a *sign* whose *meaning* was that something is wrong with the practices out of which modernist thinking emerged. Peirce diagrammed this tendency in the process of reflecting on his own modernist thinking. His pragmaticism emerged when he said, in effect, "Aha! My own merely critical thinking was an indexical *sign* that displays its *meaning* when I locate the *interpretant* that allows me to reform my precritical practices in ways hinted at in that sign. My postmodern thinking is this interpretant." The first element of Peirce's postmodern thinking that we have considered is his semiotics, in terms of which he abstracted the elemental or formal elements of his discovery, as if to say: "As a modernist, I understood my claims as signs that referred to their objects generally, apart from any particular context of meaning. Now I understand these claims as signs that deliver their meanings *to* the particular process of interpretation I am now articulating."

Principle A2: Peirce's postmodern thinking is a method of habit-change. Using the language of Peirce's semiotics, we can identify the formal properties of his postmodern thinking, viewed as an interpretive process and as part of the interpretive processes that link together his modernist criticism and his precritical practices. However, the formality of semiotics might tempt us to overlook the bodily dimension of thinking. And studying the coherence of an interpretive process might tempt us to overlook the transformational character of postmodern thinking. The bodily dimension and transformational character of Peirce's postmodernism are displayed more fully in terms of his *theory of habit-change*.

In their Metaphysical Club sessions of the 1870s, Peirce and James paid a great deal of attention to Alexander Bain's psychological studies of human habits of reasoning. In his *Principles of Psychology*, James wrote that "when we look at living creatures from an outward point of view, one of the first things that strike us is that they are bundles of habits. . . . The habits to which there is an innate tendency are called instincts; some of those due to education would by most persons be called acts of reason."[59] He added that

> the moment one tries to define what habit is, one is led to the fundamental properties of matter. The laws of Nature are nothing but the immutable habits which the different elemental sorts of matter follow

in their actions and reactions upon each other. In the organic world, however, the habits are more variable than this. . . . Organic matter, especially
nervous tissue, seems endowed with a very extraordinary degree of plasticity [meaning, "the possession of a structure weak enough to yield to an
influence, but strong enough not to yield all at once"]. . . . We may without hesitation lay down as our first proposition the following, that *the
phenomena of habit in living beings are due to the plasticity of the
organic materials of which their bodies are composed.*[60]

In the same year that James published his *Psychology*, Peirce located
the riddle of existence in this plasticity. He called it the capacity of protoplasm
to feel (and thus "to take on ideas"), to respond to stimuli (and thus "to react" or
be moved), to allow feelings to spread (and thus "to generalize" or "to grow"),
to form habits (and thus to acquire rules of behavior) and to forget or lose
excitability (and thus to "to select" certain rules of behavior and let others
go).[61] In these writings, Peirce devoted most of his attention to the phenomenon
of habit-taking, or of acquiring the capacity to act in a certain way under certain
circumstances.[62] We learn about the world, he said, not simply by forming
ideas in response to stimuli, but by forming habits of responding to the world.
This means, he concluded, that the Cartesian and Platonic picture-theory of
knowledge is inadequate: the world is not something we can depict in the way
we organize our ideas, but only something whose processual character we can
embody, and in that sense imitate, in the ways we act.[63] In these terms, a way of
thinking is a habit of thinking. If the world is viewed as a great sign, then a
habit of thinking is what Peirce called the logical, or ultimate, *interpretant* of
that sign. This means that we display the *meaning* of the world in the capacities
we acquire to act in response to the world.

But what if our habits of thinking prove faulty? In his writings on pragmaticism, Peirce directed his attention to the phenomenon of *habit-change*, or
the modification of a person's tendencies toward action. Among the sources of
habit-change, he listed "experiences forced upon" the mind; acts of will or
"muscular effort"; and "efforts of the imagination," which are ways of imagining how we might act in the future.[64] Peirce was most interested in the latter:
those "experimentations in the inner world" that enable us to test out our habits
of action without muscular effort, to examine and criticize the likely results of
our efforts and, then, to recommend to ourselves alternative ways of acting. He
claimed that, by repeating such recommendations to ourselves, we may be
able to alter our habits of action as well as we could through physical exercise.[65]

Peirce made these claims at the same time that he was framing his pragmaticism: as if he had abstracted his theory of habit-change from his own
activity of changing his merely modernist habits of thinking into postmodern
ones. We might then redescribe Peirce's postmodern thinking as a method of

habit-change—in particular, as a way of transforming his modernist habit of criticism into a habit of reforming precritical habits of action in response to modernist criticism. In this redescription, we would not characterize postmodern thinking as a mere habit, but, rather, as an activity of *habit-change*. Like modernist thinking, it is a critical activity; unlike it, it is a critique of mere criticism, and, thus, a reaffirmation—a *reforming* reaffirmation. From the attention Peirce paid to the various sources of habit-change, we may infer, furthermore, that Peirce understood his postmodern turn to be the result of his thought experiments more than of some transforming encounter or of some spontaneous act of will. This would mean that Peirce's postmodernism was, in sum, a reforming reaffirmation of his precritical habits of action, stimulated by his imaginative reflections on how his modernist criticisms actually influenced the ways he might act in the world.

Principle A3: Peirce's postmodern thinking is an activity of pragmatic inquiry. If we were to review the principles we have considered so far in terms of Peirce's phenomenology, we might say that principle A1 displays the Firstness of Peirce's postmodern thinking, its formal coherence, while principle A2 displays its Secondness, its capacity to transform actual behavior. We might then look for principle A3 to display the Thirdness of Peirce's postmodernism, or the actual and coherent process of inquiry according to which Peirce sought to transform precritical practices into reformed or postcritical practices. This is the process of pragmatic inquiry *per se*.

As Peirce argued in 1878 and continued to argue in his mature work, pragmatic inquiry begins with real doubt: in John Dewey's helpful terms, it emerges out of a "problematic situation."[66] Peirce emphasized the *reality* of this doubt to distinguish his critical commonsensism from Descartes' attempt to launch inquiry out of the academic exercise of feigning doubts. "Do you call it *doubting*," he asked, "to write down on a piece of paper that you doubt? If so, doubt has nothing to do with any serious business."[67] Peirce explained that the danger of adopting what he dubbed "paper doubts" was that, in pretending to doubt what we trust (the philosophic modernist's way of "crying wolf!"), we fall into the habit of mistrusting the very principles of reasoning we need to resolve the problems that actually confront us. On the basis of his theories of signs and of habits, he argued that *real* doubt, on the other hand, is the most reliable index of our immediate contact with reality. We may summarize his argument as follows.

If our habits of thought-and-practice are ultimate interpretants of the world as a vast symbol, then we know the world intimately only through these habits. Unlike the "sense impressions" described by the nominalistic empiricists, however, these habits are not simply forced upon us through our encounters with the world. The world is, indeed, what we actually encounter through the senses, but Peirce's critique of nominalism means that we do not *know* what we encounter simply by sensing it. Our "knowledge" of the world is the way we have learned to act successfully in it, where "success" is judged by the degree to which our interactions with the world display the effects we expect them to display. But when and how do we evaluate this success? Every time I look at a tree, do I ask myself, "Is that the way I expected it would look?" First of all, "seeing" is not the right metaphor to invoke here, because the knowledge we are discussing concerns our encountering the *realities* of things and not merely their appearances. Peirce argued early on in his work that we have acquired our conception of "reality" from scholastic usage, where *realitas* referred to the *forcible* character of the world: its insistence on being something whether I like it or not or, in Peirce's pragmatic terminology, the *difference* it makes for the way I live in the world. When I look at a tree, I do not usually ask myself what difference the tree makes in how I live; this means I am not usually interested in knowing about the tree's reality. But what if a tree falls on my house? or what if I need its lumber to warm my house and cook my food? or what if we discover that the life-sustaining character of our atmosphere depends on the tree's health? or what, finally, if I discover that the kind of creature I happen to be is one that lives well only in the company of trees? In all these cases, the tree makes a great difference in how I live. And in all these cases, I say I know the tree when my interactions with it do not surprise me. When they do surprise me, I say I want to inquire further, to find out what's there. According to Peirce, my surprise is a sign that the ways I have learned to interact with the tree are inadequate: for example, that cutting down every tree for fuel is not what I wanted to do, or that assuming that this specimen belongs to the genus *Acer* was not what I wanted to assume. According to Peirce, finally, my lack of surprise is a sign that, at this moment, the tree and I share a settled relationship. A settled relationship is one I am not concerned to examine further, which suggests that, for me, my lack of surprise would not be a sign at all, because it would be something about which I would not find myself thinking.

Pragmatists have a tendency to argue that "if belief ain't broke, don't fix it"—in other words, that we must assume our beliefs are true if we have no reason to doubt them. If we follow this maxim, however, how can we distinguish between true beliefs and potentially false yet untested ones, or between knowing truly and knowing nothing? Peirce's response was embedded in his philosophic practice but not clearly explicated. It was that the only way to know whether or not our habits correspond to the world is to *act* on them and, then, to feel reassured that the habits that work as we expect them to are *reliable* sources of knowledge and to *know* that the habits that fail to work as expected are unreliable and must be reformed. Peirce would then affirm Socrates' maxim, but in this modified way: the un*lived* and thus unexamined life is not worth living. For we cannot examine habits we have not enacted, and it is up to the world and not ourselves to declare that our habits need re-examination. The first Peircean maxim is, therefore, "Engage the world actively and without prejudgment!" The second maxim is, "Examine thoroughly whatever you have reason to doubt!" The third is, "Find within the habits you have no reason to doubt the principles that will guide you in reforming those you must doubt!" Trusting these deeper habits is what Peirce called *commonsensism.* Trusting that experience might one day call even these habits into question is what Peirce called *fallibilism.* Fallibilism is not skepticism as much as it is modesty: trusting that, as powerful as is our capacity to know the world, our capacity to grow and learn more is even greater.

For the postmodernist, modernist thinking is an index of real doubt, even if it is misinterpreted by those who display it. Misinterpreting it, modernists cannot get on with the work of the second stage of pragmatic inquiry, which is to identify and examine in detail the habits of action whose inadequacies gave rise to this doubt in the first place. This is empirical inquiry, understood pragmatically. The pragmatic inquirer is, first, a historian, who examines the biographical-social-cultural contexts of modernist doubts in order to offer reasonable hypotheses about the sorts of habits that may have informed modernists' lives. The inquirer is, secondly, a transcendental critic of a Kantian sort, who asks what a modernist must have presupposed about the world in order to have offered such and such a claim and such and such a criticism. This search for presuppositions was Peirce's critical commonsensism: manifested here as an activity of recovering the foundations of belief that underlie and are often covered over by modernist criticisms and, thus, of distinguishing just what needs to be criticized from what needs to be reaffirmed in order to respond constructively to this criticism. Linking together historical and critical research, the inquirer offers reasonable hypotheses about how the modernist's claims indicate precisely what was wrong with which inherited habits of action.

The third stage of pragmatic inquiry is to recommend ways of reforming those inherited habits of action, to respond to modernist concerns without abandoning the precritical habits out of which they emerge. The work of this stage is constructive and realistic imagination. It is to imagine new ways of acting, within the contexts of inherited beliefs and habits and as constrained by the demands of problem solving. Peirce believed the constructive imagination was guided by a logic of discovery he termed *abduction.* He said the ultimate norms guiding our discoveries may be revealed through a process of "musement," or the free play of imagination as it contemplates the orders of existence.[68] This is, in fact, the same sort of play informing the mathematical imagination that, Peirce said, underlay his phenomenology.[69] Given free play, the imagination gives uninhibited expression to the fundamental categories of our existence— Firstness, Secondness, and Thirdness—in the contemplation of which inquirers may construct norms for reforming our habits of action. The product of abduction is of practical import, because it offers possibilities that might really be enacted within our contexts of action: possibilities of real habit-change, enabling us to comprehend the world as it now displays itself. For Peirce, philosophy itself is the prototypical activity of constructively re-imagining the fundamental norms of action.

I move now from the question of what Peirce's postmodern thinking is to the question of what it tells us.

B. What Does Peirce's Postmodern Thinking Tell Us About?

Principle B1: Postmodern thinking tells us about the real. This principle brings us the reward for all our preparatory work: Peirce's claim that, *without* abandoning our modern habits of criticism and our fallibilism (and therefore reverting to *pre*modernism), we may have direct knowledge of reality. Call it a postmodern *permission.* We no longer *must* maintain what Richard Bernstein has labelled "the Cartesian anxiety." We have, indeed, discovered that our inherited traditions of belief and practice are fallible, but this discovery is not grounds for abandoning all those traditions, nor for feeling guilty whenever we suspect that, beneath all our critical training, we still have faith and trust in our capacities to know more than we admit we know. For Peirce, this suspicion—which he called our "cheerful hope"—is no merely subjective feeling, but an irrepressible index of our actual relationship to the real. Faith in this sense is no infantile wish for security, but the primary manifestation of our being in relationship to something other than ourselves and greater than ourselves, and that relationship *is* knowledge. Peirce did not read Hebrew, but the ancient Israelite term for "knowledge"—*yidiah*—may convey Peirce's claim better than any of the terms he used. For the Biblical authors, "to know" is "to have intercourse with"—with the world, with one's spouse, with God. That is, it is to enter into intimate relationship with these others, retaining one's own identity while recognizing that, in one's own being, one is not alone, but with others. To have this faith-knowledge means to recognize that, as in an argument with a lover, our errors, doubts and struggles for understanding are all aspects of our relationship to a reality that remains with us even in our moments of uncertainty.

Modern philosophers make much of the distinction between epistemology and ontology. For the postmodern Peirce, these modes of inquiry are distinguishable but not clearly distinct. Seen as a semiotic activity, the process of human knowing is not self-contained but intimately related to the processes that it interprets and the processes that interpret it. To refer to "being" is to refer to the generalizable characters of all processes with which human knowledge is potentially in relationship. To refer to "reality" is, following Peirce's adaptation of scholastic usage, to refer to that which lies outside of the knower but remains in relationship with him or her—in Peirce's terms, that "which has such and such characters, whether anybody thinks it to have those characters or not"[70] *and* that which *makes a difference* in how we think, which means in how we will act.

Contrary to what he claimed, Peirce's realism is not exactly a "scholastic realism."[71] It is, rather, what we might call a pragmatic, critical, or postmodern realism—that which remains of scholastic realism once it is made to answer the criticisms of it that are implicit in modernist thinking. For example, the postmodern realist will claim, against modern nominalists, that we can encounter and accurately describe real generality in the world—that our generalizations about the world are not merely expressive of our own desires and interests. However, this is not the generality of abstract possibility we customarily attribute to Platonic forms or essences. It is, instead, the generality of reasonable predictions, which is vague in its definition and probabilistic in its reference.[72] In Peirce's words, the purposes to which semiotic thinking refers are predictions about what *would* happen if certain conditions of experience were met. Peirce's strongest response to modern nominalism is that, as a sign of what is wrong with aspects of scholastic thinking, modernist thinking itself displays the generality of a reasonable prediction: if we were to emend scholastic thinking in such and such a way, then it would not warrant such and such a modernist objection.

The ontological implication of Peirce's postmodern thinking is, then, that human knowledge is the symbolic mode of intercourse between the processes that, from our perspective, we say take place "out there" and the processes that we say take place "in here"—the processes of human activity in the world. From the perspective of "in here," it is helpful to refer to this intercourse as a semiotic activity: viewing our thoughts as symbols of reality and viewing our efforts to connect thoughts to actions as ways of correcting and perfecting the clarity of these symbols. From the perspective of "out there," it is helpful to refer to this intercourse as a relationship among three kind of habits: "things" as habits of worldly action, our "practices" as habits of action in the world, and "thinking" as an activity of habit-change, through which the two forms of habit adjust their relations, one to the other. From these perspectives, pragmatic inquiry represents a worldly activity as much as it does a human one. As an expression of modernist practices of critical thinking, it displays to us the merely human contexts of our knowledge of reality: we do not know reality independently of the ways in which we practice our knowledge. As an expression of the postmodernist re-evaluation of modernist thinking, it reminds us that we have no reason to assume that reality could be known in any other way than this: that reality is that which, while calling attention to itself forcibly, is known fallibilistically, contextually, and relationally. As knowers, we are, in other words, part of the reality we know. In the words of the theologian Abraham Heschel, as knowers, each of us discovers that "I am that which is not mine."[73]

Principle B2: Postmodern thinking displays the realities of chance, force, and love as principles of evolution. Pragmatic realism is, thus, the principle that the elemental or indubitable characters of our own habits of thinking are also characters of the reality with which we are in relationship. The principle reflects an evolutionary conception of the adaptation of mind and world: "It seems incontestable . . . that the mind of man is strongly adapted to the comprehension of the world."[74] It is ultimately "evolution" that "made man's mind to be so constructed"[75] (although Peirce wavered on the question of whether or not natural selection was a sufficient explanation of the remarkable accuracy of our insights into Nature[76]). The upshot is that the elemental characters of our thinking are trustworthy interpretants of the reality of this world, or that, until we are shown otherwise, we expect to interact successfully with the world when our habits of action display these characters. As we have seen, Peirce discovered that he could reduce the characters of his postmodern habit of thinking to three elemental categories, which he labelled Firstness, Secondness, and Thirdness. He then found he had no reason not to assume that these categories correspond to the three elemental properties of the reality with which he was in relationship.[77]

In a series of *Monist* articles in 1892-93, Peirce claimed that the cosmos evolves in three ways: according to fortuitous variation (*tychastic* evolution), according to mechanical necessity (*anancastic* evolution), and according to creative love (*agapastic* evolution). He said "the mere propositions that absolute chance, mechanical necessity and the law of love are severally operative in the cosmos may receive the names of *tychism, anancism,* and *agapism.*"[78] I find it convenient to use these three terms to refer to the three principles according to which Peirce attributed Firstness, Secondness, and Thirdness to the experiential universe.

According to Peirce's principle of *tychism,* Firstness is a sign of the objective reality of *chance,* or spontaneity, in the experiential universe:

By thus admitting pure spontaneity or life as a character of the universe, acting always and everywhere though restrained within narrow bounds by law, producing infinitesimal departures from law continually, and great ones within infinite infrequency, I account for all the variety and diversity of the universe, in the only sense in which the really *sui generis* and new can be said to be accounted for.[79]

This *tychistic* principle is based on the point, made earlier, that the laws of nature are really habits: "the so-called immutable laws of nature . . . are not ultimate, but are the expression and indeed the outcome of tendencies, associations and habits which spread and grow."[80]

According to Peirce's principle of *anancism*, Secondness is a sign of the objective reality of brute force in the world—the direct impress of reality. Secondness displays the dyadic dimension of reality—of action/reaction, inner/outer, will and resistance—which serves as the primary index of actual existence, as opposed to essence, or merely possible being.

According to Peirce's principle of *agapism*, Thirdness is a sign of the objective reality of love in the universe: the power of ideas to attract and draw together otherwise independent or opposing actions, giving rise to communities of being whose emergence represents the end of evolutionary growth. As articulated within the vocabulary of semiotics, the attractive power of ideas is the power of symbols to elicit meaning with respect to their interpretants. In these terms, the cosmic power of love is displayed in the reality of semiosis, understood now as a cosmic process whose end is the generation of communities of interpretation. These are communities of being, with respect to which the universe is what Peirce called "a vast representamen, a great symbol of God's purpose, working out its conclusions in living realities."[81]

Peirce's metaphysics was unabashedly anthropomorphic: "I hold . . . that [humanity] is so completely hemmed in by the bounds of [its] possible practical experience, [its] mind so restricted to being the instrument of [its] needs, that [it] cannot, in the least, *mean* anything that transcends those limits."[82] "'Anthropomorphic' is what pretty much all conceptions are at bottom. . . . It is well to remember that every single truth of science is due to the affinity of the human soul to the soul of the universe, imperfect as that affinity no doubt is."[83] Consequently, Peirce's conceiving the universe as a vast symbol meant that, observing how humans create and interpret symbols, he also conceived of this symbol as the creation of a cosmic symbol-maker—God. God is therefore known to us as the author of that process of semiosis of which any understanding we have of the universe is a symbol, and of which the multifarious processes of reality are interpretants. God as creator is therefore God as symbolizer, and we do not say "God has created the world," but "God is now creating it."[84] God is here and here and here, as source of this vast symbol whose meanings we discover anew now and now and now.

As Michael Raposa has shown in *Peirce's Philosophy of Religion*, Peirce's metaphysics is thus a metaphysical theology. Because the rules of reasoning on which it is based are semiotic rather than propositional or logocentric rules, Raposa reterms it a "theosemiotics."[85] Theosemiotics is the way we conceive of God's symbol-creating activity by analogy with humanity's symbol-creating activity, which Peirce called abductive reasoning. Within Peirce's pragmatic theory of inquiry, abduction is a way of generating hypotheses about how to reform inherited habits of action. Reasoning anthropomorphically, we may then consider God's creativity to be reformatory: the creation of new ways of being out of old ways, rather than out of "nothing." If so, the symbols God creates would be symbols of new worlds, rather than icons of old ones. These symbols would have meaning for us in the way they direct us to reinterpret our worlds of experience, rather than in the way they imitate an antecedent reality.[86] The ultimate interpretants of God's symbol-making would therefore be forms of habit-change, rather than mere forms *(eide)* or the pictures we may have of God and of God's creation.

We see, therefore, the theosemiotic significance of Peirce's postmodern thinking. As a form of habit-change, this thinking qualifies as a potential interpretant of God's symbol-making activity. To imitate God is not to make claims about what the world is, but to change one's actions in a way that represents the way God changes this world. Postmodern thinking is modern thinking that has reclaimed its transformational power by reclaiming its theological, or theosemiotic, ground.

C. To Whom was Peirce's Postmodern Thinking Addressed?

Principle C1: It was addressed to the suffering self. At the outset of this essay, we noted that Peirce first offered his pragmatism as a critique of modernist conceptions of selfhood. Still working from within modernist habits of thinking, Peirce criticized as simply false the modernist conception of the self as an incorporeal substance, ultimately unknowable, self-contained, and ultimately self-referring. As stated earlier, he argued that the self, considered as a separate existence, "is only a negation."[87] As a postmodernist, however, Peirce came close to acknowledging that, behind his earlier protestations, lay a persistently modernist conception of his own selfhood. Veiling his own loneliness and distress, his complaint and his need for truth and love, he had sought to secure for himself an existence separate from the modernist selfhood he criticized. As postmodernist, Peirce no longer required this separateness. He could confess his own modernity without despairing of it, because he had acquired the resources to redeem that modernity rather than abandon it. The early twentieth-century Jewish philosopher Franz Rosenzweig clarified this confessional dimension of postmodernism in his major work, *The Star of Redemption.*[88] As interpreted by Robert Gibbs, Rosenzweig understood the Biblical injunction "You shall love the Lord your God . . ." as a prototype of the imperative that makes human relationship possible: "love me!" "Only this command is the speech of love. Why? Because the speech of the lover must itself love."[89] In speaking the words "love me," the lover calls for a response from the beloved, calling the beloved out of his or her separateness. To respond to the call to love is, however, first to acknowledge that one was indeed separate: in need of love, but not yet called to acknowledge the need. This acknowledgment is confession:

For Rosenzweig this confession is itself the process of atonement *[Ver-söhnung]*, which the soul undertakes in the presence of the lover's love. I can only come to terms with my own false self-reliance, my own illusion of completeness without love, in the presence of my lover's demand to love. And as I speak my way through this process of accepting my past as mine, as myself, even including the self that has heard the command to love, I recognize the past is not being held against me.[90]

As postmodernist, Peirce could love himself and thus recognize that his past, as modernist, was not being held against him. This is to confess the inadequacy of his self's separateness, while acknowledging, with compassion, the suffering signified by that separateness.

Interpreted this way, Peirce's postmodern thinking was addressed to the suffering self of his modernity. It was addressed to it the way a symbol is addressed to its interpretant, which means both that Peirce's thinking had *meaning with respect to* this suffering self *and* that his thinking *performed something with respect to it.* In Rosenzweig's terms, the performance was to offer it the command of love and, thus, to bring it to confess its separateness and to accept responsibility for responding to the other with whom it is in relationship. In Peirce's terms,

The Christian religion, if it has anything distinctive . . . is distinguished from other religions by its precept about the Way of Life. . . . Now what is this way of life? Again I appeal to the universal Christian conscience to testify that it is simply love. As far as it is contracted to a rule of ethics, it is: Love God, and love your neighbor. . . . The belief in the law of love is the Christian faith.[91]

Principle C2: Peirce's postmodern thinking is addressed to an antecedent and to a prospective community of inquirers. As a redeeming word, Peirce's postmodern thinking offered the modernist self permission to acknowledge its relatedness to others. In Peirce's words, "The Gospel of Christ says that progress comes from every individual merging his individuality in sympathy with his neighbors."[92] As a directive for undertaking corrective, pragmatic inquiry, Peirce's thinking offered the modernist self a procedure for reclaiming its relatedness and thus joining with its neighbor. The first step of this procedure is for the self to relate the narrative history of its suffering: that it belonged to an antecedent community of practitioners, that it grew dissatisfied with this community, that its dissatisfaction bred its self-isolation, and that its practices of dogmatic inquiry have veiled its history and thus reinforced its self-isolation. The self must confess its identity: "I am a modernist." The second step is for the self, now embodied as a modernist, to acknowledge her identity as a past member of that antecedent community. The modernist must declare this complex identity: "I have entered modernity as a scholastic, or a Catholic, or a Jew, or whatever I was when I left the community in anger." The third step is for this "modernist who once was . . ." to recognize that, while that community belongs only to the past, other communities may emerge from it, reformed through the kind of criticism she would offer. Rather than fear community, she may reclaim her criticism as part of the process of communal life and growth. The fourth step is for this "modernist who will belong again . . ." to locate those who would listen to her criticisms and join with her in the process of communal reformation. These may also be former members of her antecedent community: members now of what would become reformed scholastic, or reformed Catholic, or reformed Jewish, communities.

Peirce's postmodern thinking appears to be addressed, in particular, to a modernist in this fourth stage of corrective inquiry. I imagine that, not yet re-integrated into the reforming community for which she is searching, this modernist would first try to identify the attributes this community *would* have if she were to find it. Peirce's pragmaticist inquiry may then be re-interpreted as an abductive inquiry, whose purpose was to generate reasonable hypotheses about what these attributes would be.[93] Grounded in his mathematics of triadic relations,[94] Peirce's phenomenology suggested that such a community would be characterized by its Thirdness, or its mediational capacity. Peirce's discovery that symbols are paradigmatic Thirds suggests that the paradigmatic activity of a community may be interpretation. The community would offer its individual members interpretants (contexts of interpretation, for example, values, beliefs, narratives) with respect to which the world, as a vast symbol, has meaning. Individual members of the community would then be interrelated by way of these interpretants; the members would find their commonality in the common meanings these interpretants assigned to the world. Strictly within the terms of Peirce's semiotics, however, the community might appear to be *too* coherent a phenomenon, perhaps impervious to reform. Peirce's theory of habit-change suggested that the interpretation of symbols is a transformational, rather than a merely constitutive, activity—that is, that it establishes meaning by transforming prior meanings rather than by generating meaning *ex nihilo*. According to this theory, the concept of community displays different modalities, and we should be wary of reducing the concept to any one modality.

From the perspective of semiotics as a phenomenological and classificatory science, community appears in its Firstness as an interwoven collection of interpretants and, thus, of possible meanings. From the perspective of Peirce's theory of habit-change as a form of normative science, members of a community emerge as individuals when they suffer—that is, when their experiences of failed expectation breed doubts about communally secured meanings. From this perspective, community first appears in its Secondness, as an arena of oppositions between a disintegrated collection of dissatisfied individuals and what appears to them to be a mechanically or artificially collected block of outmoded signs. According to the pragmaticist, modernists tend to view community, exclusively, in either its Firstness or Secondness: describing community, in the former case, as an unachievably ideal state of epistemological and social integration; or, in the latter case, as the all-too-real source of the authoritarianism that restricts the free expression of the human spirit. Peirce's theory of habit-change, however, provides a perspective from which to view community in its Thirdness as well. This is to view community as the process through which individuals, stimulated by their doubts, undertake the cooperative, pragmatic inquiry through which imperfect communities of the past are transformed into the more perfect communities of the future. From this perspective, community is what Peirce called a community of inquiry, the reformed and reforming community of scientists. According to Peirce's pragmatic theory of inquiry, these scientists draw their principles of inquiry from out of the heritage of the communities they serve as both reformers and critics. To uncover these principles they must, ultimately, imitate the process of divine creativity itself. Otherwise put, pragmatic inquiry was, for Peirce, the ultimate interpretant of God's creative activity, and the community of pragmatic scientists constituted the reformed church.

Principle C3: Peirce's postmodern thinking is addressed to the universal church of pragmatic scientists. Peirce never tested his elaborate hypothesis about what the attributes of a reformed community *might be*, because he never located the reformed community to which he, in particular, belonged. For my own way of thinking, this means that, while he jumped ahead to a fifth step of pragmatic inquiry, Peirce failed to complete the fourth step. Others may argue that Peirce did complete the fourth step, because his own reformed community was either the community of pragmatic philosophers or, more broadly considered, the community of pragmatically minded scientists. I hesitate to accept this argument, because it is not apparent to me that any identifiable community of scientists or philosophers inherits the mantle of what Peirce took to be the Christian Church. I remain undecided on the question, however, and will, in closing, respect Peirce's own explicit claim. This claim may belong to a fifth step in pragmatic inquiry,[95] in which, already located in her reformed community, the modernist *cum* postmodernist interprets the principles of community to be principles that integrate individual communities as well as individual persons. She seeks to find her place in a universal church, conceived as a community of communities.[96] In Raposa's words, "It is the scientific community, after all, its members devoted to the discovery of 'God's truth,' that Peirce selected as the model for the Christian Church."[97] In Peirce's words:

Man's highest developments are social; and religion, though it begins in a seminal individual inspiration, only comes to full flower in a great church coextensive with a civilization. This is true of every religion, but supereminently so of the religion of love. Its ideal is that the whole world shall be united in the bond of a common love of God accomplished by each man's loving his neighbor. Without a church, the religion of love can have but a rudimentary existence; and a narrow, little exclusive church is almost worse than none. A great catholic church is wanted.

The invisible church does now embrace all Christendom. Every man who has been brought up in the bosom of Christian civilization does really believe in some form of the principle of love, whether he is aware of doing so, or not.

. . . Let us endeavor, then, with all our might to draw together the whole body of believers in the law of love into sympathetic unity of consciousness. . . .

To those who for the present are excluded from the churches, and who, in the passionate intensity of their religious desire, are talking of setting up a church for the scientifically educated, a man of my stripe must say, Wait if you can; it will be but a few years longer; but if you cannot wait, why then Godspeed! Only do not, in your turn, go and draw lines so as to exclude such as believe a little less—or, still worse, to exclude such as believe a little more—than yourselves. . . .

A religious civilization is a somewhat idle affair unless it be sworn in as a regiment of that great army that takes life in hand, with all its delights, in grimmest fight to put down the principle of self-seeking, and to make the principle of love triumphant. It has something more serious to think about than the phraseology of the articles of war. Fall into the ranks then; follow your colonel. Keep your one purpose steadily and alone in view, and you may promise yourself the attainment of your sole desire, which is to hasten the chariot wheels of redeeming love![98]

NOTES

1. Joseph Brent, "A Study of the Life of Charles Sanders Peirce," Ph.D. dissertation, UCLA (May 1960), 31. This is the best source of biographical information on Peirce. I have also drawn on Max Fisch, "Introduction," *Writings of Charles S. Peirce: A Chronological Edition, I, 1857-1866*, ed. Max Fisch et al. (Bloomington: Indiana University Press, 1982), xv-xxxv; and Murray Murphey, *The Development of Peirce's Philosophy* (Cambridge: Harvard University Press, 1961).

2. "The Place of Our Age in the History of Civilization" (1863), cited in *Charles S. Peirce: Selected Writings (Values in a Universe of Change)*, ed. Philip P. Wiener

(New York: Dover Publications, 1958), 13-14

3. C. S. Peirce to Smith, July 25, 1908, Scientific Correspondence. Cited in Murray Murphey, *The Development of Peirce's Philosophy*, 15.

4. Charles Peirce, "My Life written for the Class-Book," in *Writings of Charles S. Peirce: A Chronological Edition, I, 1857-1866*, 1-3.

4a. Brent, "A Study of the Life of Charles Sanders Peirce," 71.

5. He was invited to give several lecture series at Harvard: the prestigious Lowell Lectures in 1866, when he was only twenty-five; a series of lectures on logic in 1869-70; a series on pragmatism in 1903; and another Lowell series in 1903. He held one significant position, Lecturer in Logic at the Johns Hopkins University, between 1879 and 1884.

6. "Philosophical Conceptions and Practical Results," *University of California Chronicle* (September 1898), repr. in William James, *The Writings of William James*, ed. John J. McDermott (Chicago and London: University of Chicago Press, 1977), 347-48.

7. See Max Fisch's account, "Was There a Metaphysical Club in Cambridge?", *Studies in the Philosophy of Charles Sanders Peirce, Second Series*, ed. Edward Moore and Richard Robin (Amherst: University of Massachusetts Press, 1964), 3-32.

8. "Questions Concerning Certain Faculties Claimed for Man," *Journal of Speculative Philosophy* (hereafter *JSP*) 2 (1868), 103-14, reprinted in *Collected Papers of Charles Sanders Peirce*, ed. Charles Hartshorne and Paul Weiss (Cambridge: Harvard University Press, 1931-58), vol. 5, paras. 213-63 (future references to this collection will be to *CP* followed by volume and paragraph number[s], e.g., *CP* 5.213-63); "Some Consequences of Four Incapacities," *JSP* 2 (1868), 140-57, repr. *CP* 5.264-317; and "Grounds of Validity of the Laws of Logic," *JSP* 2 (1868), 193-208, repr. *CP* 5.318-57.

9. "The Universal Categories" (1903), *CP* 5.41-65, at 61.

10. "Archimedes sought only a firm and immovable point in order to move the entire earth from one place to another. Surely great things are to be hoped for if I am lucky enough to find at least one thing that is certain and indubitable" (René Descartes, "Second Meditation," in *Discourse on Method* and *Meditations on First Philosophy*, trans. Donald Cress (Indianapolis: Hackett, 1980), 61.

11. *CP* 5.214 ("Questions" [1868]).

12. *CP* 5.223 ("Questions").

13. Ibid.

14. *CP* 5.227, citing Kant's *Werke*, vii (2), 11.

15. *CP* 5.312 ("Some Consequences" [1868]).

16. Peirce overcame his earlier dogmatic logicism by arguing for a "critical"

commonsensism: the doctrine that our reasoning is guided by habits of belief that are functionally indubitable but that remain subject to future criticism.

17. As argued by David Savan in "On the Origins of Peirce's Phenomenology," *Studies in the Philosophy of Charles Sanders Peirce, First Series*, ed. Philip P. Wiener and Frederic H. Young (Cambridge: Harvard University Press, 1952), 185-94. For a similar view, see Murphey, *The Development of Peirce's Philosophy*.

18. "Illustrations of the Logic of Science," *Popular Science Monthly* 12-13 (1877-78), repr. *CP* 5.358-410, 6.395-427, 2.619-93.

19. "The Fixation of Belief" (1877), *CP* 5.358-87.

20. *CP* 5.12 (1905). See Bain's *The Emotions and the Will* (New York: Longman's Green, 1875), ch. 11.

21. *CP* 5.371, 374, 375 ("Fixation" [1877]).

22. *CP* 5.377 ("Fixation"). The citations to follow are from paragraphs 378-85.

23. As Peirce adds in an 1893 note to this article; see *CP* 5.382n.1.

24. Susan Haack, "Descartes, Peirce and the Cognitive Community," in *The Relevance of Charles Peirce*, ed. Eugene Freeman (La Salle, Ill.: The Hegeler Institute for The Monist Library of Philosophy, 1983), 238-63, at 254.

25. I take this principle to be implicit in Peirce's 1878 answer to his own question of how induction works; or, more precisely, how we come to offer reasonable hypotheses about what we experience. He wrote: "It seems incontestable . . . that the mind of man is strongly adapted to the comprehension of the world; at least, so far as this goes, that certain conceptions, highly important for such a comprehension, naturally arise in his mind. . . . How are we to explain this adaptation? The great utility and indispensableness of the conceptions of time, space, and force, even to the lowest intelligence, are such as to suggest that they are the results of natural selection" ("Order of Nature," *Popular Science Monthly* 13 [1878], repr. *CP* 6.395-427, at 417-18).

26. "How To Make Our Ideas Clear," *Popular Science Monthly* 12 (1878), 286-302, repr. *CP* 5.388-410, at 402.

27. See above, in the introductory paragraphs.

28. *CP* 5.317 ("Some Consequences" [1868]).

29. "What Pragmatism Is," *Monist* 15 (1905), 161-81, repr. *CP* 5.411-37, at 414 (emphasis added).

30. "Philosophical Conceptions and Practical Results" (see note 6, above).

31. In John McDermott's words, "this marked the beginning of the pragmatic movement" (from a note in his annotated bibliography of James' writings, appended to *The Writings of William James: A Comprehensive Edition*, ed. McDermott [Chicago:

The University of Chicago Press, 1977], 837).

32. William James, *Pragmatism: A New Name for Some Old Ways of Thinking*, ed. Bruce Kuklick (Indianapolis: Hackett Publishing Co., 1981), 26.

33. John E. Smith, *Purpose and Thought: The Meaning of Pragmatism* (New Haven: Yale University Press, 1978), 41. Smith refers the reader to James' account of concepts in William James, *Some Problems of Philosophy* (New York and London: Longman's, Green & Co., 1911), ch. 4-6.

34. Peirce's preferred spelling for "semiotics" was *semeiotic*, but for this non-technical essay I prefer to use a spelling more readers will recognize. Peirce's triadic semiotic is to be distinguished from that dyadic semiotic originated by Ferdinand de Saussure and now influencing much semiotic work on the Continent.

35. "Issues of Pragmatism" (1905), *CP* 5.438-63, at 440.

36. "What Pragmatism Is" (1905), *CP* 5.411-37, at 432. On semiotics, see the discussion below in section IV.

37. On one occasion, he labelled these first-level practices "B-reasonings" ("Why Study Logic?" [1902], *CP* 2.119-218, at 189).

38. He labelled these "A-reasonings" (ibid.).

39. As we will discuss later, one of the central principles of Peirce's pragmaticism was that the sign of the deeper or second-level practices is their indubitability. Peirce claimed that what we *mean* by "knowing reality" is equivalent to what we know of the world when our reasoning is guided by indubitable practices of reasoning, or what he also called indubitable beliefs. Peirce therefore believed that, by reaffirming our capacity to identify fundamental practices, he was reaffirming our capacity to encounter reality directly.

40. The school of Thomas Reid (d. 1796), whose response to Hume's skepticism took what would become the non-Kantian route of affirming our "original beliefs." See Thomas Reid, *Works*, 2 vols., ed. Sir William Hamilton (Edinburgh: 1846-1863).

41. *CP* 5.445 ("Issues of Pragmaticism" [1905]).

42. Ibid.

43. "Methods for Attaining Truth" (1898), *CP* 5.574-604, at 587.

44. Richard Robin, "Peirce's Doctrine of the Normative Sciences," in *Studies in the Philosophy of Charles Sanders Peirce, Second Series*, ed. Moore and Robin, 271-88, at 272.

45. See Peirce's logic of inquiry in "A Neglected Argument for the Reality of God," *Hibbert Journal* 7 (1908), 90-112, repr. *CP* 6.467-73.

46. Peirce's preferred spelling was *semeiosis*. See note 34.

47. "A Survey of Pragmaticism" (1906), *CP* 5.464-96, at 484. For the most recent argument in support of Peirce's claims for the irreducibility of triadic relations to dyadic or monadic relations, see Robert Burch, *A Peircean Reduction Thesis* (Lubbock: Texas Tech University Press, 1991).

48. "The Simplest Mathematics" (1902), *CP* 2.227-323, at 233.

49. "Three Kinds of Goodness" (1903), *CP* 5.120-50, at 148. In correspondence, Kenneth Ketner has pointed out that there were other kinds of diagrams in Peirce's system besides visual ones—"he admitted audio diagrams and tactile diagrams as well." See also Ketner, "Peirce's 'Most Lucid and Interesting Paper': An Introduction to Cenopythagoreanism," *International Philosophical Quarterly* 26 (1986): 375-92.

50. He called these the activities of *colligation, iteration,* and *erasure* (referring to the activity of *seeing* the general rule by attending to the general features of the repetitions and ignoring or erasing the other, nongeneral features). See *CP* 5.579 (1898), where Peirce notes that there are modes of deduction in which not all three of the elements are present: for example "in ordinary syllogism the iteration may be said to be absent. And that is the reason that ordinary syllogism can be worked by a machine." Ordinary syllogism, that is, lacks the creativity otherwise present in mathematical reasoning. See Kenneth Ketner, "Peirce and Turing: Comparisons and Conjectures," *Semiotica* 68/1-2 (1988), 33-61.

51. Peirce classified phenomenology (which he came to call "phaneroscopy") as the first subscience of *philosophy.* He said that philosophy "limits itself to so much of truth as can be inferred from common experience" ("An Outline Classification of the Sciences," *CP* 1.180-202, at 184). Its second subscience was "normative science," comprised of *aesthetics, ethics,* and *logic.* Its third subscience was metaphysics.

52. *CP* 5.122 ("Three Kinds of Goodness" [1903]).

53. "Phenomenology: Introduction" (1905), *CP* 1.284-94, at 284.

54. See, e.g., *CP* 1.339 (*c.* 1895).

55. "A Detailed Classification of the Sciences" (1902), *CP* 1.203-83, at 246.

56. *CP* 2.227 (*c.* 1897).

57. All three references are from *CP* 2.247-49 (1903).

58. Peirce's semiotics is, of course, a vast enterprise to which the reader is here merely introduced. See Peirce's *Semiotic and Significs: The Correspondence between Charles S. Peirce and Victoria Lady Welby,* ed. C. Hardwick (Bloomington: Indiana University Press, 1977). For some recent introductory essays, see John Dely, *Introducing Semiotic* (Bloomington: Indiana University Press, 1982), and Max Fisch, *Peirce, Semiotic, and Pragmatism* (Bloomington: Indiana University Press, 1986).

59. William James, *The Principles of Psychology* (1890; New York: Dover, 1950), vol. 1, 104.

60. Ibid., 104-05.

61. See "A Guess at the Riddle" (1890), *CP* 1.354-416, esp. 385-94. Peirce claimed that these capacities can be reduced to three, corresponding to the three categories of his phenomenology: the capacity to feel spontaneously (Firstness), the capacity to react to determining stimuli (Secondness), and the capacity to form habits (Thirdness). He viewed habit-formation as the physiological manifestation of the sign-taking capacity: habits are the ultimate interpretants of the world's signs.

62. Cf. *CP* 5.480 ("A Survey of Pragmaticism" [1905]).

63. I believe it would be more precise to say that the world is something with whose existence we can converse, *and* whose creation we can imitate, in the ways we act.

64. *CP* 5.478-81 ("A Survey").

65. By way of illustration, Peirce wrote: "I well remember when I was a boy, and my brother Herbert, now our minister at Christiania, was scarce more than a child, one day, as the whole family were at table, some spirit from a 'blazer,' or 'chafing dish,' dropped on the muslin dress of one of the ladies and was kindled; and how instantaneously he jumped up, and did the right thing, and how skillfully each motion was adapted to the purpose. I asked him afterward about it; and he told me that since Mrs. Longfellow's death, it was that he had often run over in imagination all the details of what ought to be done in such an emergency. It was a striking example of a real habit produced by exercises in the imagination." (*CP* 5.487n.1 [ibid.])

66. Peirce tended to use the terms "doubt" or "surprise," rather than the objective correlate of doubt, which, after John Dewey, I am labelling a "problem." In his 1878 papers, Peirce referred to the "doubt" that stimulates inquiry.

67. *CP* 5.416 ("What Pragmatism Is" [1905]). Peirce continued, "But do not make believe [earlier in the paragraph, he wrote 'Dismiss make-believes']; if pedantry has not eaten all the reality out of you, recognize, as you must, that there is much that you do not doubt in the least."

68. See p. 61, above.

69. See the discussions of mathematics, above, in "Principle A1" (semiotics).

70. See *CP* 5.430 ("What Pragmatism Is" [1905]), where Peirce cites Prantl, *Geschichte der Logik*, III, 91, Anm. 362.

71. In *Peirce's Philosophy of Religion* (Bloomington and Indianapolis: Indiana University Press, 1989), 16, Michael Raposa writes that "while labelling himself as both a Scotist and a scholastic realist, . . . Peirce clearly found the medieval systems to be in need of serious repair." See also Raposa, "Habits and Essences," *Transactions of the Charles S. Peirce Society* XXV/3 (1989), 251-91; and John Boler, *Charles S. Peirce and Scholastic Realism* (Seattle: University of Washington Press, 1963).

72. Peirce wrote that a *general* sign "turns over to the interpreter the right to complete [its] determination as he pleases" (*CP* 5.448 n. 1, "Issues of Pragmaticism" [1905]). The general indicates the character of a merely possible individual, representing the synthesis of a multitude of subjects. On the other hand, a *vague* sign "reserves for some other possible sign or experience the function of completing the determination" ("Consequences of Critical Common-Sensism" [c. 1905], *CP* 5.502-37, at 505). The vague denotes some of the characters of an *existent* individual, representing the synthesis of a multitude of predicates. To say that real generality is probabilistic in its reference means that the general signs that really refer to the world do not refer to discrete collections of objects, but to the probability that a certain collection would display certain characteristics. To say that real generality is vague in its definition means that general signs display these characteristics in a manner that is relative to the interpretant to which they are displayed.

73. Abraham J. Heschel, *Between God and Man*, ed. Fritz Rothschild (New York: Free Press, 1959), 61.

74. "The Order of Nature" (1878), *CP* 6.417.

75. "Pragmaticism: The Normative Sciences" (1903), *CP* 5.14-40, at 28.

76. See *CP* 6.419 ("The Order of Nature" [1878]).

77. His examination of reality with respect to these categories corresponded to Kant's verifying, through the deductions of the *Critique of Pure Reason*, the results of his Analytic.

78. "Evolutionary Love" (1893), *CP* 6.302.

79. "The Doctrine of Necessity Examined," *The Monist* 2 (1892), 321-37, repr. *CP* 6.59.

80. John E. Smith, *Purpose and Thought*, 141.

81. "The Reality of Thirdness" (1903), *CP* 5.93-119, at 119.

82. *CP* 5.536 ("Consequences of Critical Common-Sensism" [1905]).

83. *CP* 5.47 ("The Universal Categories" [1903]).

84. As suggested by the Biblical appellation for God: *ani ehyeh asher ehyeh*, "I will be there as I will be there" (Ex. 3.14). Interpreting this translation, rather than "I am what I am," Martin Buber wrote:

> And the great narrator helps us to get out of our minds the meaning of "being" *(esse)* in the use of the word by repeating in accordance with Biblical style the word *ehyeh* in the sense of "being present" *(adesse)*: he anticipates the "I will be" in question with the related "I will be with thee" (Ex. 3.12), and follows it with the related "I will be with thy mouth." Thus YHVH does not not say that He exists absolutely or eternally, but— without pledging himself to any particular way of revelation ("as I will be

there"), by which He also makes it known that He cannot be bound by any conjuration—that He wants to remain with His people, to go with them, to lead them (Martin Buber, *The Prophetic Faith*, trans. C. Witton-Davies [New York: Harper & Row, 1960], 29).

85. Michael Raposa, *Peirce's Philosophy of Religion*, 142-54.

86. Technically, these symbols display what Peirce called the irremediable *vagueness* of reality, meaning that a real thing does not simply possess a determinate character, but displays its characters relative to the other real things with which it is in relationship at a given time.

87. *CP* 5.317 ("Some Consequences of Four Incapacities" [1868]).

88. *The Star of Redemption*, trans. from the German *(Der Stern der Erlösung)* by William Halo (New York: Holt, Rinehart and Winston, 1971).

89. From chapter 3 of the unedited manuscript of Robert Gibbs' forthcoming book, *Correlations: Rosenzweig and Levinas*.

90. Ibid., 26. Rosenzweig wrote, in *The Star of Redemption*, 180: "'I have sinned.' Thus speaks the soul and abolishes shame. By speaking thus, referring purely back into the past, it purifies the present from the weakness of the past. 'I have sinned' means I was a sinner. With this acknowledgement of having sinned, however, the soul clears the way for the acknowledgement 'I am a sinner.' And this second acknowledgement is already the full admission of love."

91. "A Religion of Science," *The Open Court* 7 (1893), 3559-60, repr. *CP* 6.441.

92. "Evolutionary Love," *CP* 6.294.

93. Technically speaking, this hypothesis-making, or abduction, would correspond to a transcendental analysis of the conditions of community reformation.

94. IV.A., Principle A1, above.

95. Or, as suggested, Peirce may conflate the fourth and fifth steps.

96. Even when informed by Peirce's principles of fallibilism and of pragmatic doubt, such a conception may prove to be a totalizing or dogmatic one, in that the "principle of community" operative here is an extension of one community's conception of its own principle of integration.

97. Raposa, *Peirce's Philosophy of Religion*, 99.

98. *CP* 6.443-48 ("A Religion of Science" [1893]). Is this language of war and of desire not the language of the "modernist who will belong again . . ." but has not yet located his reforming community?

—— My thanks to David Griffin, Robert Corrington and Kenneth Ketner for suggesting improvements to various parts of this essay.

2

WILLIAM JAMES

Marcus P. Ford

"How good it is sometimes simply to *break away* from all old categories, deny old worn-out beliefs, and restate things *ab initio*, making the lines of division fall into entirely new places!"[1]

William James

William James (1842-1910) is frequently regarded as one of America's greatest psychologists, as one of the seminal founders of the philosophy of Pragmatism, and as a popular essayist. Few deny his genius. What is less commonly recognized is that James' thought, taken as a whole, constitutes a new beginning. James was more than just a brilliant modern psychologist, an important modern philosopher, and a popular modern essayist; he was one of the first postmodern thinkers. In James' writings one discovers a breaking away from old categories and the establishment of new, postmodern ones. To the extent that one fails to recognize the postmodern quality of James' thought, one invariably misses his most significant contribution to Western thought.

The modern worldview, which is to say the way reality has come to be understood in the West over the last three hundred years, rests largely upon the sensationist premise that all direct or perceptual knowledge of the world beyond ourselves is derived from sensory experience and upon one of two types of ontology: physicalism or psychophysical dualism.

The sensationist position, dominant as it has been, has not been the only basis of modern epistemology. Much modern thought has insisted that we also have nonsensory sources of knowledge, such as self-knowledge, innate ideas, and the presuppositions of knowledge and action. And on these bases have been built modern dualistic supernaturalisms and idealisms to compete with the phenomenalisms that would not go (much) beyond the data of sensory perception. In the earliest phases of modern thought these modern alternatives to sensationism represented viable epistemological options, but in the later phases of modernity, increasingly dominated by science and technology, they have not. Today it is almost axiomatic in philosophical and scientific circles that, with the important exceptions of realities that are not directly perceived *but for which there is good indirect evidence for their existence*, and general principles such as causality and the laws of nature, only those things that can be directly perceived by one or more of the senses are real.

The two modern ontologies are psychophysical dualism and physicalism. Psychophysical dualism is the metaphysical position that all of reality is comprised of one of two equally real types of substances: psychic substances and physical substances. For the physicalist, physical substance is the only type of substance. What both of these modern metaphysics agree upon is: (1) that what it means to be real is to be a substance and (2) that purely physical substances, meaning substances that occupy space and lack any psychic interior, exist. It is generally correct to say that in its initial stage modern thought was characterized by psychophysical dualism and in its later stage by physicalism. The dominance of physicalism parallels very closely the dominance of sensationism in modern thought.

James' philosophy is distinctively nonmodern in that it rejects the sensationist premise that all of our perceptual knowledge of the world beyond ourselves is derived from sensory experience, it rejects both physicalism and psychophysical dualism, and it rejects substantialism (the doctrine that the finally real units of reality are enduring substances). James' metaphysics may be described as a process panexperientialism, the view that the most fundamental units of reality are momentary, experiential events, what James sometimes called "drops of experience." His epistemological position he called "radical empiricism." The fundamental assertion of radical empiricism is that sense-perception comprises only a fraction of what is given in direct experience. Each of us has direct, first-hand experience of the world beyond ourselves which far exceeds what is given via the senses. James' break with modern philosophy on these critical issues of epistemology and ontology places him decidedly beyond the boundaries of modern philosophy.

The central objective of this essay is to demonstrate the postmodern character of James' worldview. After discussing his radically empirical epistemology and his panexperientialist metaphysics, I devote a section to his view of truth. This topic is essential because in the relativistic form of postmodernism (as discussed in the introduction to the series) it is claimed that the idea of truth as correspondence must be given up and many hold that James' pragmatic theory of truth provides an adequate alternative. I then move to more concrete issues: the nature of the physical sciences, the reality of God, and the basis of ethical behavior. In the final section I discuss James' social thought with special attention to his article "The Moral Equivalent of War."

I. THE CONCEPTUAL BREAK FROM MODERN PHILOSOPHY

A. Epistemology

A fully adequate description of all modern epistemologies would be, of course, an enormous task. One can, however, at least indicate something of the pervasiveness of the sensationist premise in modern thought by briefly considering the epistemologies of Hume, Kant, and modern science. In each of these instances, sensory perception plays a critical role.

For Hume all theoretical knowledge is based on sensation. There is nothing in the mind that was not first in one of the senses. "The mind," he writes, "has never anything present to it but the perceptions, and cannot possibly reach any experience of their connection with objects."[2] The consequence of Humean sensationism is Humean skepticism, as is clearly seen in that statement. If all knowledge is limited to sense-perception, then there can be no knowledge of external objects. Sense-experience by itself provides only a succession of sensations: one colored region succeeds another, one taste preceeds a certain odor, one taste succeeds a certain sound, and so on. (Had Hume been fully consistent, even the awareness of succession would have to be denied, for certainly one does not see, taste, feel, hear or smell succession. Either Hume simply overlooked this or he felt he needed to assume it in order to account for the notion of causation, a notion that is so basic that some account must be given of it.) On a sensationist basis, we must be skeptical about the existence of anything other than sense-data. We cannot say that these data are caused by real things. And we certainly can have no knowledge of alleged entities, such as "values" and "God," to which no sense-data correspond.

Hume recognized the limits of the sensationist premise and the skepticism that it gives rise to. As he put it:

> There is a great difference betwixt such opinions as we form after a calm and profound reflection [philosophical knowledge], and such as we

embrace by a kind of instinct or natural impulse, on account of their suitableness and conformity to the mind. If these opinions become contrary, 'tis not difficult to forsee which of them will have the advantage. As long as our attention is bent upon the subject, the philosophical and study'd principle will prevail; but the moment we relax our thoughts, nature will display herself, and draw us back to our former opinion.[3]

In other words, in addition to theoretical or *philosophical knowledge*, which is limited to sensory knowledge, there is *instinctual knowledge*, which Hume links to "habit" and "custom." From a sensationist perspective there is no alternative but to doubt the reality of everything except what is revealed by the senses, but where philosophy requires doubt, instinct (or habit or custom) supplies a basis for action. "Practice" comes to the rescue of "theory."

Kant sought to move philosophy beyond Hume, not by rejecting sensationism, but by supplementing sensationism with transcendental aesthetics and categories of understanding and by formalizing Hume's distinction between theoretical knowledge and practical knowledge. Practical reason enabled one to know precisely those things that Hume concluded we must doubt (or knew only instinctually or as a matter of habit): an external world, causation, values, and God. Kant, then, is in agreement with Hume on this important issue: external realities, causation, values and God are not given in direct perception.

What I am calling the "sensationist premise" was much less dominant in the earliest stages of modern science than it is today. In the seventeenth, eighteenth, and nineteenth centuries, scientists were less sensationist than most of their twentieth-century counterparts. Copernicus, Kepler, Galileo, Newton and Boyle, to name but a few of the early modern scientific giants, all regarded sensory experience as important but all would have been incredulous at the suggestion that all knowledge is a result of sensory experience. In addition to sense-derived knowledge they knew that there is a God, that this God created the world, that human beings are free not only to act as they choose but free to choose, that truth, beauty, and goodness exist and can be realized, that nature can be described mathematically, that there is a world that corresponds to sense impressions, that the future will resemble the past, and that things are causally connected.

In the last hundred years scientific thought has become more sensationist in its understanding of what constitutes knowledge. (I distinguish "scientific thought," in the sense of the public discourse of the scientific community, from the private beliefs of individual scientists.) This is not to say that twentieth-century scientific thought excludes all nonsensory knowledge. Modern scientific thought, for the most part, accepts the existence of real objects that correspond to sense-impressions, causation, and predictable patterns of behavior that may be described mathematically. Contemporary scientific thought even accepts the existence of entities that have never been, and may well never be, directly perceived when there is sufficient empirical or rational evidence to warrant it. But twentieth-century scientific thought excludes the existence of God and objective values (with the important and theoretically inexplicable, although practically understandable, exception of the value of truth) and has great difficulty with the idea that there exists anywhere in the universe real freedom. A full accounting of this shift in the scientific outlook involves many factors, one of which is the scientific community's increasing commitment to the sensationist premise that sensory perception is the necessary basis for all true knowledge of existence.

This more sensationist brand of "scientific empiricism" was on the way to becoming orthodoxy during James' lifetime. James fought against this view for two complex, interrelated reasons. On the one hand, James was concerned with the moral and religious implications of this scientific empiricism—the fact that it provides no basis for the reality of God, the existence of value, free will, and life after death. On the other hand, he was convinced rather early in his life that so-called scientific empiricism was not sufficiently empirical. Why limit the analysis of experience to sense-data? What about memory and the vague feeling of "something there" which underlies sensation? What about the feelings of relations and the feelings of worth, intentionality, and responsibility? And what about mystical experiences, hallucinations, drug-induced trances, and what James called the "fringes" of experience, which surround normal waking consciousness? What is given in experience greatly exceeds what is given through the senses. Why limit oneself to sensation? If empiricism is to be radical, it must take, as James put it in 1903, "the concrete data of experience in their full completeness. The only fully complete data are, however, the successive moments of our own several histories, taken with their 'objective' deliverance or 'content.'"[4] The content of human experience, the only sort of experience directly available to humans, is much, much more than sensations.

Although James did not use the term "radical empiricism" before 1903, he made use of this approach already in *The Principles of Psychology* (1890), his Lowell Lectures on "Exceptional Mental States" (1896), and *The Varieties of Religious Experience* (1902). In *The Principles of Psychology*, for example, he states that clear conscious experience is always "fringed" with vague awareness, and that the experience of relatedness is included in this vague awareness.

> Let us use the words *psychic overtone*, *suffusion*, or *fringe*, to designate the influence of a faint brain-process upon our thought, as it makes it aware of relations and objects but dimly perceived.[5]

In *The Varieties of Religious Experience* he writes:

> It is as if there were in the human consciousness a *sense of reality, a feeling of objective presence, a perception* of what we may call '*something there*,' more deep and more general than any of the special and particular 'senses' by which the current psychology supposes existent realities to be originally revealed.[6]

At the base of human experience is the awareness that there is more to reality than what is given by way of the senses. Our experience includes the nonspecialized experience of "something there."

But nothing is simply "there" in some general and abstract way. Everything is wherever it is in some specific way, and the experience of it includes its particularity, its particular relatedness to other things. Experience is not limited to isolatable objects, if indeed there are such things; experience includes the awareness of relations. In *The Principles of Psychology* James states:

> We ought to say a feeling of *and*, a feeling of *if*, a feeling of *but* and a feeling of *by*, quite as readily as we say a feeling of *blue* or a feeling of *cold*. Yet we do not: so inveterate has our habit become of recognizing the existence of the substantive parts alone, that language almost refuses to lend itself to any other use. The Empiricists [sensationists] have always dwelt on its influence in making us suppose that where we have a separate name, a separate thing must needs be there to correspond with it; and they have rightly denied the existence of the mob of abstract entities, principles, and forces, in whose favor no other evidence than this could be brought up. But they have said nothing of that obverse error . . . of supposing that where there is *no* name no entity can exist.[7]

Experience includes the experience of the connectedness, the disjointedness, the alongwithness, the hypotheticalness, and the like, just as surely as it includes colors and temperatures.

Memory and religious experiences provide two other illustrations of the fact that much of the objective content of human experience is not derived solely from the five senses. In memory, one has an example of nonsensory experience, because memory is the present experience of past events. One does not *see* with one's eyes a sight seen in the past, or *hear* with one's ears a tune heard long ago. One simply remembers such things. The words "memory" and "remember" point to a form of nonsensory perception. James writes, "Remembrance is like direct feeling; its object is suffused with a warmth and intimacy to which no object of mere conception ever attains."[8] In memory, one feels the past directly.

Sensationist empiricists have either ignored memory or tried to account for it in terms of association and inference. When one "remembers" something one saw, one is merely associating some present sense-data with some previous sense-data. But, as Whitehead points out in his analysis of Hume, this type of association does not *explain* memory; rather, it *presupposes* it. For unless one remembers past experiences, one cannot associate present sensations with past ones.

Memory is a particularly important example of direct experience in that, for James, it is memory that provides the basis of the notion of causation. "The 'original' of the notion of causation," he writes, "is in our inner personal experience, and only there can causes in the old-fashioned sense be directly observed and described."[9] One knows oneself as related to the past because one directly experiences this relatedness: one feels past facts shaping one's present experience. This experience that our present is to some degree caused by events in the past is the basis for the more general notion of one thing's causing another.

Looking at Hume's explanation of the idea of causation helps us appreciate the difference between Hume's sensationist empiricism and James' radical empiricism. Hume bases his explanation of causation on human memory: causation is an inference from past experience. The idea of causation is derived from the constant association of two types of experiences. When the experience of A is perceived constantly to precede the experience of B, one comes to think of A as the cause of B. This explanation, however, rests upon awareness of past facts, which is to say, memory. But if Hume's account of memory is faulty (because association of present sensation with past sensations presupposes rather than explains memory), then his explanation of the idea of causation is without foundation.

In contrast to Hume, James, who does not limit experience to sensory experience, maintains that in memory one experiences past facts directly. Memory need not be explained in terms of sensation. What is given in memory is even more fundamental than what is given through the senses. In memory one *feels* the weight of the past acting on the present, and this, James maintains, is the direct experience of causation. Not all causation, then, is an inference; some of it is part of the immediate content of human perception.

Religious experience provides yet another important example of nonsensory experience for James. The experience of God is another case of "realities directly apprehended." What is unique about religious experiences, from the perspective of radical empiricism, is not that they represent a form of direct, nonsensory, experience, but only their content. In *The Varieties of Religious Experience*, James writes:

> The further limits of our being plunge, it seems to me, into an altogether other dimension of existence from the sensible and merely "understand-

able" world. Name it the mystical region, or the supernatural region, whichever you choose. . . . God is the natural appellation, for us Christians at least, for the supreme reality, so I will call this higher part of the universe by the name God.[10]

Clear, conscious experience shades off into various degrees of semiconscious and then unconscious experience. It is only at these lower levels that most people's experience includes God. Some individuals, to be sure, are capable of extraordinary religious experiences. James focused upon these people in *The Varieties of Religious Experience*. But his conclusion was that these experiences are only exaggerated examples of what is ordinary. In *A Pluralistic Universe*, he contends that each conscious self is surrounded by an unconscious "more" which in turn forms the margin of a superhuman intelligence with whom the individual conscious self may be coconscious if the threshold of consciousness is sufficiently lowered. "The absolute," he says, "is not the impossible being I once thought it. Mental facts do function both singly and together, at once, and we finite minds may simultaneously be coconscious with one another in a superhuman intelligence."[11]

Humean and scientific empiricists, with their focus on sensation, cannot accept religious experiences for what they seem to be, that is, as experiences of a numinous reality beyond the experiencing individual. They must either deny the reality of religious experiences outright, or explain them solely in terms of sensations, which has the result of denying their religious content.

James, then, sides neither with Hume nor with Kant, the two thinkers who, in many respects, define the range of modern philosophy. He affirms what Hume denies (except to "instinct"): the knowledge of external realities, of the past, of causal relatedness, and of God. But, unlike Kant, he grounds his affirmation not in reason's transcendental categories and in merely practical reason, but in direct human experience. The differences between James and Hume, and James and Kant, are too profound to permit one to see radical empiricism as one more form of modern epistemology. James' radical empiricism is best regarded as a postmodern epistemology which rejects both of the modern alternatives in favor of a new type of empiricism.

B. Metaphysics

James' metaphysics is as revolutionary as is his epistemology. Just as he rejected sensationism, he rejected both of the two orthodox modern metaphysics: physicalism and psychophysical dualism. Moreover, he rejected the doctrine of substances that is common to both of these modern metaphysical positions.

The modern worldview began, at least from a philosophical perspective, with (Cartesian) psychophysical dualism and ended with physicalism. As the language indicates, one significant point of agreement between these two metaphysical schools of thought is the concept of physicality. Both views hold that at least some things are purely physical. In addition to this important point of agreement, these two worldviews agree that everything actual is a substance. Psychophysical dualists maintain that there are two types of substances whereas physicalists contend that there is only one type, but they agree that what it means to be actual is to be a substance, meaning an actuality that is self-contained and self-sufficient (except possibly for its dependence on God who, as completely self-sufficient, was for Descartes the substance *par excellence*). Individual substances do not include other substances. They do not interpenetrate, or overlap, or essentially depend upon each other. Substances are related to other substances only externally. Relations are never *internal*, meaning *constitutive*.

For Descartes, the world consisted of two irreducible types of actualities that had nothing in common (save their dependence on God). There were minds, defined as thinking, feeling, perceiving things that lack all spatial extension. And there were physical substances, defined as spatially extended things that lack all feeling, perceiving, and thinking. Most things, including all non-human animals, were regarded as more or less complex arrangements of extended, nonfeeling things. The apparent feelings and intelligence of nonhuman animals were dismissed as illusory. What appears to be a feeling of pain in a dog, for example, is actually only a complex physical mechanism.

Human beings, however, were said to be metaphysically different. For in addition to being spatially extensive, human beings have a psyche or soul, meaning a nonextended, thinking, feeling, perceiving, willing substance. Unlike nonhuman animals, human beings feel, entertain concepts, and make free decisions. Human beings have, in addition to their physicality, a subjective interior. And by virtue of their capacity for making decisions, human beings, unlike all other earthly creatures, are morally accountable for their actions.

Descartes' way of understanding human beings as an association of two metaphysically distinct types of actuality gave rise to the problem of explaining how these two types of actualities can interact. It was apparent to Descartes that the feelings in the mind bore some relation to the events in the physical body, on the one hand, and that the thoughts, feelings and decisions in the psyche produced effects in the body, on the other. Descartes' solution, if one can call it that, was to suggest that the pineal gland has properties in common with both thinking and extended substances and can thereby mediate between them. But this is manifestly impossible, because the two types of actualities have no qualities in common. In order for the pineal gland to mediate between the mind and the body, it would have to be both nonextended and extended, both feeling and unfeeling, both thinking and unthinking, both active and inactive.

Descartes recognized the difficulty in his position but underestimated its significance to his general metaphysics. There were others who recognized the profound implications of this nonsolution and who proposed other explanations that did not involve the pineal gland. One solution, put forth by Arnold Geulincx, had God do the work of the pineal gland moment by moment. On Geulincx's view, God keeps the mind informed of the occurrences in the body, moment by moment, requiring the mind to react to the body's demands. God likewise requires the body to do what the mind wants it to do, moment by moment. This explains, he said, how mind and body appear to interact. Another solution, advanced by Nicolas Malebranche, had God doing the work of the pineal gland all at once, in the beginning. God created the mind and the body in such a way that the two would appear to work in perfect harmony, though in fact they had absolutely no effect upon one another. The first position was called "occasionalism" in reference to the moment-by-moment activity of God; the second was termed "parallelism," because mind and body were said to run along in parallel without ever touching. (Malebranche is usually portrayed as an occasionalist, against whom Leibniz proposed a form of parallelism. But that merely reflects Malebrache's popular presentation of his position. As a staunch Augustinian, he could not think of God as interacting moment by moment with the world process.)

In the judgment of history these solutions have come to be regarded as completely implausible. With the rise of science and its assumption of the autonomy and machinelike regularity of nature, and the widespread dominance of sensationist epistemology, people were increasingly less willing to rely on God to explain anything, let alone something so commonplace as the interaction of the mind and the body. Furthermore, if the interaction of mind and body is not comprehensible, how is the influence of God on physical substances any more so? Better to stick with earthly mysteries than to violate the sensationist doctrine and employ divine assistance.

Even more fatal to the theories of occasionalism and parallelism than the increased skepticism regarding the existence of God was the broader tension between Cartesian dualism and sensationist empiricism. With the increasing intellectual and social dominance of science and its brand of sensationism, the Cartesian dualism of minds and bodies became increasingly problematic. Descartes' mental substances, or minds, are no more empirically verifiable than is God, when empiricism is taken to mean *sensate* empiricism. And without minds there is no mind-body problem (or at least so it seems). Occasionalism and parallelism were ad hoc philosophies, conceived solely to solve the mind-body problem. Without minds they stood as answers to a question that no one was asking.

Physicalism is the metaphysical position that all reality is comprised of extended, nonperceiving substances. (It can be thought of as mindless Cartesianism in that it affirms only one of the two Cartesian substances.) This view has become increasingly influential in the last hundred years. To a very large extent this is a consequence of the ever-expanding importance of science in the late nineteenth and twentieth centuries and its brand of sensationist empiricism. If all that can be known about reality is what can be known through the five senses, then nothing can be known of nonphysical realities—and what cannot be known might just as well not exist. (Of course, as I pointed out before, it is equally true that if one limits oneself to sensory data, nothing can be known of physical realities either and of causal interaction between them; but scientists have seldom been aware of this implication of sensationism.)

While physicalism has the advantage over psychophysical dualism of avoiding the mind-body problem (or at least appearing to), it is not without problems of its own, as James was acutely aware. One problem that James found particularly vexing was how to explain thoughts and feelings and free decisions in purely physical terms. Or to raise the same question from an evolutionary perspective: How does one explain the evolution of life from nonliving matter?[12] Another problem James had with physicalism was how it could be reconciled with moral responsibility. "Materialism," he writes, ". . . ceases to supply any moral incentive to my heroic devotion to truth. It remains mere *taste*, which, as its results are unpleasant, I need not follow."[13]

James' difficulty with physicalism was not purely theoretical. It was first and foremost an existential matter. If everything is physical through and through, then all meaning evaporates. What can possibly be meant by right and wrong, good and bad, brave and cowardly, beautiful and ugly, and so on? James' difficulties, both existential and theoretical, were such that he abandoned physicalism, first in favor of psychophysical dualism, and then in favor of panexperientialism, which he called "panpsychism."

James first calls himself a panpsychist in a course he taught at Harvard in 1902-03. In his course outline he states that "pragmatism would be his method and 'pluralistic panpsychism' his doctrine," and proceeds to explain that by "pluralistic panpsychism" he means the doctrine that "material objects are 'for themselves' also."[14] But one can point to earlier statements that show his favorable predisposition toward, or even advocacy of, this doctrine long before he endorsed it by name. For example, in *The Principles of Psychology* (1890), he writes:

The demand for continuity has, over large tracts of science, proved itself to possess true prophetic power. We ought therefore ourselves sincerely to try every possible mode of conceiving the dawn of consciousness so that it may *not* appear equivalent to the irruption into the universe of a new nature, non-existent until then.

Merely to call the consciousness "nascent" will not serve our turn.

It is true that the word signifies not yet *quite* born, and so seems to form a sort of bridge between existence and nonentity. But that is a verbal quibble. The fact is that discontinuity comes in if a new nature comes in at all. The *quantity* of the latter is quite immaterial. The girl in "Midshipman Easy" could not excuse the illegitimacy of her child by saying, "it was a small one." And Consciousness, however little, is an illegitimate birth in any philosophy that starts without it, and yet professes to explain all facts by continuous evolution.

If evolution is to work smoothly, consciousness in some shape must have been present at the very origin of things.[15]

And in *The Varieties of Religious Experience* (1902), written just before he called himself a panpsychist, he writes:

A conscious field *plus* its object as felt or thought of *plus* an attitude toward the object *plus* the sense of a self to whom the attitude belongs— such a concrete bit of personal experience may be a small bit, but it is a solid bit as long as it lasts. . . . It is a *full* fact, even though it be an insignificant fact; it is of the *kind* to which all realities whatsoever must belong; the motor currents of the world run through the like of it; it is on the line connecting real events with real events.[16]

He does not say that all realities must be *exactly the same as a bit of human experience*, but that they must be akin to it. In 1903, he says virtually the same thing, only this time he speaks of *complete* realities, saying that they must be conceived "after the analogy" of a moment of human experience.

The only fully complete concrete data are, however, the successive moments of our own several histories, taken with their subjective personal aspect, as well as with their "objective" deliverance or "content." After the analogy of these moments of experiences must all complete reality be conceived. Radical empiricism thus leads to the assumption of a collectivism of personal lives (which may be of any grade of complication, and superhuman or infrahuman as well as human), variously cognitive of each other, variously conative and impulsive, genuinely evolving and changing by effort and trial, and by their interaction and cumulative achievements making up the world.[17]

All "complete reality" must be conceived "after the analogy" of the "successive moments of our several histories," which is to say, our experiences. For our experiences are the "only complete data" available to us. To say that reality, or parts of reality, are completely different from the only bit of reality we know directly, by *being* it, is to make a purely negative statement, and one of doubt-ful meaning. What could it possibly mean to say that some things are com-pletely different from everything we directly know?

No one doubts that James was a panpsychist in 1902-03 when he explic-itly says he was, but the vast majority of James scholars believe that he turned away from panpsychism the following year and never returned.[18] A close read-ing of James' work, however, renders this conclusion extremely unlikely. It is true that in some essays written in 1904 and 1905, later published as *Essays in Radical Empiricism*, he equivocated somewhat in his commitment to panpsy-chism, adopting at times a position that has been labelled "neutral monism." (This is the position that everything actual is potentially either "physical" or "mental" but in fact neither, and that it only becomes physical or mental as it functions in a specific context. For example, the difference between an idea of a pen and a real pen is that they function differently; the idea comes and goes by thinking of it or not thinking of it and does not write on real paper, while the real pen is much more stable and writes on real paper.) But to whatever degree James adopted neutral monism during this period, he soon returned to his panpsychic metaphysics. In lectures for a course he taught in 1905-06, he writes:

> Our only intelligible notion of any object *in itself* is that it should be an object *for* itself, and this lands us in panpsychism and a belief that our physical perceptions are effects on us of "psychical" realities. . . .*That* something exists when we as individuals are not thinking it, is an inex-pungable conviction of common sense. The various stages of idealist reflection are only as many successive attempts to define *what* the something is that thus exists. The upshot tends pretty strongly towards something like panpsychism. But there are various shades of opinion here.[19]

Only panpsychism, he maintains, provides one with an intelligible notion of what something is in itself.

In 1908, in his "Miller-Bode" notebook (which he kept principally to respond to the charge that his philosophy was antirealistic), he writes:

> The world *is* business . . . but the "agent" (element, substance, subject) which grammar and thought require, can be expressed as the potentiality of residual business. . . . Turning to my own particular puzzle, how shall we translate all this? The "pen," as a living real, is the name of a business centre, a "firm." It has many customers, my mind, e.g., and the physical world. To call it the *same pen* both times would mean that although my mind and the physical world can and may eventually figure in one and the

same transaction, they need not do so . . . and that in respect of this particular pen-experience neither *counts* in the transaction which the other is carrying on. Neither is *counted* by the other, neither is *for* the other. All such coming and going and alteration connects with the general notion of being counted, observed, associated, or ignored and left separate. These are essentially psychic expressions so that the constitution of reality which I am making for is of [the] psychic type.[20]

In *A Pluralistic Universe* (1909), he alludes favorably to "the great empirical movement toward a pluralistic panpsychic universe, into which our own generation has been drawn,"[21] and in *Some Problems of Philosophy*, a work James began in 1909 and never completed, he writes: "Meanwhile, the concrete perceptual flux, taken just as it comes, offers in our own activity-situations perfectly comprehensible instances of causal agency. . . . If we took these experiences as the type of what actual causation is, we should have to ascribe to cases of causation outside of our own life, to physical cases also, an inwardly experiential nature. In other words we should have to espouse a so-called 'panpsychic' philosophy."[22] And in "Final Impressions of a Psychical Researcher," his last publication before his death in 1910, he writes: "Not only psychic research, but metaphysical philosophy, and speculative biology are led in their own ways to look with favor on some such 'panpsychic' view of the universe as this."[23]

The view, first put forth by Ralph Barton Perry, that James flirted with panpsychism prior to 1904 but then moved away from it never to return, stands in direct opposition to all of these statements. Time and again James states that he is strongly inclined in the direction of panpsychism or flatly declares that his metaphysical position is the panpsychic position. Not to recognize this important break with modern thought is to miss one of the most essential aspects of James' thinking. Modern thought is modern largely by virtue of the fact that it has rejected panpsychism. Psychophysical dualism and physicalism, the two modern metaphysics, are in complete agreement as to the nature of matter—matter is dead, devoid of experience and inner activity. James' affirmation of panpsychism places him well beyond the boundaries of modern philosophy.

An equally fundamental break with modern metaphysics is the *process* element of James' thought. James' panpsychism or panexperientialism is not simply a new type of substance philosophy. His metaphysics is a process metaphysics. For James the basic units of reality are momentary. Reality is comprised of experience, and experience "comes in drops." And, unlike substances, which do not include one another, experiences necessarily include other experiences. In some respect, experiences overlap, interpenetrate, and include other experiences. The basic units of reality are thus internally related to, constituted by, other such units.[24] In the same entry in his Miller-Bode notebooks in which James says "the constitution of reality I am making for is of [the] psychic type," he says: "At bottom it seems nothing but this . . . that neither world nor things are finished, but in process, and that process means *more's* are continuous yet novel."[25]

The first expressions of James' process metaphysics are in *The Principles of Psychology*. Here James openly criticizes a variety of substance psychologies and puts forth a process view of the self. The self, for James, is not a Kantian ego or a Cartesian substance, nor is it a Humean collection of sensory data or impressions. The self is rather a series of psychic events or, as he sometimes calls it, "a stream" of consciousness. James contends that the conscious self, "as a psychological fact, can be fully described without supposing any other agent than a succession of perishing thoughts, endowed with the functions of appropriation and rejection and of which some can know and appropriate or reject objects already known, appropriated or rejected by the rest."[26] One need not posit a substance that thinks thoughts or feels feelings or makes decisions or that unifies a host of sensations into a single experience. All that one needs to suppose is that "thinking goes on," or more generally, that "experience goes on."

In *The Principles of Psychology* James referred to the succession of experiences that comprise the self sometimes as "drops" or "droplets," sometimes as "buds" and sometimes as the "stream of experience." Of these various metaphors it is the image of the stream that has enjoyed the most popularity, giving rise to, among other things, one of the characteristic literary styles of the twentieth century. But it is the imagery of drops (or droplets) that best portrays James' overall position on the nature of experience. The imagery of a stream suggests an undivided continuum. The imagery of a series of drops, however, does not. Drops may merge—they may include other drops—but drops are discrete. They come whole or not at all. In *Some Problems of Philosophy*, James makes it clear that he understands experience in terms of unitary events. He writes:

> "*Infinitum in actu pertransiri nequit*," said scholasticism; and every continuous quantum to be gradually traversed is conceived as such an infinite. The quickest way to avoid the contradiction would seem to be to give up that conception, and to treat real processes of change no longer as being continuous, but as taking place by finite not infinitesimal steps, like the successive drops by which a cask of water is filled, when whole drops fall into it at once or nothing. This is the radically pluralist, empiricist, or perceptualist position, which I characterized in speaking of Renouvier. . . . We shall have to end by adopting it in principle ourselves, qualifying it so as to fit closely to perceptual experience.[27]

Later in the same chapter he concludes that what has often been taken to be cases of continuous growth or change is in fact a succession of

> drops, buds, steps, or whatever we please to term them, of change coming wholly when they do come, or coming not at all. Such seems to be the nature of concrete experience, which changes always by sensible amounts, or stays unchanged. The infinite character we find in it is woven into it by our later conception indefinitely repeating the act of subdividing any given amount supposed. The facts do not resist the subsequent conceptual treatment; but we need not believe that the treatment necessarily reproduces the operation by which they were originally brought into existence.[28]

For James, reality came in drops, drops of experience. These experiences include previous experiences, and it is the inclusion of past experiences in present experiences that constitutes the relatedness of these discrete events. In the preface of *The Meaning of Truth* he states that the "generalized conclusion of radical empiricism," what he termed its "metaphysical statement," is that "the parts of experience hold together next to next by relations that are themselves parts of experience." "The directly apprehended universe," he continues, "needs . . . no extraneous transempirical support [i.e., no substances], but possesses in its own right a concatenated or continuous structure."[29] One finds similar statements in *A Pluralistic Universe*, and *Essays in Radical Empiricism*.[30]

    In adopting a process philosophy in which apparent substances are actually processes of various types of experiential entities, James once again breaks with modern philosophy, putting forth a postmodern alternative. James' process panexperientialism and his radical empiricism are not simply new examples of modern ways of thinking. The break with modern philosophy is too profound. Instead, they constitute a postmodern approach to understanding reality.

II. POSTMODERN SCIENCE AND RELIGION

James' postmodern perspective is evident in his writings on science (especially in his critique of science for dismissing psychical research before looking at the evidence) and in his writings on God and the moral life. His critique of modern science and his interest in psychic phenomena have been generally ignored (at least until quite recently, as the modern worldview has begun to lose its grip). His views on religious issues, though less often simply ignored, have enjoyed no greater success among most modern thinkers. Most modern thinkers today are true descendants of David Hume. On matters such as the reality of

God, genuine religious experiences, life after death, and the existence of values, the only legitimate conclusion is a skeptical one. In many cases skepticism has passed over to the outright assertion of nonexistence. There are many today who are quite certain that God does not exist and hence that genuine religious experiences are impossible, that there is no life after death, and that there are no values which exist independently of specific cultures and specific individuals. James, however, because of his radical departure from sensationism, and because of his adoption of a process panexperientialism, brings a new perspective to both science and religion.

A. On Science

James was, at one and the same time, a great admirer of modern science and an insightful and persistent critic. As a medical doctor, a professor of anatomy, and the author of *The Principles of Psychology*, he was a scientific "insider." He was a scientist who was aware of the intellectual achievements of modern science and the power of the scientific method, properly applied, to increase human knowledge. "Science," he writes, has made "glorious leaps in the last three hundred years, and extended our knowledge of nature so enormously both in general and in detail."[31] Elsewhere he writes that "to pass from mystical to scientific speculation is like passing from lunacy to sanity. Our debt to science," he says with clear hyperbole, "is literally boundless, and our gratitude for what is positive in her teachings must be correspondingly immense."[32]

These statements notwithstanding, his regard for modern science had its limits. Modern science has developed close ties to both physicalism and sensationism. By virtue of James' rejection of both of these doctrines, he was critical of modern science. Some of his writings on science take the form of noting the fundamental inadequacy of the philosophical presuppositions of modern science. Others take the form of proposing a postmodern science, one built upon panexperientialism and radical empiricism.

As early as 1878, James expressed his judgment against a science based on physicalism and a sensationist epistemology.

> Many persons nowadays seem to think that any conclusion must be very scientific if the arguments in favor of it are all derived from twitching of frogs' legs—especially if the frogs are decapitated—and that, on the other hand, any doctrine chiefly vouched for by the feelings of human beings—with heads on their shoulders—must be benighted and superstitious. They seem to think too, that any vagary or whim, however unverified, of a scientific man must needs form an integral part of science itself; that when Huxley, for example, has ruled feeling out of the game of life, and called it a mere bystander, supernumerary, the matter

is settled. The lecturer [James] knows nothing more deplorable than this indiscriminating gulping down of everything materialistic as peculiarly scientific. Nothing is scientific but what is clearly formulated, reasoned and verified. An opinion signed by the Pope, if it have these merits, will be a thoroughly scientific opinion. On the other hand, an opinion signed by Professor Huxley, if it violate these requirements, will be unscientific. To talk of science as many persons do whose mental type is best presented by the *Popular Science Monthly* is ridiculous. With these persons it is forever Science against Philosophy, Science against Metaphysics, Science against Religion, Science against Poetry, Science against Sentiment, Science against all that makes life worth living.

The truth is that science and all these other functions of the human mind are alike the result of man's thinking about the phenomena life offers him. No mode of thinking is *against* any other, except false thinking and illogical thinking. If we think clearly and consistently in theology or philosophy we are good men of science too. If, on the contrary, our thought is muddled in one field, it is worthless in all the rest. It must be that truth is one, and thought woven in one piece. I, for one, as a scientific man and a practical man alike, deny utterly that science compels me to believe that my conscience is an *ignis fatuus* or outcast and I trust that you too . . . will go away strengthened in the natural faith that your delights and sorrows, your loves and hates, your aspirations and efforts are real combatants in life's arena, and not impotent, paralytic spectators of the game.[33]

I have quoted James at such length because this passage represents the heart of James' discontent with modern science—and because the language is so wonderfully impassioned and the imagery so vivid. Speaking in more measured tones, James raises many of the same objections to modern science in his essay "What Psychical Research has Accomplished":

Although in its essence science only stands for a method and for no fixed beliefs, yet as habitually taken, both by its votaries and outsiders, it is identified with a certain fixed belief,—the belief that the hidden order or nature is mechanical exclusively, and that nonmechanical categories are irrational ways of conceiving and explaining even such things as human life.[34]

Correctly understood, science is only a method. It need not adhere to physicalism or to sensationism. And to the extent that it does, it has critical limitations. A science wedded to physicalism and one that is overly sensationist fails for at least four reasons: (i) it cannot explain the evolution of conscious beings such as ourselves; (ii) it must deny free will because there is no empirical evidence for it; (iii) it thereby must deny genuinely ethical decisions; and (iv) it must deny the radical-empirical evidence of one's own experience. More often than not, James focused mainly on the moral implications of a mechanistic view of reality, but he raised all four of these objections in various places in his writings.

Given the limitations of physicalism and sensationism and modern science's historical ties to these doctrines, James envisioned two proposals for saving science. The first amounts to *supplementing* scientific knowledge with other types of knowledge (what James sometimes called "personal" or "romantic" knowledge). The second proposal consists of *reconceptualizing* science so as to replace physicalism with panexperientialism and to expand its empiricism so as to include radical empiricism. This second proposal amounts to a call for a postmodern science. I will examine both proposals, beginning with the proposal to supplement scientific truths with other types.

Modern science, James maintained, presents one with a view of reality built upon a limited set of abstractions important for particular purposes. "Physics," he says,

> is but one chapter in the great jugglery which our conceiving faculty is forever playing with the order of being as it presents itself to our reception. It transforms the unutterable dead level and continuum of the "given" world into an utterly unlike world of sharp differences and hierarchic subordinations for no other reason than to satisfy certain subjective passions we possess.[35]

Science, illustrated here by physics, is human enterprise rooted in certain human desires, the desire to know some of the formal and predictable aspects of reality. But there is more to reality than those aspects of it that interest (modern) scientists. In addition to its formal aspects, there is the *content* of reality: the inner nature of things. And in addition to the predictable aspects, there are the unpredictable: those parts of nature where individual choices make real differences. Science provides only half truths. The full truth includes scientific truth but is not limited to it.

> Religious thinking, ethical thinking, poetical thinking, teleological, emotional, sentimental thinking, what one might call the personal view of life to distinguish it from the impersonal and mechanical, and the romantic view of life to distinguish it from the rationalistic view, have been, and even still are, outside of well-drilled scientific circles, the dominant forms of thought.[36]

The scientific perspective on reality requires the balance provided by the personal (religious, ethical, poetical, teleological, emotional, sentimental) perspective. Apart from these additional perspectives, scientific knowledge is incomplete and misleading.

In *A Pluralistic Universe* James makes roughly the same point. "Rationality," he contends, "has at least four dimensions, intellectual, aesthetic, moral and practical." The rational judgment is the one that allows for "the maximal degree *in all these respects simultaneously*."[37] Insofar as modern science, with its sensationist and physicalist orientation, discounts the moral, the practical, and (for the most part) the aesthetic dimensions, it needs to be supplemented with other approaches to understanding reality. Modern science, at its best, is incapable of getting at the full truth of the universe. Its "truths" must be factored into the final analysis, but because of its very limited approach it is incapable of arriving at the full truth about anything. The most rational perspective, James sometimes says, is one that *supplements* scientific truths with aesthetic and moral truths.

But James also put forth a second means of saving science from the limitations that result from its physicalist and sensationist perspective. One could replace its physicalism with panpsychism and include its sense-knowledge within a wider, more radical, empiricism. In other words, modern science could be reconceptualized. Unlike modern science, which requires supplementation by the personal or experiential view, a postmodern science would include the experiential view in its very foundation.

In his article entitled "What Psychical Research Has Accomplished" (1896), James prophesied that future generations may well look back at modern science in amazement for its systematic exclusion of "the only form of thing that we directly encounter"—human experience.

> The only form of thing that we directly encounter, the only experience we concretely have, is our own personal life. . . . And this systematic denial on science's part of personality as a condition of events, this rigorous belief that in its own essential and innermost nature our world is strictly an impersonal world, may, conceivably, as the whirligig of time goes round, prove to be the very defect that our descendants will be most surprised at in our own boasted science, the omission that to their eyes will most tend to make *it* [science] look perspectiveless and short.[38]

If science is to live up to its calling, if science is to be knowledge or knowing (as its name means), it must adequately account for the "only form of thing that we directly encounter," namely, human experience.

James was quick to point out that there are ways of including the personal and the romantic into one's metaphysics that do not constitute an advance of knowledge, especially in the area of the natural sciences. "Wholly unchecked by impersonal rationalism," the romantic and the personal view of nature may lead into what he called "Central African Mumbo-jumboism."[39] One way to avoid this fate is to allow for the apparent great differences among the types of experience that constitute various realities. As noted above, the panexperiential metaphysics that James endorsed recognizes "a collectivism of personal lives (which may be of any grade of complication, and superhuman or infrahuman as well as human), variously cognitive of each other, variously conative and impulsive, genuinely evolving and changing by effort and trial and by their interaction and cumulative achievement making up the world."[40] Rocks, trees, animals, and God are similar insofar as each has some experience, but the levels of experience—the content and presumably the clarity of the respective experiences—differ enormously. James might have done more to account for the seemingly vast differences between things such as clouds and rocks, on the one hand, and animals and God on the other. For example, he might have anticipated the distinction between individuals and aggregates made by Whitehead and Hartshorne, which is based on a distinction made long ago by Leibniz. (This distinction is developed by David Griffin in the chapter on Hartshorne below.) Nonetheless, the type of panexperientialism he endorsed recognizes an exceedingly wide range of experiencing actualities.

One of the practical differences between modern science and a panexperiential, radical empirical, postmodern science would be the latter's openness to investigating what have come to be called psychic, parapsychic, parapsychological, or paranormal phenomena. Throughout his life James was interested in various types of abnormal psychological phenomena, including drug-induced hallucinations, apparent thought-transference (or telepathy), and apparent communication with the dead. Not only was modern science unable to explain these phenomena to James' satisfaction; modern science dismissed the reality of such phenomena without even considering the evidence. "Why do so few 'scientists' even look at the evidence for telepathy, so-called?" James asks. "Because," he answers, "they think, as a leading biologist, now dead, once said to me, that even if such a thing were true, scientists ought to band together to keep it suppressed and concealed. It would undo the uniformity of Nature and all sorts of other things without which scientists cannot carry on their pursuits."[41] In other words, science turned a blind eye to anything that contradicted its materialistic, sensationistic paradigm. Rather than investigating such phenomena, it excluded them *a priori*. Writing to Carl Stumpf, James says, "I believe there is no source of deception in the investigation of nature which can compare with a fixed belief that certain kinds of phenomenon are *impossible*."[42]

On one level, it is perfectly understandable that modern science, with its historical ties to physicalism and sensationism, excludes parapsychic events.

A science that cannot account for any instance of psychological reality, even the everyday type that we all know by being an instance of it, is clearly incapable of accounting for exceptional mental states. The biologist to whom James refers is partially correct: admitting the existence of exceptional mental states (of the parapsychic type) would undo the uniformity of modern scientific theory. One cannot simply add psychic phenomena to an otherwise materialistic universe, nor can one simply add nonsensory perception in an ad hoc fashion. Parapsychic phenomena represent a direct challenge to modern science.

James' postmodern attitude to psychic phenomena can best be described as "open to the facts." In some cases he believed that the facts were there, in other cases that they were not. In a letter to Henry William Rankin in 1879 on the matter of demoniacal possession, he writes:

> I am not as positive as you are . . . in the belief that the obsessing agency is really demonic individuals. I am perfectly willing to adopt that theory if the facts lend themselves best to it, for who can trace limits to the hierarchies of personal existences in the world?[43]

And in his notes to his Lowell Lectures on "Exceptional Mental States," he writes: "Whether supernormal powers of cognition in certain persons may occur is a matter to be decided by evidence." He continues:

> I believe that Hodgson, Myers, and Sidgwick in obstinately refusing to start with any theories, in patiently accumulating facts, are following in the footsteps of the great scientific tradition of Mosely. I myself am convinced of supernormal cognition and supernormal healing. The facts are there.[44]

James was fully aware that psychic research was "a field in which the sources of deception are extremely numerous,"[45] but he was also aware that reports of psychic phenomena are as old as human records and occur in every culture. Those committed to physicalism and sensationism must reject psychic phenomena, for their worldview precludes the existence of nonsensory experiences. James, however, because he was neither a physicalist nor a sensationist, was free to be open to the facts whatever they might prove to be.

James' view of communication with the dead and life after death is in keeping with his general position regarding parapsychic phenomena: if the facts warrant such a position, so be it. Apart from carefully examining all the evidence, it would be irrational to take a stand for or against such occurrences. "Happy you," he wrote to G. H. Howison in 1901, "with such confident assurance of more life beyond! I find that I myself am growing more and more into a feeling of the probability of the same."[46] But this feeling of probability never

became a feeling of certainty. Eight years later, less than a year before his
death, James published a long report on attempts to communicate with Richard
Hodgson (a psychical researcher who had died in 1905). James concluded his
lengthy report with these words:

> *I myself feel as if an external will to communicate were probably there*,
> that is, I find myself doubting, in consequence of my whole acquain-
> tance with that sphere of phenomena, that Mrs. Piper's [the medium's]
> dream-life, even equipped with "telepathic" powers, accounts for all the
> results found. But if asked whether the will to communicate be Hodg-
> son's, or be some mere spirit-counterfeit of Hodgson, I remain and await
> more facts, facts which may not point clearly to a conclusion for fifty or
> a hundred years.[47]

The facts, as yet, were not in.

It is clear in "What Psychical Research Has Accomplished" that James
realized that psychical research requires more than a simple expansion of modern science's scope of inquiry. Psychical research requires a fundamental recon-
ceptualization of science.

> Science, so far as science denies such exceptional occurrences, lies pros-
> trate in the dust for me; and the most urgent intellectual need which I feel
> at present is that science be built up again in a form in which such things
> may have a positive place.[48]

If science is to understand parapsychic occurrences, it must be reconsidered
from the ground up, "built up again in a form in which such things may have a
positive place." It cannot simply be extended to include such phenomena, nor
can it merely be supplemented by other truths.

A science grounded upon panexperientialism and radical empiricism
would be a science in which paranormal events would have a positive place,
along with normal events. If reality consists of nothing but experiential entities,
and if there are modes of experience that are more fundamental than sensory
experience, then all sorts of explanations for parapsychic phenomena are possible. Equally important, such a science could account for such hard-core com-
mensense notions as personal experience, the existence of realities other than
oneself, and causation. These are notions that modern science necessarily presupposes, but for which no explanation can be given so long as one limits oneself to the doctrines of physicalism and sensationism.

It would be false to say that James' principal objection to modern science
stemmed from its inability to deal with apparent parapsychic events. James' primary objection to modern science, at least initially and for most of his adult life,

was that the epistemology to which it was allied provided no support for the ethical, religious, and aesthetic dimensions of reality and, indeed, tended to deny those aspects of reality. Insofar as ethical intuitions, free decisions, and religious experiences (and, one might add, experiences of relations, and the nonsensory awareness of something there) are counted as parapsychic experiences—that is falling outside the realm of modern psychology—it *is* modern science's inability to account for parapsychic phenomena that rendered it "prostrate in the dust" before James. But this is not the customary usage of the term "parapsychic." James' primary objection to modern science was its inability to account for the personal aspect of reality, the aspect of reality that is the subject matter of religion, poetry, ethics, and aesthetics. Modern science's refusal to consider paranormal experiences was just one more example of its commitment to physicalism and sensationism.

Of James' two proposals—to supplement modern science with other truths, or to reconceive science in a postmodern way—it is unclear which James preferred. The obvious advantage of the first proposal is that it does not require any fundamental change on the part of science. All that is required is a recognition that its truths are by nature limited and partial. The advantage of the second proposal is that it would result in a more adequate science, a science that can support the reality of ethical intuitions, free will, emotions, religious experiences, aesthetic enjoyment, the feeling of causality and other relations, the direct awareness of a real world, and nonsensory perceptions, including parapsychic ones. In short, the advantage of the second proposal is that it allows for an integrated understanding of reality in all its experienced complexity. I suspect James preferred this approach, at least in his more radical or postmodern moods, and that he proposed the first approach in his more conservative or modern moments.

B. On God and Ethics

The issue of morality in general was raised above; James' postmodern perspective is also evident in his thinking about the relation of God to the moral life in particular. From a modern perspective God and the moral life are highly problematic topics of discussion. If everything is finally physical, and if all knowledge comes via the physical senses, what possible meaning could it have to talk about God or about right and wrong? But if, as James maintained, nothing is simply physical, if everything has some personal/experiential aspect, and if sense-mediated experience is only a small fraction of human experience, talk about God, and about morality, and the relation of one to the other, can be meaningful.

Each of us, James maintained, has direct experience of God. Some people have had particularly vivid religious experiences, but all of us experience

God at some level. "The further limits of our being plunge," James states, "into an altogether other dimension of existence from the sensible and merely 'understandable' world. Name it the mystical region, or the supernatural region, whichever you choose. . . . God is the natural appellation, for us Christians at least."⁴⁹ God's existence is not merely a postulate. For James, God's existence is an empirical fact. God is said to exist because God is perceived, albeit not through any of the five senses.

James seems to argue that, even if there were no empirical evidence for God, one would have the right to believe in God, and that it is healthy, normal, and intellectually defensible to have such a belief. He concludes his essay "The Will to Believe" (which he regretted not calling "The Right to Believe"⁵⁰) with these words:

> If a man chooses to turn his back altogether on God and the future, no one can prevent him; no one can show beyond reasonable doubt that he is mistaken. If a man think otherwise and acts as he thinks, I do not see that anyone can prove that *he* is mistaken. Each must act as he thinks best; and if he is wrong, so much the worse for him.⁵¹

Belief in God is legitimate, in part, because it cannot be shown to be false.

But the right to believe in God is derived also from the fact that it is, or can be, positively useful. Belief in a certain concept of God—a finite God who works alongside us for good—inspires within us the very useful sentiment of the "strenuous mood."

> The capacity of the strenuous mood lies so deep down among our natural human possibilities that even if there were no metaphysical or traditional grounds for believing in a God, men would postulate one simply as a pretext for living hard, and getting out of the game of existence the keenest possibilities of zest. . . . Every sort of energy and endurance, of courage and capacity for handling life's evils, is set free in those who have religious faith. For this reason the strenuous type of character will on the battle-field of human history always outwear the easy-going type, and religion will drive irreligion to the wall.⁵²

The belief in a certain kind of God is useful in that it renders life both challenging and meaningful and provides one with the wherewithal to live vigorously.

As far as I know, James never linked his position that belief in God is rationally defensible and useful with this position that belief in God's existence is justified on radical-empirical grounds. He did argue that belief in God was normal and healthy and he argued, in "The Sentiment of Rationality" and in "Reflex Action and Theism," that in philosophy one must take into account all human faculties, so that the fact that we need the world to be a certain way is some evidence that it is that way. But he never explicitly stated that it was rationally defensible and useful (and normal and healthy) to believe in God because God was a part of every individual's experience at some level. Had he done so, the judgment that James' primary argument for the existence of God is found in "The Will to Believe" would certainly be less widespread than it currently is. In fact, James' primary "argument" for God's existence, if one wishes to employ that term, is a complex argument predicated on the direct experience of God.

The fact that James' worldview included God does not, in itself, make this worldview postmodern. Indeed many thinkers would assume that his inclusion of God shows him to have been somewhat *premodern*. What makes his thinking about God postmodern is his particular understanding of God. James concluded that God is not all-powerful, that God is not wholly transcendent, and that God is not unaffected by human activity. In rejecting God's omnipotence, absolute transcendence, and impassibility, James rejected three of the central tenets of premodern theism.

James never seems to have thought it intelligible to doubt God's goodness. If there is evil in the world—and James thought it was impossible to deny that there is—the explanation for it had to entail God's limited ability to control events. "I believe that the only God worthy of the name," he writes, "*must* be finite."[53] In *A Pluralistic Universe* he states,

> The only way to escape the paradoxes and perplexities that a consistently thought-out monistic universe suffers from . . .—the mystery of the "fall," namely, of reality lapsing into appearance, truth into error, perfection into imperfection, of evil, in short . . .—the only escape, I say, from all this is to be frankly pluralistic and assume that the superhuman consciousness [God], however vast it may be, has itself an external environment, and consequently is finite.[54]

Were God all-encompassing, were God responsible for everything that happens in every detail, one would have to hold God responsible for all the sins of commission and omission that litter human history. God acts in the world, but God is not the sole actor.

While making this unambiguous affirmation of God's limited power, and of the correlative powerfulness of nondivine beings such as ourselves, over against traditional theism, James also stressed God's involvement in the world. He rejected the position of that somewhat Hegelian, transcendental monism that assigned to God no power to produce effects in the world. James never denied that God was in some respects transcendent, but he believed that God is, at the same time, immanent. Were God wholly transcendent, God could not be experienced; nor could God act. James writes:

Transcendentalists are fond of the term "Oversoul" but as a rule they use it in an intellectualist sense, as meaning only a medium of communion. "God" is a causal agent as well as a medium of communion, and that is the aspect which I wish to emphasize.[55]

God is not only *over* the world; God is in the world. James makes this point again in the following passage.

For them [the monists] the world of the ideal [God] has no efficient causality, and never bursts into the world of phenomena at particular points. The ideal world, for them, is not a world of facts, but only of the meaning of facts; it is a point of view for judging facts. It appertains to a different "———ology," and inhabits a different dimension of being altogether from that in which existential propositions obtain. It cannot get down upon the flat level of experience and interpolate itself piecemeal between distinct portions of nature, as those who believe, for example, in divine aid coming in response to prayer are bound to think it must.[56]

The only God to whom James can attest is one who can be experienced and who exercises efficient causality—one who "get[s] down upon the flat level of experience" and produces effects.

A final feature of James' postmodern concept of God to be noted is that God is affected by the free actions of nondivine beings. Classical theologians have long thought of God as impassible, incapable of feeling in response to the world. To maintain that God could suffer, that God could thus feel, was to affirm that God is in some sense dependent—for the feeler is dependent upon what is felt—and dependency has long been regarded as inferior to self-sufficiency. But, if human beings are incapable of affecting the divine life, if God is indifferent to human decisions, activities, and feelings, James reasoned, then finally nothing matters. In "Is Life Worth Living?" he writes:

I confess that I do not see why the very existence of an invisible world order may not in part depend on the personal responses which any one of us may make to the religious appeal. God himself, in short, may draw vital strength and increase of very being from our fidelity. For my own part, I do not know what the sweat and blood and tragedy of this life mean, if they mean anything short of this.[57]

If what we do does not have some effect on the only being who endures forever, then nothing that we do matters, ultimately. Rather than envisioning God after the fashion of classical theology as wholly self-contained, James viewed God as drawing "vital strength and increase of very being from our fidelity." God affects the world and is in turn affected by the world.

Because of James' postmodern belief that human beings are essentially free beings, that they are not simply physical realities obeying the mindless laws of nature, and that God exists, is active in the world, and is affected by human activity, morality was not as problematic for James as it is for more modern philosophers. In "The Moral Philosopher and the Moral Life," he concludes:

> It would seem . . . that the stable and systematic moral universe for which the ethical philosopher asks is fully possible only in a world where there is a divine thinker with all-enveloping demands. If such a thinker existed, his way of subordinating the demands to one another would be the finally valid casuistic scale; his claims would be the most appealing; his ideal universe would be the most inclusive realizable whole. If he now exist, then actualized in his thought already must be that ethical philosophy which we seek as the pattern which our own must evermore approach.[58]

In this particular essay James leaves us with this hypothetical statement; he does not go on to claim that because God does in fact exist, there is an ethical order to the universe (though he did say that "would-be philosophers . . . must postulate a divine thinker, and pray for the victory of the religious cause").[59] If, however, one takes this assertion in conjunction with James' unambiguous claims in *The Varieties of Religious Experience* and in *A Pluralistic Universe* attesting to the reality of God, one may conclude that for James the way things ought to be, the correct moral order, is the way God judges that they ought to be.

One final point regarding James' postmodern perspective as it pertains to ethics. His metaphysics and epistemology contain two important implications for moral philosophy that James himself never developed. First, panexperientialism allows us to posit intrinsic value in all things. If everything actual experiences, then everything has some intrinsic value—that is, some value for itself—quite apart from whatever instrumental value it may have for something else. This type of philosophy provides, in contrast with dualism and physicalism, a basis for an ecological ethic. Second, radical empiricism allows for the *perception* of intrinsic value. Even if things beyond ourselves, including so-called physical things, have intrinsic value, one could never know this if all knowledge were mediated through the senses. Our senses are attuned only to external qualities or appearances of physical things—their color, sound, taste, smell, and texture, Radical empiricism, however, allows for the awareness of intrinsic value. For example, in feeling bodily pains and pleasures, we are getting an inkling of the type of intrinsic value (or disvalue) our bodily members are experiencing. Although James did not develop these two aspects of his postmodern philosophy, he laid the foundation for those extensions.

III. James' Pragmatic Theory of Truth

James' pragmatic theory of truth is widely regarded as an alternative to both the correspondence and the coherence theories of truth. Ellen Kappy Suchiel, in *The Pragmatic Philosophy of William James*, writes: "In the philosophical tradition we find that there have been three major theories of truth: the correspondence, the coherence, and the pragmatic. James develops his pragmatic theory of truth as an alternative to the other two. . . . This theory represents James's most important contribution as a philosopher and lies at the heart of his philosophy."[60] Looking for an hour through the various "introduction to philosophy" textbooks in my office, I was able to locate six additional texts that put forth a similar interpretation of James' theory of truth.[61] One can also point to Richard Rorty, who has argued at great length the position that truth is not a correspondence between statements and the way things really are. Until quite recently he maintained that in holding this position he was only agreeing with James. Rorty still holds this position, but now no longer claims that it necessarily corresponds (!) to James' position.[62]

There is no denying that James made a host of statements that seem to indicate that by "truth" he meant something other than the agreement between a thought or a statement and some specified object or condition in the world, and one needs to account for all of these statements in one way or another. But time and time again James insisted that his pragmatic theory of truth involves a correspondence theory of truth. In the preface to *The Meaning of Truth*, he states, in rather unambiguous terms:

> Altho in various places in this volume I try to refute the slanderous charge that we deny real existence, I will say here again, for the sake of emphasis, that the existence of the object, whenever the idea asserts it "truly," is the only reason in innumerable cases, why the idea does work successfully.[63]

This assertion, forcibly stated and strategically placed in the preface, cannot be easily overlooked or dismissed. Nor is it the only textual support one can cite to show that James understood truth to mean an agreement between the way things are and the way they are thought to be. In "The Will to Believe" (1896), for example, he writes, "But in our dealing with objective nature we obviously are recorders, not makers of truth. . . . Throughout the breadth of physical nature facts are what they are quite independently of us."[64] In his review of F. C. S. Schiller's *Humanism* (1903), he writes,

> Grant . . . that our human subjectivity determines *what* we shall say things are; grant that it gives the "predicates" to all the "subjects" of our

conversation. Still the fact remains that some subjects are there for us to talk about, and others are not there; and the further fact that, in spite of so many different ways in which we may perform the talking, there still is a grain in the subjects which we can't well go against, a cleavage-structure which resists certain of our predicates and makes others slide in more easily.[65]

Writing to his friend Charles Strong in 1907, James vigorously objects to Strong's accusation that his theory of truth is not sufficiently realistic.

You are the man who has least right to misrepresent me, for to no one have I talked so fully; and with epistemological realism at the very permanent *heart and centre* of *all* my thinking, it gives me a queer "turn" to hear you keep insisting that I shall and must be treated as an idealist.[66]

In a subsequent letter James admitted that he may have made some "verbal slips" and once again affirms his commitment to realism. He writes: "I have always intended (though I may have made verbal slips) to be realistic, and to be called an idealist . . . makes me feel queer."[67] And, writing to Schiller the following year about a philosophical meeting James had just attended where Schiller's position was being discussed, James writes,

I, being radically realistic, claimed you to be the same, but no one believed me as to either of us. Wouldn't you subscribe to the paper I enclose ["The Meaning of Truth"]? Isn't the ὕλη [substance] which you speak of as the primal bearer of all our humanized predicates, conceived by you epistemologically as an independent *that* which the *whats* qualify, and which (in the ultimate) may be decided to be of any nature whatsoever? I hope so; for that position seems to me invulnerable.[68]

These statements, taken together, clearly show that James intended his theory of truth to be a correspondence theory. If this is the case, then some explanation is needed for those statements that suggest otherwise.

Of importance equal to that of these textual citations is the fact that James clearly intended his pragmatic theory of truth to support both his metaphysics and his epistemology. In his words, "it seems to me that the establishment of the pragmatic theory of truth is a step of first-rate importance in making radical empiricism prevail."[69] A noncorrespondence theory of truth would support neither. A correspondence theory of truth supports both. James can have a correspondence theory of truth because his panexperientialism allows him to conceive of a world existing in its own right and because his radical empiricism allows him to account for how this world can be known.

If James' pragmatic theory of truth is, at heart, a correspondence theory, how is it that it has been so widely misunderstood? In addition to the "verbal slips" that he willingly acknowledged, James is guilty of three additional confusions in his writings on truth. These are (1) his misunderstanding of F. C. S. Schiller's humanism, (2) his failure most of the time to distinguish clearly between truths about the past, which are true independently of human actions, and "truths" about the future, which are not already true but, depending on human actions, may *become* true, and (3) his repeated confusion of truth and knowledge. (In some cases, these failures may have been instances of "verbal slips," but in the majority of instances the problem seems to have been more profound.) I will examine these three confusions in order.

James found much to agree with in Schiller's *Humanism*. Like Schiller, James was convinced that human consciousness is inescapably culturally conditioned. The human mind is not a "mirror of nature"—an undistorted, uninterpreted reflection of what is out there. Quite to the contrary, human experience is always teleological and socially constructed. James writes:

> Our nouns and adjectives are all humanized heirlooms, and in the theories we build them into, the inner order and arrangement is wholly dictated by human considerations, intellectual consistency being one of them. . . . We plunge forward into the field of fresh experience with the beliefs our ancestors and we have made already; these determine what we notice; and what we notice determines what we will do; what we do again determines what we experience; so from one thing to another, altho the stubborn fact remains that there is a sensible flux, what is *true of it* seems from first to last to be largely a matter of our own creation.[70]

Truth is, in a sense, "largely a matter of our own creation." That is, what we notice, how we understand it, and how we act upon our understanding, are all greatly influenced by our cultural and personal past. But this is, for James, not the whole story. Ponder again James' remarks in his review of Schiller's *Humanism*:

> Grant . . . that our human subjectivity determines *what* we shall say things are; grant that it gives the "predicates" to all the "subjects" of our conversation. Still the fact remains that some subjects are there for us to talk about, and others are not there; and the further fact that, in spite of so many different ways in which we may perform the talking, there still is a grain in the subjects which we can't well go against.[71]

For Schiller, there were no extracultural "stubborn facts" to be taken account of. Human consciousness was not *largely* a cultural construct, but a cultural construct through and through. James' identification of "pragmatism" with Schiller's "humanism" led others, who understood Schiller better than James did, to infer that James, too, was not a realist and therefore that pragmatism did not involve a correspondence theory of truth.

A second source of misunderstanding of James' pragmatic theory of truth lies in his failure clearly to distinguish between truth as it pertains to past facts, and truth as it pertains to events in the future. Time and again James says that, in relation to the objective world and the past, *it is the existence of the objective fact that makes a true statement true.* As stated in the preface of *The Meaning of Truth,* "the existence of the object, whenever the idea asserts it 'truly,' is the only reason in innumerable cases, why the idea does work successfully."[72] But in saying this, James is also indicating that, in some cases, it is *not* the existence of an object that makes an idea true. These are the cases where the truths are about future events. Because the future does not exist (and James never waivered on this point), *a "true" belief about what will happen cannot be true in the same sense that a statement about the past or the objective world can be true.* One cannot hold a correspondence theory of truth with regard to nonexistent realities, which is precisely what the future is comprised of.

On a number of occasions, James speaks of some beliefs—such as, "You will become my friend," "I can escape this dangerous situation," and "My life is meaningful"—as being true, not because they correspond to already existing facts, but because they are useful in bringing about the desired facts. Some facts depend upon human actions. If we fail to act, those facts will never come into existence. What we believe affects how we act. If, to use James' example of the endangered hiker, we feel certain that we cannot make the necessary leap across the chasm, we increase the likelihood that we will not. James made this point repeatedly throughout his career: our beliefs matter because at least part of the future depends on what we do, and what we believe largely deter-mines what we do. James' failure to distinguish clearly between beliefs about the future (or "truths" about future events, which are not already true but can become true), and truths about the past (which are true because they correctly characterize some actuality or collection of actualities), has led many inter-preters to conclude that, for James, truths about past events, like truths about future events, do not depend on already existing facts. A careful reading of James, however, does not allow this interpretation. James held that the past is irrevocably what it is, and our ideas about it are *useful* insofar as they accurately *correspond* to those past facts.

A third reason for the frequent misunderstanding of James' pragmatism is his tendency to confuse "truth" with "belief" or "judgment" about the truth.[73] James' discussion of the counting of the stars in Ursa Major provides an exam-ple. Was it true that there were seven stars in Ursa Major prior to anyone's actu-ally counting them?

Were they explicitly seven . . . before the human witness came? Surely nothing in the truth of the attributions drives us to think this. They were only implicitly or virtually what we call them, and we human witnesses first explicated them and made them "real." A fact virtually pre-exists when every condition of its realization save one is already there. In this case the condition lacking is the act of the counting and comparing mind. But the stars (once the mind considers them) themselves dictate the result. The counting in no wise modifies their previous nature, and, they being what and where they are, the count cannot fall out differently. It could then *always* be made. *Never could the number be questioned*, if the question were *once raised*.

We have here a quasi-paradox. Undeniably something comes by the counting that was not there before. And yet that something was *always true*. In one sense you *create* it, and in another sense you *find* it. You have to treat your count as being true beforehand, the moment you come to treat the matter at all.[74]

James' language of "virtually pre-existent facts" stems from his confusing "truth" with "belief," or what is taken to be "knowledge." Before anyone counted seven stars in Ursa Major it was true, given what and where the stars are, that those seven bodies existed, just as it was true that the earth was round (or nearly so) prior to anyone's knowing it. What comes with counting and circumnavigating is a change not in the *truth* about the facts but in the *beliefs* that we take to be knowledge about the facts, which "in no wise modifies" the "previous nature" of that which is now known. Speaking of "virtually pre-existent facts" is simply a confusing way of talking about unknown truths.

James' tendency to confuse truth (true propositions) with knowledge (justified belief in true propositions) requires him to say, or nearly say, that truths about the past and truths about the present are always changing, for certainly human knowledge is always changing. "Experience," he says, ". . . has ways of *boiling over*, and making us correct our present formulas. . . . We have to live to-day by what truths we can get to-day, and be ready to-morrow to call it falsehood." He likewise says: "Truth lives . . . for the most part, on a credit system. . . . You accept my verification of one thing, I yours of another. We trade on each other's truths."[25] Had James said, "we have to live today by what beliefs or judgments we have today, by what we take to be knowledge, and be ready tomorrow to call it falsehood," and "we trade on each other's beliefs and judgments, each other's knowledge," his theory of truth would have been less open to misunderstanding. No one can deny that beliefs and judgments about the past and the present are subject to change. But by confusing truth with knowledge, and especially with beliefs and judgments about the truth that subsequently are realized to be unwarranted, James often appears to say that what was once true can become false. When asked point blank, however, in 1907, if truths about the past can change, James replied,

> I can frame no notion of the past that doesn't leave it inalterable. Truths involving the past's relations to later things can't come into being till the later things exist, so such truths may grow and alter, but the past itself [hence the truth about the past] is beyond the reach of modification.[76]

It would be wrong to suggest that James had a fully adequate correspondence theory carefully worked out. His writings on truth are arguably his most careless and confused. Nevertheless, it seems clear that James always intended his pragmatic theory of truth to involve a type of correspondence theory (except when applied to beliefs about the future), and that this interpretation fits neatly with his metaphysics and his wider epistemological views. If, as James maintained, the world exists independently of some external perception of it, and if each of us has, via experience taken radically, a direct apprehension of reality, then it makes perfectly good sense to understand truth as the correspondence of the meaning of an assertion with an existing fact. True ideas are verifiable and work because they accurately characterize some feature of reality, that is, they correspond to the way things are.

IV. SOCIAL RAMIFICATIONS

One last topic needs to be raised to round out this brief overview of James' postmodern philosophy, and that is the social dimension of this worldview. James was often deeply engaged in the social issues of his day. This is perhaps most evident in his famous essay "The Moral Equivalent of War," in which he was responding to America's involvement in the Spanish-American War. But his social or political philosophy is by no means limited to this one essay.[77]

Speaking broadly, there are four important characteristics of James' social philosophy: his concern for the physical well-being of all; his commitment to economic and social justice; his protest against "bigness"; and his desire for peace. These are, of course, not unrelated matters, but simply different dimensions of the same moral concern. It is useful, however, to look at James' social philosophy from each of these perspectives in turn.

James was troubled by the fact that so many human beings, often through no fault of their own, lack the physical means for life, or live perilously close to the edge of starvation.

> That so many men, by mere accidents of birth and opportunity, should have a life of *nothing else* but toil and pain and hardness and inferiority

imposed upon them, should have *no* vacations, while others natively no more deserving never get any taste of this campaigning life at all—*this* is capable of arousing indignation in reflective minds.[78]

For James, to sit by while other human beings struggle to survive is morally inexcusable. Whatever actions can be taken to rectify this situation must be taken.

James was also concerned with the vast disparity of wealth so apparent in the United States. The gap between the rich and the poor (or the "haves" and the "have nots") is inexcusably and unjustifiably wide. In "What Makes a Life Significant?" (1898), he concludes his analysis of the labor problem with the prediction that American society will move towards some "newer and better equilibrium, and the distribution of wealth has doubtless got to change."[79]

A third dimension of James' social philosophy was his critique of "bigness" and his conviction that individuals need to be rooted in appropriately sized communities. In a letter to Mrs. Henry Whitman, he put it quite forcibly:

I am against bigness and greatness in all their forms, and with the invisible molecular forces that work from individual to individual, stealing in through the crannies of the world like so many soft rootlets, or like the capillary oozing of water, and yet rending the hardest monuments of man's pride, if you give them time. The bigger the unit you deal with, the hollower, the more brutal, the more mendacious is the life displayed. So I am against all big organizations as such, national ones first and foremost; against all big successes and results; and in favor of the eternal forces of truth which always work in the individual and immediately unsuccessful way, under-dogs always, till history comes, after they are long dead, and puts them on the top.[80]

When Santayana said of James, "He was one of those elder Americans who were still disquieted by the ghost of tyranny, social and ecclesiastical,"[81] it was to this aspect of James' thought that he was referring. "Bigness"—social bigness but also what might be termed "philosophical" or "theological bigness"—inevitably tyrannizes the individual. James was for the individual, especially the poor and the overlooked, the "under-dogs."

But he was *not* an individualist pure and simple. Human beings are social creatures. Individualism in the extreme is neither possible nor desirable. James only advocates individuals when the alternative is one or another form of "bigness." Between "bigness" and radical individualism lies the view of the individual in appropriately sized communities. There are scores of passages in James' writings to support the claim that James is not a radical individualist, but one particularly clear passage is found in a letter he wrote to Ernest Howard Crosby. Here James says that he is convinced that the best way to maintain freedom, as well as to protect the rights of the individual, remains "for lovers of the ideal [of freedom] to found smaller communities. . . . Through small systems, kept pure, lies one most promising line of betterment and salvation." He asks, "Why won't anarchists get together and try it?"[82] The alternative between "bigness" and radical individualism, then, is the individual-in-community.

James opposes bigness in all its forms, be it American imperialism or Royce's brand of Absolute Idealism, because it necessarily undercuts individual freedom, responsibility, and worth. Where "bigness" prevails it is the Absolute, or History, or American Foreign Policy, or the University, or Whatever, that decides, that acts, and not men and women. Individual men and women are acted upon. And without power, without the ability to make a difference for good or for ill, there is no room for moral responsibility. In a big system, individual men and women are not accountable for their actions because they are incapable of action. And, incapable of action and responsibility, unreal in any meaningful sense, individuals have no worth. Only the Absolute, the Whole, the System, the Whatever, has worth.

Each of these dimensions of James' social thought—his concern for the physical well-being of humanity, his commitment to economic and social justice, and his affirmation of individual human beings living and working together in small communities, along with his desire for a world without wars—is evident in his justly famous essay "The Moral Equivalent of War."

War, James argued, has its aesthetic and moral appeal. Despite its ugliness and its horrors, war excites and inspires us. It thrills us and provides us with challenges. It calls for heroism, hardiness, and sacrifice. It requires us to transcend ourselves. Pacifists who overlook this aspect of war, focusing only on war's undeniable destructiveness, overlook what is noble and good about war. And when these same pacifists go on to offer consumerism and self-indulgence as alternatives to war, they offer a way of life that is in many respects less aesthetically and morally appealing. War, and the preparation for war, will continue so long as there is no equally attractive alternative—no moral equivalent—to war.

Let us, James proposed, replace military conflict with a war on absolute poverty.

> If now, and this is my idea—there were, instead of military conscription, a conscription of the whole youthful population to form for a certain number of years a part of the army enlisted against *Nature*, the injustice would tend to be evened out, and numerous other goods to the commonwealth to follow.[83]

The world is full of people who live miserable lives, who are ravished by famine or left homeless by floods and earthquakes. The fighting spirit that military adventures depend on could just as easily, and much more profitably, be sparked by the rightful indignation that is the proper response to such gross unfairness.

James' vision of a world without war, a world in which the wealth is shared more equally, in which efforts are made to eliminate undeserved suffering, and in which individuals thrive in appropriately sized communities, needs to be seen as part and parcel of his postmodern philosophy. This vision, this social idea, presupposes that there is free will (which in turn logically entails some form of panexperientialism), and it presupposes a relational view of reality.

Physicalism requires determinism. If all of reality can be understood in terms of the interaction of bits of matter, then everything is as it must be. As a panexperientialist, James did not have to subscribe to determinism. In fact, one of the reasons he turned to panpsychism or panexperientialism in the first place was to avoid determinism. Because all true individuals are, in addition to their physicality, also experiential, each entity is free, within limits, to determine itself and, in doing so, to decide something for the future. As a panexperientialist James was freed from any deterministic philosophy of history and of war. "The fatalistic view of the war function," he wrote, "is to me nonsense, for I know that war-making is due to definite motives and subject to prudential checks and reasonable criticism, just like any other form of enterprise."[84] Wars are made by individuals (usually men). And individuals, having free will, need not choose to make war. Any view that wars are inevitable is incompatible with the postmodern view that all individuals have some degree of freedom.

One also finds in this essay a reaffirmation of James' belief that human beings are inherently social. This view, while not unique to postmodern modes of thought, is in James' case grounded in his claim that reality itself is relational. Nothing actual is cut off from everything else. War, whatever else it may be, is a communal affair and this is why consumerism, for example, which is less social, can never be the moral equivalent of war. "All the qualities of man acquire dignity," James writes, "when he knows that the service of the collectivity that owns him needs them. If proud of the collectivity, his own pride rises in proportion."[85]

The modern worldview has emphasized individualism as opposed to individuals within appropriately sized communities. In the extreme case, when individuals are thought to be like substances requiring nothing but themselves in order to exist, community is all but denied. James, however, holds a postmodern view of individuals and communities. Individuals exist in a dialectical relation with other individuals. Individuals are social, though not only social; they are also unique and private, and possess some degree of self-determination. Given a process panexperientialist metaphysics such as James', both distinctness and relatedness can be affirmed. If individuals are not substances but rather units of experience that include other experiences, then every individual is in its very being social. It is not merely social, however, because, in addition to experiencing other actualities, it is *its experience of them*, which is to say that it is a unique individual.

James did not view himself as a great system builder, and there is more than ample justification for this self-assessment. Nowhere does he explicitly make the connections that I have made here between his metaphysics and his social thought. Still, the connections are there to be made.

Much more could be said about James' social philosophy. Here only a bare outline of this aspect of his thought has been sketched. My purpose has been to give a fuller account of the character and the scope of James' thought and to argue, though briefly, that his social thought is not separate from his postmodern perspective.

V. Conclusion

The modern worldview rests on one of two substance philosophies—dualism and physicalism—and the dominant epistemologies have been sensationist. James rejected all of these modern alternatives. Instead of a substance philosophy he offered a process philosophy; instead of either dualism or physicalism he adopted panexperientialism; and instead of sensationism he put forth radical empiricism. His departure from modern thought is too profound to regard him as just another modern.

James' break with the modern worldview is embodied in his proposals for a postmodern science, a postmodern view of God and ethics, and a postmodern alternative to war. If the fundamental units of reality are drops of experience and if sensory perception is not fundamental but rather derivative, then modern science is predicated on mistaken assumptions. If the self-determining power of the experience of the things being studied is sufficiently small so as to be practically irrelevant, or if one is interested only in some external aspect of certain realities, the mistaken assumption of modern science does not constitute a problem. Within certain limits, modern science is useful. Beyond those limits, however, it is positively misleading and unhelpful. Normal everyday human experience goes beyond those limits, as do paranormal experiences of the type that James was interested in. James wavered between merely recognizing the limits of modern science and supplementing its truths with other truths—religious, moral, poetic, teleologic, and emotional truths—and the more radical option of replacing modern science with a postmodern, process, panexperiential science.

His break with modern philosophy, especially the atheistic variety that has superseded the various theistic versions, allowed him to include God in his worldview. God is, at best, a useless hypothesis if one accepts physicalism and sensationism. But as a panexperientialist and a radical empiricist, James could incorporate a certain understanding of God in his worldview. James understood God, for the most part, as a divine being working for good in the universe. God is not wholly transcendent, nor all-powerful, nor unaffected by human activity. Rather, God is—in addition to whatever transcendence is rightly attributed to God—present in all human experience; explicitly religious experiences are only an extreme example of what is always and everywhere the case. And unlike classical theists, James understood God to be both limited in power and directly affected by human activity. Were God all-powerful and entirely good, there could be no evil in the world. Being unwilling to give up either God's goodness or the reality of evil, James concluded that God's power is not complete. This conclusion was also forced—though James never, so far as I know, made it explicit—by the radical-empirical fact that each person knows him- or herself to be powerful, to decide to do one thing rather than other. God cannot be *all*-powerful if each individual has *some* power.

James' postmodern vision is also incorporated in his proposed alternative to war. The division of the world into nation-states with conflicting interests has been the assumed basis for global political and ethical thinking in modern times. To suppose that wars could be avoided altogether is considered by most to be unrealistic, which it is from a modern perspective. From a postmodern perspective, however, war can be avoided. The energies that have been directed toward fighting one another can and should be redirected to combating natural forces that inflict undeserved suffering. All the benefits associated with war—the excitement, the challenge, the unity, the need to be needed—can be obtained in the struggle to improve the lives of the least fortunate among us while avoiding all of the evils of war.

To try to understand James as a modern, as a representative of that complex philosophic tradition which began with Descartes and is in one form or another still dominant today, is to miss the central focus of his thought. As James said in *A Pluralistic Universe*: "A man's vision is the great fact about him."[86] James' vision was postmodern.

NOTES

1. Ralph Barton Perry, *The Thought and Character of William James*, 2 vols. (Boston: Little Brown and Company, 1935), vol. II, 606.

2. W. T. Jones, *A History of Western Philosophy: Hobbes to Hume*, vol. II (New York: Harcourt Brace Jovanovich, Inc., 1969), 301.

3. Ibid., 258.

4. William James, *Collected Essays and Reviews*, ed. Ralph Barton Perry (New York: Longmans, Green and Co., 1920), 443-44.

5. William James, *The Principles of Psychology*, vol. I (New York: Longmans, Green and Co., 1890), 258.

6. William James, *The Varieties of Religious Experience* (New York: Longmans, Green and Co., 1902), 58.

7. James, *The Principles of Psychology*, I, 245-46.

8. Ibid., 239.

9. James, *The Varieties of Religious Experience*, 502 n. 1.

10. Ibid., 515-16.

11. William James, *A Pluralistic Universe* (London: Longmans, Green and Co., 1912), 292.

12. James, *The Principles of Psychology*, I, 146-50. See also Perry, *The Thought and Character of William James*, I, 490.

13. Perry, *Thought and Character*, I, 503; II, 25-33.

14. Ibid., II, 745; see also 373.

15. James, *The Principles of Psychology*, 148-49.

16. James, *The Varieties of Religious Experience*, 499.

17. Perry, ed., *Collected Essays and Reviews*, 443-44. (See note 4 above.)

18. Bruce Kuklick, *The Rise of American Philosophy: Cambridge, Massachusetts, 1860-1930* (New Haven: Yale University Press, 1977), 333.

19. Perry, *Thought and Character*, II, 446.

20. Ibid., 764.

21. James, *A Pluralistic Universe*, 141-42.

22. William James, *Some Problems of Philosophy* (New York: Longmans, Green and Co., 1911), 218.

23. William James, *Memories and Studies* (New York: Longmans, Green and Co., 1912), 204.

24. For a somewhat extended treatment of James' understanding of both constitutive (or internal) and nonconstitutive (or external) relations, see chapter 6 of my book, *William James' Philosophy: A New Perspective* (Amherst: University of Massachusetts Press, 1982). James did not work out a general theory of relations, but he clearly believed in both constitutive and nonconstitutive relations.

25. Perry, *Thought and Character*, II, 764.

26. James, *The Principles of Psychology*, I, 341-42.

27. James, *Some Problems of Philosophy*, 172.

28. Ibid., 185.

29. William James, *The Meaning of Truth* (Cambridge: Harvard University Press, 1975), 7.

30. In "Does 'Consciousness' Exist?" James says: "'Mind' or 'personal consciousness' . . . is the name of a series of experiences run together by certain definite transactions, and an objective reality is a series of similar experiences knit by different transactions" (*Essays in Radical Empiricism* [Cambridge: Harvard University Press, 1976], 39). See also "The Continuity of Experience" in *A Pluralistic Universe*.

31. William James, *The Will to Believe* (Cambridge: Harvard University Press, 1979), 49.

32. Ibid., 239.

33. Perry, *Thought and Character*, II, 30-31.

34. James, *The Will to Believe*, 239.

35. Ibid., 103.

36. Ibid., 239.

37. James, *A Pluralistic Universe*, 55.

38. James, *The Will to Believe*, 241.

39. Ibid., 239.

40. See note 17 above.

41. James, *The Will to Believe*, 19.

42. *Letters of William James*, vol. I (Boston: Atlantic Monthly Press, 1920), 248; or John J. McDermott, *The Writings of William James* (New York: Random House, 1967), 787.

43. Eugene Taylor, ed., *William James on Exceptional Mental States* (Amherst: University of Massachusetts Press, 1984), 109; or *Letters of William James*, vol. II (Boston: Atlantic Monthly Press, 1920), 55.

44. Taylor, *Exceptional Mental States*, 91-92.

45. McDermott, *The Writings of William James*, 787.

46. Perry, *Thought and Character*, II, 217.

47. William James, *Essays in Psychical Research* (Cambridge: Harvard University Press, 1986), 358.

48. James, *The Will to Believe*, 236.

49. James, *The Varieties of Religious Experience*, 515-16.

50. Edward H. Madden, *Chauncey Wright and the Foundations of Pragmatism* (Seattle: University of Washington Press, 1963), 69. See also *Letters of Chauncey Wright*, ed. J. B. Thayer (Cambridge: John Wilson and Son, 1878), 341-43, and H. S. Thayer's preface to the Harvard edition of *The Meaning of Truth*.

51. James, *The Will to Believe*, 33.

52. Ibid., 161.

53. James, *A Pluralistic Universe*, 60.

54. Ibid., 140.

55. James, *The Varieties of Religious Experience*, 516-17 n. 2.

56. Ibid., 521.

57. James, *The Will to Believe*, 55.

58. Ibid., 161.

59. Ibid.

60. Ellen Kappy Suchiel, *The Pragmatic Philosophy of William James* (Notre Dame, Ind.: University of Notre Dame Press, 1982), 91.

61. The six additional texts I located with no difficulty are:

Charles Landeman, *Philosophy: An Introduction to the Central Issues* (New York: Holt, Rinehart and Winston, 1985). See 272-74.

Arthur Minton and Thomas Shipka, *Philosophy: Paradox and Discovery* (New York: McGraw-Hill Book Company, 1982). See 177-84.

Jeffry Olan, *Persons and Their Worlds: An Introduction to Philosophy:* (New York: Random House, 1983). See 281-82.

Jack B. Rogers and Forrest E. Baird, *Introduction to Philosophy: A Case Method Approach* (San Francisco: Harper and Row, 1981). See 172.

Gerald Runkle, *Theory and Practice: An Introduction to Philosophy* (New York: Holt, Rinehart and Winston, 1985). See 431-42.

Robert C. Solomon, *Introducing Philosophy: Problems and Perspectives* (New York: Harcourt Brace Jovanovich, Inc., 1981). See 179-85.

62. In "Comments on Sleeper and Edel" (*Transactions of the Charles S. Peirce Society* XXI [Winter 1985], 39-48) Rorty retracted his claim that his position is the same as that of Dewey and James. He writes, "I can only say that my references to pragmatism were an effort to acknowledge my own lack of originality rather than an attempt to make new bottles look good by claiming that they held old wine."

63. James, *The Meaning of Truth* (Cambridge: Harvard University Press, 1975), 8.

64. James, *The Will to Believe*, 26.

65. *Collected Essays and Reviews*, 451.

66. Perry, *Thought and Character*, II, 549.

67. Ibid., 550.

68. Ibid., 509.

69. James, *The Meaning of Truth*, 6.

70. William James, *Pragmatism: A New Name for Some Old Ways of Thinking* (Cambridge: Harvard University Press, 1975), 122.

71. *Collected Essays and Reviews*, 451.

72. See note 63 above.

73. See Michael D. Bybee's excellent article, "James' Theory of Truth as a Theory of Knowledge," in *Transactions of the Charles S. Peirce Society* XX/3 (Summer 1984), 253-68.

74. James, *The Meaning of Truth*, 56 (his emphasis).

75. James, *Pragmatism*, 100, 106-07.

76. Perry, *Thought and Character*, II, 478.

77. For a detailed analysis of James' social philosophy, see George Cotkin's excellent book, *William James: Public Philosopher* (Baltimore: The Johns Hopkins University Press, 1990). Much of what I have put forth here draws upon this book.

78. McDermott, *The Writings of William James*, 669.

79. William James, "What Makes a Life Significant?," in *Talks to Teachers on Psychology* (Cambridge: Harvard University Press, 1983), 166.

80. William James to Mrs. Henry Whitman, 7 June 1899, in *Letters of William James*, ed. Henry James (Boston: Atlantic Monthly Press, 1920, vol. 2, 90). Note here James' references to "the eternal forces of truth" working for good in the world. This counts as still another piece of evidence that, for James, truth has some objective status.

81. George Santayana, *Character and Opinion in the United States: With Rem-*

iniscences of William James and Josiah Royce and the Academic Life in America (London: Constable and Co., 1920), 91.

82. William James to Ernest Howard Crosby, 23 October 1901, in *William James: Selected Unpublished Correspondence: 1885-1910*, ed. Frederick J. Down Scott (Columbus: Ohio State University Press, 1986), 266. Quoted by Cotkin on p. 174.

83. McDermott, *The Writings of William James*, 669. James today would surely be a strong advocate of ecological ethics (see my comments on p. 116, above), and therefore would not make his point by speaking of a war against "Nature."

84. Ibid.

85. Ibid., 667.

86. James, *A Pluralistic Universe*, 14.

3

HENRI BERGSON

Pete A. Y. Gunter

I. INTRODUCTION

The philosophy of Henri Bergson (1859-1941) captured the spirit of his time. His appearance in New York in 1913 was heralded as an event of signal importance. Daily papers carried articles on his "new philosophy"; philosophers, artists, theologians vigorously debated his ideas. A traffic jam—reputed by one authority to be the first in the history of the new world[1]—choked the avenues to Columbia University as prosperous New Yorkers hurried to hear him speak. Who, asked John Dewey, as he introduced the visiting celebrity, has not been influenced by Bergson?[2] Dewey might have mentioned Bergson's "influence" on former British prime minister Lord Balfour[3] and former American president Theodore Roosevelt.[4] Both had devoted articles to the philosophy of "creative evolution."

The same outpouring of interest had already marked Bergson's career in France. His lectures were filled to overflowing by an international audience of journalists, students, fashionable matrons. In the words of one observer:

His lecture room is the largest in the College de France, but it is too small to accommodate the crowd which would hear him. A cosmopolitan crowd it is that on Wednesday awaits the lecturer, talking more languages than have ordinarily been heard in the same room at any time during the period from the strike on the Tower of Babel to the universal adoption of Esperanto. French, Italian, English, American, Yiddish and Russian are to be distinguished among them; perhaps the last predominates among the foreign tongues for young people of both sexes come from Russia in swarms to put themselves under his instructions. This may rouse in us some speculation, even apprehension.[5]

The spectre of a Bergsonized Russia had to give way, however, to more pressing concerns. Auditors began to arrive in the lecture hall two to three hours early, causing problems for professors lecturing then: "Ladies and gentlemen," one remonstrated when a violent quarrel broke out over a seat, "before hearing M. Bergson, I insist that you listen to me in silence."[6] One wag finally suggested—half seriously—that Bergson's lecture be held in the Paris Opera. The philosopher resolved the problem in the end by retiring from public lectures.

Meanwhile the vogue associated with Bergson's name continued to be paralleled by his impact on serious academic philosophers. Gabriel Marcel, Georges Sorel, Jacques Maritain, Gaston Bachelard, Eugene Minkowski, Alfred Schutz, and most of the thinkers with whom he shares the focus in this volume constitute an incomplete list indeed of twentieth-century thinkers whose thought was significantly shaped by contact with Bergson's philosophy.[7]

But if the *Zeitgeist* gives, it also takes away. The cultural disaster of the First World War created an atmosphere in which philosophies that promised, or even seemed to promise (Bergson was not blindly optimistic, as I point out later), happy resolutions of human ills were given short shrift. Evolutionary optimism scarcely prevailed amid the grisly slaughter in the trenches, or in the sombre aftermath of a presumed "war to end all wars." If Bergson's thought enjoyed wide currency as almost the emblem of an age, it was to be a victim of that age's demise. *Passé.*[8]

Even in the period of his acclaim and influence, however, Bergson paid a price for the de facto alliance of his writings with the current climate of opinion. It is tempting to define a philosophy not by its texts but by its entourage, and this approach to definition was often applied to the French "intuitionist." One would be careful not to interpret Wittgenstein through the precious statements of some of his followers and, hopefully, one would refuse to understand Nietzsche through the declamations of "pop" Nietzscheans. To an unusual degree, Bergson was not extended these conceptual courtesies. He achieved both fame and influence but, in influential philosophical circles, not always a fair hearing.

Today Bergson's thought is undergoing serious reassessment. If this is so, it is because of a widespread disillusionment with the ideas that led to his downfall in the first place. These ideas can be lumped together under the heading of "modernism." They include an insistence on mechanistic (reductionistic) categories, a dogmatic faith in formal (logical/mathematical) language, an anti- or a-religious attitude, a domineering attitude towards nature, and a mind-body theory that wavers unsteadily between sharp dualism and strict reductionism. To these might be added an intolerant belief in technology and economic "progress." Against all of these, Bergson registered his protest, beginning with his doctoral dissertation *(Time and Free Will)*[9] and ending with his profound explorations of the sources of morality and the function of religious experience *(The Two Sources of Morality and Religion)*. It is to the former that we will now turn.

II. THE EARLY DUALISM: INNER FREEDOM/OUTWARD SPACE

Bergson's first work, *Time and Free Will* (1889), is an exploration of "inner duration," a concept that, along with William James' "stream of conscious- ness," forms an important basis for subsequent process philosophies. By show- ing that mathematical and geometrical thought fail to do justice to the experi- ence of inner duration or the stream of consciousness, both thinkers sought to demonstrate the freedom and the reality of the individual.

There were many who refused to take such claims seriously. Modern thought, then as now, fairly bristles with presumed proofs that human beings are machines and, like machines, strictly predictable in their behavior. The temp- tations to such reductionism are strong in an age of science and technology. But, Bergson argues, views like these rest on a common error. They conceive of time as a kind of space. They "spatialize" time.

If we examine our experience attentively, Bergson notes, we do not find a series of sharp breaks. (Imagine, for example, listening to a melody or fol- lowing a conversation.) Rather, we find a continuous transition which involves both the persisting influence of the immediate past and the upwelling of the immediate future. We live "through" and "in" our personal time, which is thor- oughly dynamic, qualitative, and expresses itself—at least, exceptionally—in acts that are free and unpredictable.

How different from this inner duration with its "interpenetration"[10] of past and present are our time-measuring concepts: the instant and the "unit" of time. An instant, for example, has no breadth—any more than does a spatial point. Nor does it have the slightest dynamism. It is a mathematical, static knife-edge, cleanly severing past from future. A series of such knife-edges, no matter how many, scarcely conveys experienced change. If we try to create a moving real duration out of static instants, we commit a "fallacy of compo- sition": the change not present in the instants themselves cannot be found in the time we make up of instants—not without surreptitiously introducing our lived, experienced time to put the instants in "motion."

Similarly with "lengths" of time: minutes, hours, seconds. The experienced present does contain real breadth; this is a factor that distinguishes it from a point-instant. But this breadth is thoroughly dynamic; its qualities exhibit ceaseless change, as the parts of a mathematical time-length do not. Still more striking is the fact that, while *no* two moments of experienced duration are alike (my present, even at its most monotonous, differs from its predecessors, if only because it is conditioned by them), *all* mathematical time-units are identical. Our lives are lives precisely because they do not repeat the same features forever, whereas mathematical time units, being nothing but segments of space, are paradigms of endless repetition.

If our "inner duration" cannot be conceived consistently as repeating itself, or as made up of units that repeat, then there is something about duration that is unpredictable by its very nature. And if this is so, then one ought to be cautious about claiming that human behavior is the result of mechanical causes:

> To say that the same inner causes will reproduce the same effects is to assume that the same cause can appear a second time on the stage of consciousness. Now, if duration is what we say, deep-seated psychic states are radically heterogeneous to each other, and it is impossible that any two of them should be quite alike, since they are two different moments in a life-story.[11]

This may not be especially true of ordinary, habitual, superficial behavior. But if we probe our experience in depth, Bergson argues, we find there profound inner causes which produce their effects once and for all, and will never repeat them. It is precisely such causes that ground, and express, our freedom.

If Bergson's explorations of inner duration in *Time and Free Will* provide both a searching critique of mathematical time and the basis for a spirited defense of individual autonomy, they also leave unsolved a basic—and inescapable—problem. "Inwardly," Bergson insists, we are potentially (sometimes actually) free. Well and good. But if our inner freedom cannot be expressed in "outward," voluntary behavior, then it would appear that it can never be expressed, either through our bodies or with respect to the other people who make up our social worlds. It is not possible here to go into a detailed analysis of the ways in which Bergson makes this problem so difficult to solve. The major difficulty, however, clearly rises from his very sharp distinction between "inner" duration and "outer" space: "Outside us, mutual externality without succession; within us, succession without mutual externality."[12] Until this almost Cartesian (and thoroughly "modernist") dualism is relaxed, until its two poles are allowed to come into communication with each other, the possibility of self-determining behavior is rendered unintelligible.

III. MEMORY AND A NEW VIEW OF MATTER

The goal of Bergson's next major work is to dissolve this quasi-Cartesian dualism. *Matter and Memory*[13] (1896) does this in two ways: first, by reconceiving the physical world as a mode of duration and therefore as having psychological characteristics. If this is so, then mind and physical nature (including the brain) have a common pulsational nature. Second, it is possible on this basis to develop a mind-body theory that conceives the brain not as a storehouse for memories but as an organ adapted for action.

One of Bergson's most fundamental departures from modernist thought is his extension to matter of the basic characteristics of psychological duration. The extent to which his bold move presaged the discoveries of classical quantum physics, nearly thirty years later, is astonishing, although it is not yet widely recognized. For Bergson, matter is not comprised of inert Newtonian mass particles but of "modifications, perturbations, changes of tension or of energy and nothing else."[14] Matter thus becomes pulses of energy bound together by a thread of ''memory,''[15] and, Bergson urges, these pulses ought to exhibit measurable indeterminism.[16] If this is true, then the rhythms of consciousness and those of matter do not comprise entities entirely different in kind.[17] They can be said to be different only in degree, and we can begin to understand, at least in principle, how they may be able to influence each other.[18]

It is fascinating, from the vantage-point of the late twentieth century, to observe Bergson struggling at the end of the nineteenth century to criticize and to overcome basic concepts of Newtonian physics—concepts that were then widely believed to be unassailable. Newton's physics was, Bergson reasoned, for all its extraordinary success, paradoxically lacking in the very features that made its success possible in the first place. Unlike the Greeks who opted for changeless form as fundamental, Newton and his followers, drawing on the insights of Galileo, were the first to introduce the dynamic concept of *acceleration* into physics as a fundamental datum, and to create a new mathematics (the "calculus") to depict this datum. Yet once Newton's physics was formalized, it lacked any trace of process, duration, "fluxion." The word "time" was often pronounced by Newtonian physicists, but the inert mass particles, instantaneous gravitational attractions, rigid space, abstract motion, and mathematical time of Newton reduced without exception to radically unchanging instants, points, lines, solids. Matter and motion, Bergson saw, had been spatialized by the ruling paradigm. Duration—though necessary to physics in the first place—had been, strangely, eliminated. It would, sooner or later, he held, be reintroduced in a new form.

In attempting to go beyond Newtonian mechanism, Bergson certainly did not produce the equations of relativity or quantum physics. He did, however, create a theory that strongly suggests features of both of these viewpoints:

Matter thus resolves itself into numberless vibrations, all linked together in uninterrupted continuity, all bound up with each other, and travelling in every direction like shivers through an immense body. In short, try first to connect together the discontinuous objects of daily experience; then resolve the motionless continuity of their qualities into vibrations on the spot; finally fix your attention on these movements, by abstracting from the divisible space which underlies them and considering only their mobility. . . . [Y]ou will thus obtain a vision of matter, fatiguing for your imagination, but pure, and freed from all that the exigencies of life compel you to add to it in external perception.[19]

In dealing with nature in the large (the macrocosm), Bergson was proposing a field theory in which force and mass are conceived as aspects of one fundamental reality, in which distinct objects are construed as aspects of a fundamental physical interconnectedness, in which there are different rhythms of duration, and in which motion is less the translation of a distinct body through an empty space than the transformation of an entire situation. These factors and others demonstrate tendencies in his thought that (although he was in *Duration and Simultaneity*[20] to attack certain of Einstein's ideas) bear a real resemblance to relativity physics.

In dealing with the microcosm (nature in the small), Bergson devised concepts of matter and of motion that—as quantum physicist Louis de Broglie has pointed out[21]—more clearly foreshadow central concepts of quantum physics. Most essentially, Bergson's ideas that in order for there to be motion there need not be a static *thing* which moves, and that "matter" is comprised of consecutive pulses of energy, each having a finite breadth of duration, were remarkably prophetic, as was his recommendation (noted above) that physicists look for measurable indeterminism in the behavior of very small "units" of matter. There are in these and other closely related Bergsonian notions both *precise* and *specific* anticipations of the course of twentieth-century physics.[22]

Thermodynamicist Ilya Prigogine (like de Broglie, a Nobel laureate) stresses the fact that Bergson was well-placed, historically, to make telling criticisms of the Newtonian system. Comparing Bergson's philosophy of nature to Hegel's, Prigogine states that, "unlike Hegel, he had the good fortune to pass judgement upon science that was, on the whole, firmly established—that is, classical science at its apotheosis, and thus identified problems which are still our problems."[23] Prigogine argues, in the light of the direction twentieth-century philosophy has taken, that Bergson's metaphysics based on intuition has not materialized. But he heralds Bergson's critique of Newton as providing "a program that is beginning to be implemented by the transformation science is now undergoing."[24]

It is not only Bergson's critique of classical Newtonian physics that has been helpful to Prigogine. It is also Bergson's idea of "duration," with its stress on novelty, indeterminism, and holism, that has provided, Prigogine asserts, an "inspiration" to his own thinking. Bergson's philosophy is thus associated with a promising approach in the sciences, one that may provide keys to the understanding of the emergence of life, the dynamics of the cell, the evolution of biological form, and the temporality of the nervous system and brain.

Besides the general solution of finding "duration" in "matter," however, a satisfactory mind-body theory must also deal with thought and behavior in a more detailed manner. In Bergson's day, the most intensively studied psychological/neurophysiological phenomena were the aphasias: the maladies of memory. According to the prevailing theory, memories (now called "engrams") are simply stored in the brain. Loss of memory was presumed to be due to injury to tissues containing them. A survey of aphasiology, however, convinced Bergson that, in spite of its plausibility, this theory is not valid. It rests on both a simplistic notion of memory and an artificial notion of brain function.

Memory, Bergson urges, is twofold, with one side (habit memory) representing the brain and the other side (spontaneous memory) representing the mind. Habit memory involves, for example, the ability to recite the multiplication table or to give the date of John F. Kennedy's assassination. Established by effortful repetition in the past, it consists of behaviors performed in the present. By contrast, spontaneous memory involves, say, the recollection of grade-school experiences, or of what one was thinking or feeling when one heard of the president's assassination. Habit memory is programmed into the brain and consists of automatic or semi-automatic tendencies towards behavior. Spontaneous memory, although it may depend on brain mechanisms for its realization, is not physical.[25] It is mental, and as such it is capable (as habit memory is not) of generating both reflection and free, creative acts.

Any study of habit memories leads us quickly to the realization that they, like the brain and nervous system of which they are a part, have a practical and not a theoretical function. They are structured so as to enable us not to think in general, speculative terms, but to cope with the reality around us. They help orient our "attention to life."[26]

"Attention to life" is both a central and a subtle concept. It is central because it grounds Bergson's philosophy in a kind of "life-world" beyond whose boundaries, he holds, philosophical questions become hopelessly scholastic and ill-formed. It is subtle because it contains (among other things) a dual reference: inward, towards spontaneous memory and will, and outward, towards perception and action. In attending to life—that is, in coping—we fuse inner and outer in a single circuit. In this circuit, the brain is a necessary, but not a sufficient, condition of behavior.

The brain assists spontaneous memory, first, by filtering out those memories that are not apropos of some present situation. All our memories, even the oldest, are preserved and, Bergson holds, without some filtering mechanism we would be overwhelmed by a flood of spontaneous reminiscence. Damage to the brain is thus a direct cause of many (though not all) cases of mental illness. Destruction of or injury to the filter renders concentration or effective memory impossible. The aphasic is unable to recall a word or, confronted with it, can not determine its meaning. In senile dementia the patient remembers the past, but is unable to deal with or even recognize the present.

Memory is only part of thought, however. The second function of the brain, Bergson argues, is to make action possible. The brain's focus on action is clear from its immediate ties to the "efferent" nerves and the body's motor system. Without the capacity for specific physical acts, and for choice between these acts, the mind would remain at the level of reverie or unconsciousness.[27] The brain with its ritualized, automatic "memory" thus makes possible—to a certain extent compels—reflective discriminating thought, as well as focused, effective behavior. It should go without saying that "action" here includes what we have now come to call "speech acts."

One last filtering operation is performed by the brain (and sense organs). If the world around us seems so "pictorial" (comprised of distinct images of presumably solid objects), this is because our nervous system and sense organs delete from our environs what we cannot make use of. In reality, Bergson concludes, a physical object is never simply located at any one place, but is connected by fields of energy to all parts of nature. In a sense, it is everywhere. Our neurosensory system, however, is inevitably pragmatic, shutting out the unmanageable welter of the outer world, leaving us a clear field of action, much as the brain excludes the profusion of memory images to allow only useful recollections.

Clearly then, for Bergson, no precise thought, focused reflection, or significant action can be carried on without the brain. But there is also spontaneous memory. Whenever habitual, stereotyped behavior ceases to function effectively, spontaneous memory emerges, furnishing us with images through which to make comparisons, and then act—or not act—effectively. (Reading, for example, is as much interpretation as it is sensation. Is the word before us in the stream of the sentence "autism" or "altruism"? When we are uncertain, an interplay of word-memory and perception gives us an answer, and we move on.) This means that memories must be capable, perhaps through some sort of rhythmic similarity, of merging with selected brain "mechanisms." If this is indeed possible, then it is a very ordinary occurrence, and our ordinary experience involves a real interpenetration of mind and brain: hardly a conclusion genial to late modern thought!

Usually when we try to recall something—a word, an event—we talk about it as if we were trying to reach back to the past. The opposite is the case. In spontaneous memory we place ourselves in an attitude through which memories *can come to us*. Memory is thus active. It is vectored towards the present. But memory is active not only in acts of cognition (reading, recollecting, recognizing). It is active in the fundamental choices of our lives, in the choices by which we shape our own character. We may think with only a part of our past, Bergson urges, but we act out of our entire past. Here he rejoins the insights of *Time and Free Will*, but now from the standpoint of an embodied consciousness:

> Not only, by its memory of former experience, does . . . consciousness retain the past better and better, so as to organize it with the present in a newer and richer decision; but, living with an intenser life, contracting, by its memory of the immediate experience, a growing present duration, it becomes more capable of creating acts of which the inner indetermination . . . will pass more easily through the meshes of necessity.[28]

The mind, dependent on matter for the percepts on which it feeds (and on the brain for both clear consciousness and clearly distinguished means and objects), is capable of responding to its percepts with acts: "movements which it has stamped with its own freedom."[23]

Bergson's theory in *Matter and Memory*, which he maintains in all subsequent works, thus depicts mind and body as constituting not a sharp dualism but a duality or even polarity. Distinguishable ideally, they are in fact always intermingled. If we are tempted to treat them as one thing, it is not because they are identical but because they *function* as one.

IV. PSYCHE AND PSI

In 1913 Bergson, then president of the British Society for Psychical Research, gave a talk with the rather baroque title "'Phantasms of the Living' and Psychical Research."[30] It may seem a long way from the theories of *Matter and Memory* to the problems of parapsychology, but the two are in fact closely related.[31] Bergson's concept of mind-body relations, with its "filter" theory of perception and its supposition that nature everywhere "interpenetrates," gives rise quite naturally to a theory both of how "psi phenomena" are possible and why we are ordinarily unaware of them.

Most of us have enough trouble dealing with our own thoughts. Suppose that we had, through telepathy, to deal with everyone else's? The results would be, literally, unthinkable. Our brain and sense organs must therefore function with respect to any supposed "psi" phenomena, Bergson reasons, in the same way that they function with regard to our physical surroundings: they must exclude, and simplify, making concentration on ordinary problems possible. That is, if we are in most cases unaware of psychic influences, perhaps that is because we are structured both physically and psychologically so as to wall them out.

It seems unlikely that the influences that give rise to telepathy, for example, are intermittent. (Bergson believes that telepathy is a well-enough attested fact to make such speculations worthwhile.) Telepathic communications, he posits, must be as ubiquitously present as radio waves or x-rays, and—whatever they may turn out to be—like radio waves they are beyond the ordinary range of our senses. Also like x-rays and radio waves, their existence may someday be verified.

Just how such verification might come about is implicit in Bergson's approach to parapsychology as well as to the mind-body problem, and is made explicit in his essay on dreams (1901).[32] When are we least caught up in the "coping" mechanisms of the brain, sense organs, and motor system? Clearly, in reverie, dreams, deep sleep, states in which attention to life is withdrawn. There is no special superiority in such states—quite the opposite. But in them we are significantly freed from our habitual conceptual and perceptual blinders. Research involving such states may well prove difficult. But Bergson clearly believes that "especially appropriate methods" can be devised to cope successfully with the difficulties they pose.

V. CREATIVE EVOLUTION

Creative Evolution (1907), which catapulted Bergson into international fame overnight, develops his earlier mind-body duality in terms of a theory of the origin and development of life. He begins his biology with a heresy: Neo-Darwinism is inadequate; it cannot explain the major steps in evolution. Whatever one may think of this heresy, it is based on a clear-cut critique of the newly arisen neo-Darwinism, a critique widely influential in its time.

Neo-Darwinian theory, Bergson argues, falls victim to a dilemma. Either it will explain evolution through individual mutations somehow working collectively to produce new organs and organisms; or it must appeal to macromutations suddenly producing new organs or organisms (since termed "hopeful monsters") all at once. The first alternative cannot explain how useful mutations can be produced and *accumulated* in the right order at the right time. (The "wrong" mutations will cause pathology or death.) The second solution seems less a scientific explanation than an appeal to a kind of miracle. It is equally unsatisfactory.

But then what does explain evolution? Bergson's response seems to crown heresy with mystery. Rejecting mechanistic explanations, he introduces the *élan vital*, a life force, which, he insists, is responsible for the incessant creativity of life. It is *élan vital* that drives evolution up the steep slope of entropy, overcoming matter's drift towards randomness and disorder. Life has a "non-mechanistic" explanation. I have argued elsewhere that there is more to Bergson's critique of Darwin than is commonly believed, and that his life force is less a mystery than an effort to suggest new, fruitful, but nonmechanistic directions in biology.[33]

In any case, the critique developed in *Creative Evolution* came at a propitious time, reinforcing doubts about the adequacy of neo-Darwinism. Some biologists in succeeding decades (J. Arthur Thompson, Julian S. Huxley, R. A. Fisher, C. Lloyd Morgan, T. Dobzhansky, Sewall Wright, Wm. M. Wheeler, among others) retained their faith in Darwin, but sought to reinterpret evolution in less mechanistic ways. At the same time, many of these felt it necessary to reformulate neo-Darwinism in the face of the skeptical challenge. The result, developed in the 1930s, is termed "Darwinism, the modern synthesis." Julian Huxley, one of its formulators, could thus state in 1943: "it is with this reborn Darwinism, this mutated phoenix risen from the ashes of the pyre kindled by men so unlike as Bateson and Bergson, that I propose to deal in succeeding chapters of this book."[34] On the negative, critical side, then, Bergson played a role in biology not unlike that of George Berkeley in mathematics, whose criticisms, along with others, forced a reformulation of the infinitesimal calculus. Karl Popper makes such dialectical interactions intelligible: the attempt to *falsify* a science may provoke renewed creativity on the part of scientists.

But the critical side of Bergson is also accompanied by a constructive side, as we have already seen with regard to physics. Bergson's biological ideas were to inspire some of the first experimental studies of biological time, by Alexis Carrel (cytological time) and Pierre Lecomte du Noüy (physiological time).[35] It was also to spark studies of evolutionary and anthropological time by François Meyer.[36] These studies point to the centrality of time in biological processes at all levels, and are closely related to more recent proposals in theoretical biology concerning temporal hierarchy, pattern formation, and the temporal communication of biological information.[37]

Although much more could be said concerning the relations between Bergsonian metaphysics and scientific biology, I must now deal with a different, in many ways a broader, question: What, for Bergson, is humankind? More particularly, what philosophical anthropology can be found in *Creative Evolution*?

VI. Instinct and Intuition: Humanity's Place in Evolution

In part, the answer to this question can be found by examining humanity's place in evolution, which, for all its complexity of detail, has proceeded in only a handful of major directions. In animal evolution there are two such directions: the invertebrates, culminating in the elaborate societies of the social insects, and the vertebrates, culminating in human beings and other higher primates. Insects have emphasized instinct, an unlearned knowledge which, Bergson observes, is focused on life. By contrast, vertebrates have emphasized intelligence, which is focused not on life but on nonliving matter and increasingly involves the capacity to fashion tools. The human being is, *par excellence*, the tool-using animal, and should be termed not *Homo sapiens* but *Homo faber*.

But if we are tool-using, machine-creating creatures, it is no accident that we construct mechanical models of matter, spatialize time, and construct industrial societies. Mechanism is our *métier*. At the same time, however, mechanism is our limitation. The fact that there is art suggests, Bergson argues, that this limitation is vaguely felt by most of us. Similar corroboration can be found in the extraordinary wholeness of evolution. The various forms of life depend on each other, have evolved together, and derive ultimately from common ancestors. Hence Bergson's claim that each sort of organism bears implicitly within it aspects—tendencies—of others far removed from it on the evolutionary tree, rather, we might now say, as a holograph[38] bears in each of its components information detailing the state of all others. In the case of human beings, Bergson urges, our evident intellectual abilities are haunted by a memory, however vague, of instinctive tendencies once possessed by the common ancestors of both vertebrates and invertebrates.

These capacities—dormant and usually neglected—might help us understand aspects of life that otherwise remain opaque to us. They might help, that is, if they could be developed and made reflective. The recovery of these lost "data" and their development into reflective awareness Bergson terms "intuition." It is clear that in *Time and Free Will* and *Matter and Memory* Bergson was already, without using the word, utilizing a concept of "intuition"—usually characterized as "immediate awareness" or "pure perception"—in his exploration of inner duration and personal memory. He first introduces intuition as a technical term in *An Introduction to Metaphysics* (1903),[39] contrasting it, as we might expect, with "analysis": a spatial, static, atomistic (but very useful) mode of thought. In *Creative Evolution*, intuition is defined in a biological context and, as suggested above, connected with instinct: "It is to the inwardness of life that *intuition* leads us—by intuition I mean instinct that has become disinterested, self-conscious, capable of reflecting on its object and enlarging it indefinitely."[40]

Bergson has been widely criticized for introducing the concept of intuition, and especially for relating it to biology. Bertrand Russell, for example, proclaimed that "intuition" must lead to tribal primitivism and hence jibed that "intuition is at its best in bats, bees and Bergson."[41]

Such misunderstandings should be forestalled at the beginning. Bergson does not hold that humans have specific instincts (for monogamy or polygamy, for example, or for competition or cooperation). He is suggesting that we have capacities for sympathy with all forms of life. We are possessed not of a racial unconscious in C. G. Jung's sense, but of a universal biological unconscious.[42] Ideally, we feel a kinship with everything that lives—a kinship which ought to allow us to understand living things more fully.

Bergson is thus scarcely pleading for a return to primitivism. (Indeed, as we will see in *Two Sources of Morality and Religion*, he is trying to get away from it.) He is simply pleading for a fuller understanding of life. Equally, even the most superficial reading of his treatment of instinct and intuition reveals that intuition has fundamental characteristics that instinct lacks. The special instincts of the insects (on which Bergson largely bases his notion of instinctive knowledge) are limited in scope, stereotyped, and are the source of automatic behavior—features antithetical to everything that, for Bergson, typifies intuition. The sphex, a digger wasp, which "knows" how to sting a cicada precisely on its nerve centers so as to paralyze but not kill it, has a special insight, but this insight concerns only one aspect of one kind of organism. It has no breadth of application. Moreover, while intuition tends towards increasing reflectiveness, instinct—little more, Bergson holds, than a stimulus to behavior—tends towards unconsciousness.[43]

Bergson's intuition, therefore, for all its connections with instinct, is *not* instinct. It is a kind of reflection that distances us from mere feeling or sensation while integrating us more fully within the web of life. Social custom and exigency force the repression of this sympathy, forbidding its development. But in a John Muir, an Henri Fabre, or a Saint Francis, we find the failure of this repression and the flowering into reflective knowledge of an originally "instinctive" sense of kinship. Human beings are not isolated in the stream of life; they are part of its fabric both physically and psychologically. Those who meditate on the possibility of a postmodern world, and who understand our ability to plunder, diminish, and ultimately destroy the biosphere, ought to consider how to revive and intensify this felt commonality. Bergson's biological theory of knowledge could form a basis for the realization that not only nothing human, but also nothing living, is alien to us.

VII. BERGSON'S SOCIOBIOLOGY OF RELIGION

In *The Two Sources of Morality and Religion* (1932), Bergson, while retaining his earlier psychological and biological orientation, approaches the human predicament from a new standpoint.[44] No longer does he explain humanity's alienation from nature and itself simply through the misapplication of mechanistic categories and the consequent repression of human sensitivity. Indeed, it remains a good question what role these previous criticisms play, from the vantage-point of his later philosophy.

The conclusions proposed in *Creative Evolution* are here reshaped by new questions: What sorts of human societies are there, and how do these relate to the possible sorts of religion? What are the sources of religion, and of religious conflicts? Is religion a feature of an earlier, barbaric age, or is it destined to endure—and if so, in what form? If the answers that Bergson gives to such questions are both new and striking, this is in part because of his radical insistence that we must see anthropology, history, and sociology against an evolutionary background. Charles Hartshorne has rightly insisted that in *The Two Sources of Morality and Religion* Bergson is writing as a kind of sociobiologist.[45]

Among the animals, we recall, evolution has resulted in two culminating achievements: the societies of ants and bees, dominated by instinct, and human societies, directed by intelligence. In *The Two Sources of Morality and Religion*, Bergson retains this contrast while deepening its significance. We have seen that instinct provides an innate but radically limited knowledge of life, while intelligence provides general knowledge, but at the price of fragmentation and superficiality; that instinct provides order, but without progress, while intelligence provides change, but at the cost of instability. Is it possible to go further? An instinctive being (although Bergson contends that it experiences some form of awareness) does not reflect, and hence cannot conceive its own good apart from that of its community. It simply acts so as to carry out biologically preordained functions. (The ant works for and defends the ant hill, even if that should involve its death.) An intelligent creature, however, will sooner or later reflect and discover that it can pursue its own good separately. It might relax and let others work; it might retire to safety while others fight and die.

In our present mass societies, such egoism, if widespread, will be socially demoralizing. In the small groups of early humankind, the results could well have proved fatal. Some ready means therefore had to be present to guarantee social cohesion, social survival. It is not clear, even today, that utilitarian arguments (that the good of the society is the good of the individual, and vice versa) could have produced the requisite results. They have not, Bergson notes, convinced all philosophers, much less the mass of humankind. Something far simpler, far more direct, had to occur: forbidding images, arising from the human unconscious, conditioning behavior:

> If intelligence now threatens to break up social cohesion at certain points—assuming that society is to go on—there must be a counterpoise, at these points, to intelligence. If this counterpoise can not be instinct itself . . . the same effect must be produced by a virtuality of instinct . . .: it can not exercise direct action, but, since intelligence works on repre-

sentations, it will call up "imaginary" ones, which will hold their own against the representation of reality and will succeed, through the agency of intelligence itself, in counteracting the work of intelligence.[46]

At a later stage in human development the forbidding image will be that of a god of the city, demanding obedience. In the beginning, however, things need not be—and could not have been—so elaborate. It does not take unusual psychological insight to see that an "intentional resistance" or even a "vengeance" may appear to us as self-sufficient entities. The beings, Bergson hypothesizes, that haunted early human beings and held them back from the brink of revolt were neither merely physical forces nor fully realized personalities. They were simply "presences," forbidding or encouraging. But they were sufficient to establish the taboos which regulated social life.[47] Through their agency the problem of the recalcitrant individual could be solved, the spectre of social disintegration banished.

The second major problem that the intelligent animal must face is of a very different kind. It is conceivable that some other animals (Bergson cites cases of animal suicide) have the idea of death; it is entirely unlikely that they have the idea of death's inevitability. The other animals appear to live in an all-consuming present; we alone conceive of events outside the present and (like death) inescapable. The result is, Bergson holds, not fear but depression. The awareness of death "interrupts" the forward movement of life. There are both social and individual reasons why this depressant must be overcome. In the small societies of primitive humanity, for example:

A society already civilized is supported by laws, by institutions, even by buildings constructed to defy the ravages of time; but primitive societies are simply "built" up of human beings: what would become of their authority if people did not believe in the enduring character of the individualities of which they are composed?[48]

The "hallucinatory image" called for in this instance is not a forbidding presence, but the presence of the dead: "In its beginning, intelligence simply sees the dead as mingling with the living in a society to which they can still do good or ill."[49] Such shades or phantoms are in the beginning little more than images; as they develop they will take on purposes and a vitality of their own.[50] Ancestor worship will emerge later. Meantime there is palpable reassurance. (These reflections, of course, concern only the social *uses* of the belief in immortality, not its validity. Bergson's mind-body theory did convince him, however, that the survival of the mind after bodily death is a real possibility.)

Whether early humankind, therefore, is called on to resolve problems of social solidarity or of its reaction to the inescapability of death, the solutions are provided by images emerging from the human unconscious. The "purpose" embodied in this process is rational—the continued survival of the group, and hence of the species. But the means are, Bergson is clear, irrational—or infra-rational. To those who find it strange that the human race should have acted in this way, he replies that at this early stage in human evolution there was no other way. The gods, and the predecessors of the gods, are inescapable components of the early stages of human history. The human being begins its reflective life as a religious creature.

It is clear, however, that the tensions that give rise to the rudimentary forms of religion do not cease at that point to provoke new human responses. Humanity's myth-making genius gradually develops a rich drama involving not shadowy beings but gods of increasingly marked personality. Bergson notes two interesting features in this process. The first is the thoroughly utilitarian character of the gods; the second is their ready replaceability.

The gods of ancient polytheism are not allowed to wander at will but are yoked to useful tasks: one is to take care of the harvests, another to tend to justice, another to war. Bergson points out:

> The gods of pagan civilization are indeed distinguishable from older entities, elves, gnomes, spirits, which popular belief never actually abandoned. The latter were the almost direct products of that myth-making faculty which is natural to us; and they were naturally adopted, just as they had been naturally produced. They conformed to the need from which they sprang.[51]

If this is not surprising, the arbitrary existence of each of these gods, taken singly, certainly is: "The pantheon exists independent of man, but on man depends the placing of a god in it, and the bestowal of existence on that deity."[52] Pagan gods could be replaced, abolished, enlarged, diminished almost at will, yet still be believed in. Pagan faith—which moved in an atmosphere quite unlike our own—was "limitless in its compliance."[53]

The myth-making process is in many respects haphazard, hit-or-miss. But it leads in the long run to the expression of basic human (one might say, all-too-human) character. Bergson terms this sort of belief "natural religion,"[54] depicting it as the inevitable response of an intelligent, reflective being to the demands of social existence. One might almost describe natural religion as prefigured in the human brain and nervous system, not in the sense that it is literally innate there, and certainly not in the sense that consciousness is not involved, but in the sense (amply documented in *Matter and Memory*) that only a creature with a brain and nervous system as complex as ours can realize the problems of egoism and death. And only such a creature can respond to them in a specifically religious fashion.

Before proceeding, it is important to point out that Bergson is not either saying that natural religion is the only form of religion or *recommending* that we should embrace it. To the contrary, he is simply describing the history of religion, pointing out its tendency to take on a particular, human form. If natural religion creates social cohesion, it is through social pressure.[55] If it strengthens and stabilizes the social order, it is at the cost of a "closed society."[56] The result of this closure, inevitably, is conflict. Each society, with its natural religion, organizes itself as an absolute and opposes its gods to the gods of other societies. Outsiders are strictly excluded. (One recalls the Greek contempt for "barbarians.") War is thereby not only justified—it is virtually necessitated. Let us be frank about it. The religion that begins as a set of "defensive reactions"[57] against anarchy and individual melancholy ends as a defensive reaction against change, openness, transformation.

VIII. OPEN SOCIETY/DYNAMIC RELIGION

Bergson's almost surgical dissection of "natural religion" is far more detailed than our description suggests. His analyses of magic, totemism, mana, chance, prayer, and sacrifice as they operate in natural religion are extensive and repay close examination. Even so, one closes an exploration of Bergson's description of this form of religion with a sense of insufficiency, of incompleteness. Surely there is more to the phenomenon of religion than this elaborate ruse supported by social pressure. And surely this more is "essential." Social pressure and tribal solidarity—no matter how large the tribe—surely cannot exhaust the teachings of a Buddha, a Ramakrishna, or a Jesus of Nazareth.

Not surprisingly, Bergson's response to this criticism is affirmative. If natural religion is a reflection of our all-too-human nature, there is another possibility. Religion may call on us to transcend ourselves: to rise above tribalism (hence certainly above racism), above the divisions between nations and classes, above egoisms personal or collective. Indeed, this alternative exists. It is dynamic religion, the expression of an open society.[58] It finds its source in Jesus of Nazareth and the Jewish prophets who preceded him. It finds its continuing development in the Christian saints and mystics.

A glance at humanity's evolutionary context shows that some such leap beyond the closed societies of natural religion was bound to occur sooner or later. The continuing creativity which has led through the many branchings of the evolutionary tree to the higher primates and humankind seems unlikely suddenly to halt at the achievement of closed human societies. The human brain and nervous system, moreover, make possible not only reflection (and the problems it poses) but also flexibility, innovation, change. Bergson puts the situation as follows:

Man, fresh from the hands of nature, was a being both intelligent and social, his sociability being devised to find its scope in small communities, his intelligence being designed to further individual and group life. But intelligence, expanding through its own efforts, has developed unexpectedly. It has freed men from restrictions to which they were condemned by the limitations of their nature. This being so, it is not impossible that some of them, specifically gifted, should do, at least for themselves, what nature could not possibly have done for mankind.[59]

These privileged individuals are revolutionaries, for they "break down the gates of the city."[60] From the vantage-point of Bergson's speculative biology, they seem to have "placed themselves again in the current of the vital impetus."[61] Leaders of humankind, they have drawn human beings after them.

The characteristics of the new religious spirit are precisely the contraries of those of natural religion. Against the closed, the open; against the static, the dynamic; against social pressure, aspiration; against the mass, the individual; against fear, love. Judaism, an avowedly ethnic and nationalistic religion, becomes in Christianity a religious movement intended to reach out to all humankind: against the particular, then, the universal.

The effects of this new spirit, Bergson argues, are all around us, but we have become so accustomed to them that we have forgotten how radical they were in the beginning. Impelled by an extraordinary energy and by a vivid conviction of both the value of humanity and the reality of their God, the early Christians spread their message throughout Europe and beyond its borders. They abolished slavery: an extraordinary act, one only waveringly conceived by previous religions, and conceived of by previous philosophies (notably Stoicism) only as an ideal impossible of fulfillment.

The same evangelical zeal that led to the abolition of slavery was to be revived again and again, not merely as rebirths of social and emotional intensity (factors that "natural religion" already stressed), but as intuitions that have enlarged and enriched our idea of justice. There are "geniuses of the will," Bergson argues, as well as geniuses of the intellect. To the moral genius of the great Christian mystics we owe a tremendous debt.

The extent of this debt can be seen by comparing the idea of "justice" sustained by the classical *polis* with our present conceptions. In the closed societies of the ancient world, the idea of justice, like other obligations, met a clear social need: "and it was the pressure of society on the individual which made justice obligatory. This being so, an injustice was neither more nor less shocking than any other breach of the rules."[62] There was no justice, Bergson points out, for slaves, except an optional, relative justice. For the sake of social order, the most draconic laws could prevail and be enforced without compunction: "Public safety was not merely the supreme law, as indeed it has remained, it was furthermore proclaimed as such; whereas today we should not dare to lay down the principle that it justifies injustice."[63] Bergson, to bring home the contrast, asks what we would do today if we learned that for the common good, for the continued existence of humankind, a decent, an innocent person were to be submitted to unending torment? Perhaps little, if we were able easily to forget it. But if we were compelled to know that this person's hideous torture were the price of our existence, what would be our response? "No! A thousand times no! Better to accept that nothing should exist at all!"[64] Our protest is a clear revelation of the fact that something fundamental has transformed, enlarged, and deepened our concept of justice.

A similar transformation has occurred in our political conceptions. If the closed society could sum itself up in a slogan, it would be "authority, hierarchy, immobility."[65] Democracy, precisely by contrast, proceeds under a banner emblazoned "liberty, equality, fraternity." It is the third of these three ideals, fraternity, that is central, Bergson argues, and that reconciles the other two. It is for the sake of fraternity that we have preached liberty and equality. And if this is so, we can say

that democracy is evangelical in essence and that its motive power is love. Its sentimental origins could be found in the soul of Rousseau, its philosophic principles in the works of Kant, its religious basis in both Kant and Rousseau: we know how much Kant owed to his pietism, and Rousseau to an interplay of Protestantism and Catholicism. The American Declaration of Independence (1776), which served as a model for the Declaration of the Rights of Man in 1791, has indeed a Puritan ring.[66]

The religious origins of the democratic ideal are too easily forgotten, along with the evangelical zeal of those who introduced that ideal into the mainstream of political life—a mainstream prepared by centuries of inculcation in Christianity to understand and accept it.

IX. A FEW OBJECTIONS—AND SOME ANSWERS

There are innumerable objections to Bergson's account of religion. It will help in explaining his viewpoint to discuss some of them here. The first, which I have often encountered from students, concerns Bergson's intentions. Is he trying to start a new religion? Does *he* think he has the final truth? The answer to these questions is straightforward. What Bergson is doing is studying the phenomenon of religion. The result of this study is a series of distinctions, insights, suggestions. He does not consider himself a prophet. Nor is he starting a movement. As for the *final* truth, on his own grounds there is no such thing.

Dynamic religion, if it continues fundamental insights, is always reaching out for increased scope, increased understanding, increased concern.

Another objection involves Bergson's attitude towards contemporary religious practice. Does he really believe, in the light of the sometimes bizarre, sometimes regrettable (often merely forgettable) behavior of many Christians in this century, that there is such a thing as an active, outgoing mysticism at work in our world? Recently "reborn" Biblical and Islamic fundamentalisms are dynamic no doubt, and certainly "mystical," yet they point towards mutual suspicion, closure, war. But, Bergson cautions, ordinary religion, in the modern world, is a "hybrid," containing elements of both static and dynamic:

> Thus may arise a mixed religion. . . . The contrast is striking in many cases, as for instance when nations at war each declare that they have God on their side, the deity in question thus becoming the national god of paganism, whereas the God they imagine they are invoking is a God common to all mankind, the mere vision of Whom, could all men but attain it, would mean the immediate abolition of war.[67]

In most of "Christdom," then, we have a mixture, if not a confusion, of two very different religious impulses. It is in most cases, however, not difficult to separate out the element of closure, tribalism, defense-reaction. It is more difficult to single out the truly open, dynamic, outgoing impulse. And in our time, Bergson admits, that impulse has reached a kind of impasse.

Still another objection—more likely to be posed by scholars than students—strikes at the supposed "irrationalism" of Bergson's position. This is a complex matter, which cannot be dealt with here in detail.[68] Bergson notes that "natural religion" is essentially infra-intellectual. It develops what is implicit in its origins, but is not, or is only minimally, creative; it gives rise not to new ethics or new concepts, but to modes of social control with provincial, not universal, scope. "Dynamic religion" is described by contrast as "supra-intellectual." It has broadened and deepened—and universalized—our *concept* of justice; it has transformed our *theologies*; it has given rise to new political *philosophies*. The "emotion" that has given rise to dynamic religion thus has unique noetic content. "Mystical intuition" results, Bergson argues, not only in action—a thing that concepts by themselves seem unable to provoke—but in concepts appropriate to that action, which express its essential character. But, then, if they lead to a humanity more free, more reflective, more concerned, and with ideas that express this concern and freedom, why should we term them "irrational"?

A similar criticism centers on Bergson's treatment of the mystic as both a moral genius and a leader of humankind. The study of such "leaders" shows, it will be objected, personal instability and even neurotic symptoms; the history of charismatic figures exhibits more than its share of fanatics, phonies, irrationalists. Surely, it will be objected, we would be better off without them. Bergson's response is that such a conclusion, like the purported set of facts on which it is based, is superficial. If we take the great Christian mystics (a St. Paul, a St. Theresa, a St. Catherine of Sienna, a St. Francis, a Joan of Arc),

> we can but wonder how they could ever have been classed with the mentally diseased. True, we live in a condition of unstable equilibrium; normal health of mind, as of body, is not easily defined. Yet there is an exceptional, deep-rooted mental healthiness, which is readily recognizable. It is expressed in the bent for action, the faculty of adapting and readapting oneself to circumstances, in firmness combined by suppleness, in the prophetic discernment of what is possible and what is not, in the spirit of simplicity which triumphs over complications, in a word, supreme good sense.[69]

Is not this supreme good sense, he asks, precisely what we find in the mystics mentioned above? Could not they provide the very definition of intellectual vigor?

But, the objection will be continued, the fact is that these "paradigms of intellectual vigor" describe their own abnormal states for us: visions, ecstasies, raptures—and deep depressions, "darkest midnights of the soul."[70] Bergson's response is perceptive, and contains the germ of an important insight. If we look carefully at the lives of these persons, he cautions, we discover that these "abnormal" states are simply "way stations," functions of the difficulty of what they have tried to achieve:

> They have been the first to warn their disciples against visions which were quite likely to be pure hallucinations. And they generally regarded their own visions, when they had any, as of secondary importance, as wayside incidents; they had to go beyond them, leaving raptures and ecstasies far behind, to reach the goal, which was the identification of the human will with the divine will.[71]

To pass from the static to the dynamic, the closed to the open, from the city gates to the mystic life, is a shock (and, Bergson might have added, involves every sort of insecurity). It does not follow that what is psychologically "abnormal" is necessarily morbid.

The ultimate achievement of the great mystics is therefore not only to pass beyond visions, raptures and similar states, or even simply to participate in the divine being. The sort of "mysticism" whose ultimate exclusive goal is mystical contemplation is, Bergson argues, "incomplete."[72] But a "complete mysticism"[73] involves the impulse to action. It is outgoing. It is a concrete manifestation of love for one's fellow creature. There is thus no inherent contradiction between a complete mysticism and *caritas*: a charity both spiritual and human. Indeed, mysticism and social concern are profoundly compatible.

(I am reminded, at this point, of a conversation with the formal axiologist Robert S. Hartman on precisely this issue. "The mystics," I pondered, "leave society and dwell apart. They do little." Professor Hartman exclaimed: "But you, with your Bergson, should know better than this. For Bergson mysticism *is* social action!")

X. Cash Value for a Postmodern World

William James often spoke of the "cash value" of ideas. He did not mean to propose some crudely financial concept of truth. He meant only to ask: After all the weighing, debating, footnoting, publishing, and writing are done, *what difference will it* (an idea, an attitude, an approach) *make*? We are right to ask, sooner or later, for a philosophy's cash value—and to be puzzled if none is forthcoming.

What cash value, then, has a philosophy like Bergson's, and specifically, what "cash value" for a postmodern world? Can a philosophy presumably the expression of the turn-of-the-century *belle epoque* outlive its own demise to become a guidepost towards a wholly different sort of world? I believe it can, and should. The problem, however, is that there are so many possible fruitful consequences of Bergson's philosophy. One can deal here with only a few.

The first is a useful conceptual distinction that helps make sense of the confusing welter of contemporary religious life. I refer to Bergson's distinction (made popular by Karl Popper)[74] between the closed and the open. In so many religious struggles the point of dispute becomes clear when the open/closed distinction is applied. Otherwise—if we do not see the element of openness combatting perpetual closure—the struggles within religions seem pointless furors.

The open/closed distinction has another use. It indicates that the usual condemnations of religion (as anti-intellectual, primitive, warlike, cruel . . . *ad infinitum*), although valid within their limits, are literally one-sided. They fall on natural religion with its strong tendencies towards tribalism and closure. They ignore the universal, the humane, the giving impulse within the Judeo-Christian (as well as other) traditions, without which our profoundest ethical and political convictions are unintelligible.

They ignore another factor in our present situation: the extent to which our very technological success is allowed not only needlessly to complicate our lives, but to breed a set of false needs which end by dominating us. "Never, indeed, do the satisfactions with which inventions meet old needs induce humanity to leave things at that; new needs arise just as imperious and increasingly numerous. We have seen the race for comfort proceeding faster and faster, on a track along which are surging ever denser crowds. Today it is a stampede."[75] It is wrong, however, to blame technology for our excesses. It is what we have done—and *not* done—with our machines (and by implication, our economy) that stands to blame. We have allowed our technology, instead of answering to basic human wants, to create desires that are artificial. If we were willing to make the effort, we could begin simplifying our existence with as much frenzy as we have devoted to complicating it.

Bergson does not say so explicitly, but his treatment of the "baubles which amuse us, the vain shadows for which we fight"[76] strongly implies the emptiness which is so profound a feature of modern life. It was once taken for granted that industrialism and mechanization would bring happiness to humankind.[77] Those who reasoned thus, he asserts, understood neither the limitations of technology per se nor its capacity, if adequately directed, to free us. But in order to be free it is not enough to invoke a more balanced use of technology. For that we require the will, the vision, the inspiration, to transform our lives and our world.

But this leads finally to an essential question raised at the beginning of this essay. Is religion a primitive phenomenon, one destined to die out as the great wave of scientific and technological progress surges on? If Bergson's analysis is correct, no such disappearance can be expected. The foreseeable future fairly teems with uncertainties, insecurities, increasing complexities of every kind—many of these the result of our technologies and the uses to which they are put. Science, technology, philosophy itself, scarcely lay to rest the fundamental insecurities: death, social disintegration. Indeed, they seem in our present and foreseeable situation to intensify them.

One would be more accurate, therefore, to predict the resurgence rather than the disappearance of religion. The problem, of course, is the sort of religion being reborn. Islamic and Christian fundamentalisms clearly exemplify closure, suspicion, anger, whatever their verbal professions of concern for humanity.

In this era of television evangelism, we do not have to look far to find the religion of the closed society. Media fundamentalism does seek to reinforce unravelling institutions, to dissolve rootlessness, to combat nihilism. No special insight is needed, however, to see the tribalism at its roots. It puts us Christian "insiders" against those accursed "outsiders." It proclaims America God's chosen nation; the others will just have to wait—and suffer. Against enemies (Communism, or whatever comes next) we must sustain an ever more sophisticated war machine. Membership, moreover; has its privileges. For those with solid club credentials, it is no longer necessary to worry: about war, pestilence, famine, hatred, prejudice, sexism, environmental degradation. And, in the event of universal destruction, the "in" group will be wafted up into a heaven of harps and cherubim; the others will be plunged into a sort of gigantic Patterson, New Jersey, there to suffer forever.

But there is also the religion of the open society, the only religion that can on a planetary scale—the scale a postmodern world imposes on us—unify without degrading, heal without closure, love without excluding. Indeed, the resurgence of closed societies with their potential for friction, suspicion, and war creates a vacuum which only the religion of the open society is suited to fill.

We have once again mentioned war. The supreme task of the human spirit today, Bergson urges, is its elimination. This is the central practical preoccupation of *The Two Sources of Morality and Religion*. The advance of military technology, if nothing else, now renders the abolition of war absolutely necessary. Here the glory and resulting misery of the human being, the successful machine-maker, become all too painfully apparent. Thus Bergson warns, in 1932:

> At the pace at which science is moving, that day is not far off when one of the two adversaries, through some secret process which he was holding in reserve, will have the means of annihilating his opponent. The vanquished may vanish off the face of the earth.[78]

That he is referring here to the possibility of nuclear weapons seems inescapable. Only twenty-five pages later[79] he refers explicitly to the possible peaceful uses of atomic energy. We recall that as far back as 1896 he had defined matter as a form of energy.

One suspects many pacifists and peace-oriented movements of naive optimism. But if Bergson is an optimist, his optimism is at least not naive. One by one he lists the obstacles to peace. Among the pressing "practical" problems that lead to conflict are overpopulation, the subjugation of women (a major cause of the desire for luxuries), the failure to improve agriculture (in the rush towards industrialization), the lack of an international government capable of settling disputes:

> We repeat, no single one of these difficulties is insurmountable, if an adequate portion of humanity is determined to surmount them. *But we must face up to them, and realize what has to be given up if war is to be abolished.*[80]

If we have failed to be creative in the abolition of war, it is because we have failed to be realistic about both war's immense cost and the radical nature of the measures necessary to overcome it.

Beyond these social and political obstacles, there are obstacles even more deeply rooted in human nature. If modern humanity under the joint impetus of the Judeo-Christian tradition and a new, potentially liberating technology has increasingly proclaimed "liberty, equality, fraternity," we must never forget that the primitive humankind we carry within us proclaims just as insistently "authority, hierarchy, immobility."[81] The closed society, by a tremendous effort towards openness, can be overcome, can be "repressed or circumvented."[82] But let us not fool ourselves. It will take a tremendous effort.

What will lead us to *make* that effort? William James' notion of a "moral equivalent of war," useful as it is, and even necessary in some fashion to a sustainable peace, is not radical enough. Political doctrines based on class warfare do not reach deeply enough into human psychology. Economic dogmas based on the quest for more consumer goods and pleasures only make the problem worse. Perhaps we will be favored by the emergence of some privileged individual, some moral genius capable of drawing humanity after him or her, of opening what is closed, of outflanking what is primitive. Perhaps some other force will open our minds and hearts to the possibility of a transcendent value, in the light of which our rush towards materialism and our frantic clutching at sensuality will pale into insignificance. Barring either of these alternatives, we will simply have to put up as we have with makeshift solutions: muddling precariously on the sharp edge of annihilation.

Two more points of application of Bergson's philosophy—points already suggested above—should be stressed here: the coherence of his philosophy with feminism and its consistency with environmentalism. Bergson does not say so in as many words, but it is clear that a society whose implicit motto is "authority, hierarchy, immobility" is going to be one that, to put it nicely, finds that biological functions define women: *Kinder, Küche, Kirche*. An open society, however, makes possible the liberation of woman, and thereby (at least potentially) helps solve the problem of the ever-increasing demand for luxury. Speaking of overblown sexuality and commercial sex appeal ("the keynote of our whole civilization"), Bergson insists:

> Here again science has something to say, and it will say it one day so clearly that all must listen: there will no longer be pleasure in so much love of pleasure. Woman will hasten the coming of this time according as she really and sincerely strives to become man's equal, instead of remaining the instrument she still is, waiting to vibrate under the musician's bow. Let the transformation take place: our life will be both more purposeful and more simple. What woman demands in the way of luxuries in order to please man, and, in the rebound, to please herself, will become to a great extent unnecessary.[83]

If one reflects seriously on this passage one sees its *lack* of condescension; it is not man who will make woman free, but woman who will be able to free herself. Being free, she will no longer need the bribe of luxuries to feel herself complete. And one more step will have been taken towards a simplified society, a simplified life.

Today a powerful feminist movement seems, temporarily at least, to have stalled, divided within itself and uncertain of its acceptance among those who might otherwise be expected to support it. If one broadens Bergson's brief remarks on feminism, one sees a new possibility. Feminism will succeed not when it bases itself primarily on economic goals or even on economic fairness, not when it bases itself on strident demands for one sex or complaints against another, but when it embodies a powerful love, one that reaches out to all humanity, male or female. (Among Bergson's "mystical geniuses" there are as many women as men.) It will succeed when it is clear that it is part of a movement that seeks to raise, transfigure, humanize us all.

I have argued elsewhere that process-relational philosophies like those of Bergson, James, and Whitehead are ideally suited to deal with environmental problems.[84] If it is true, as it now appears, that we are capable of disbalancing the climate of our planet—with potentially horrendous results for all of us— then the question of how we humans are to conceive of and approach our environment is a matter of great importance. Two factors, at least, dictate the usefulness of process postmodern philosophies to environmentalism: the appeal to process as the fundamental reality out of which things are made, and, second, the insistence on the organic (profoundly relational) nature of reality. It is as if these philosophers had developed their conception of reality precisely to parallel the character of ecosystems, in which a change in one part necessarily involves changes in others, and in which "parts" are defined through their relations. It should come as no surprise, then, that in the period 1900-1950 two of the few major professional philosophers to mention problems of food, population, and environmental degradation were Bergson and Whitehead.[85]

There is a further insight to be gained from this. The problems of the abolition of war, of environmental degradation, and of feminism are precisely postmodern problems. Bergson was the first to see—or at any rate the first to say explicitly—that these problems are bound together by a common effort to overcome the closed society, paternalism, "natural religion." He was also the first to see that no one of them can be solved apart from the others. We face, as this darkest of centuries wanes, a threefold task which is yet one task. Perhaps at the center of it is a new religious consciousness, a turning of the spirit still unrealized. Perhaps we have yet to conceive the theology that will liberate us.

NOTES

1. Geraldine Joncich, *The Sane Positivist: A Biography of Edward L. Thorndike* (Middletown, Conn.: Wesleyan University Press, 1968), 334.

2. John Dewey, "Introduction," *A Contribution to a Bibliography of Henri Bergson* (New York: Columbia University Press, 1913), ix.

3. Arthur Balfour, "Creative Evolution and Philosophic Doubt," *Hibbert Journal* 10, Part 1 (October 1911), 1-23, reprinted in *Living Age* 271 (December 2, 1911), 515-27. See also "Bergson and Balfour Discuss Philosophy," *Review of Reviews* 44/1 (1912), 107-08.

4. Theodore Roosevelt, "The Search for Truth in a Reverent Spirit," *Outlook* 99 (December 22, 1911), 819-26.

5. Edwin E. Slosson, "Twelve Major Prophets of Today. II. Henri Bergson," *The Independent* 70/3262 (June 8, 1911), 1246.

6. "Threatened Collapse of Bergson Boom in France," *Current Opinion* 56/5 (May, 1914), 371.

7. For a more comprehensive list of writers and philosophers influenced—diversely indeed—by Bergson, see Pete A. Y. Gunter, "Intuition and its Expressions: An Introduction to the Bergson Literature," in *Henri Bergson: A Bibliography*, 2nd ed. (Bowling Green, Ohio: Philosophy Documentation Center, 1986), 1-13. See also Paul Douglass, *Bergson, Eliot and American Literature* (Lexington: University Press of Kentucky, 1986), 210.

8. Two examples of this attitude: J. W. Scott, "Bergsonism in England," *Monist* 27/2 (April 1917), 179-204; Albert Schinz, *French Literature of the Great War* (London and New York: D. Appleton and Co., 1920), 433.

9. Henri Bergson, *Time and Free Will*, trans. F. L. Pogson (London: Allen and Unwin, 1950) (henceforth *TFW*), 252.

10. *TFW*, 1.

11. *TFW*, 220.

12. *TFW*, 227.

13. Henri Bergson, *Matter and Memory*, trans. N. M. Paul and W. S. Palmer (London: Allen and Unwin, 1950) (henceforth *MM*), 339.

14. *MM*, 266.

15. *MM*, 268.

16. See Milič Čapek, *Bergson and Modern Physics* (New York: Humanities Press; Dordrecht, Holland: Reidel, 1971), 414.

17. For a recent re-evaluation of Bergson's mind-body duality, see Milič Čapek, "Bergson's Theory of the Mind-Brain Relation," in *Bergson and Modern Thought: Towards a Unified Science*, ed. A. C. Papanicolaou and P. A. Y. Gunter (New York: Harwood Academic Publishers, 1987), 129-48. For some further recent re-evaluations of Bergson's mind-body theory, see Karl H. Pribram, "Bergson and the Brain: A Bio-Logical Analysis of Certain Intuitions," and Andrew C. Papanicolaou, "Aspects of Henri Bergson's Psycho-Physical Theory," in *Bergson and Modern Thought*, 149-74 and 56-128, respectively. See also Yuasa Yasuo, *The Body: Toward an Eastern Mind-Body Theory*, ed. T. P. Kasulis (Albany: State University of New York Press, 1987), 161-201.

18. *MM*, 276-77

19. Henri Bergson, *Duration and Simultaneity*, trans. L. Jacobson (Indianapolis: Bobbs-Merrill Company, 1965), 190.

20. Louis de Broglie, "The Concepts of Contemporary Physics and Bergson's Ideas on Time and Motion," *Bergson and the Evolution of Physics*, ed. and trans. Pete A. Y. Gunter (Knoxville: University of Tennessee Press, 1969), 45-62.

21. Milič Čapek, "Bergson's Theory of Matter and Modern Physics," *Bergson and the Evolution of Physics*, 362 n. and throughout, 297-330.

22. Ilya Prigogine and Isabel Stengers, *Order out of Chaos: Man's New Dialogue with Nature* (New York: Bantam Books, 1984), 92-93.

23. Ibid., 93.

24. In a review of *Bergson and Modern Thought* (see n. 17, above), Prigogine says: "I want however to mention the fact that Bergson's views have undoubtedly influenced my own work on nonlinear processes" ("Nobel Chemist Examines Essays on Bergson," *Texas Books in Review* 8/3 [Fall 1988], 12). In conversation, Prigogine responded affirmatively to my observation that he had "Bergsonized chemistry." For a discussion of the relations between Bergson and Prigogine, see my "Bergson and Non-Equilibrium Non-Linear Thermodynamics: An Application of Method," *Revue Internationale de Philosophie* 45/177 (October 1991), 108-21.

25. *MM*, 86-105.

26. *MM*, 226.

27. *MM*, 198.

28. *MM*, 332.

29. Ibid.

30. Henri Bergson, "'Phantasms of the Living' and Psychical Research," in *Mind-Energy: Lectures and Essays*, trans. H. Wildon Carr (New York: Henry Holt and Company, 1920), 75-103.

31. For a recent historical account of the relations between Bergson's thought and parapsychology (and, more generally, "occultism"), see R. C. Grogin, *The Bergsonian Controversy in France, 1900-1914* (Calgary, Alberta, Canada: University of Calgary Press, 1988), 222.

32. Henri Bergson, "Dreams," in *Mind-Energy*, 104-33.

33. Pete A. Y. Gunter, "Philosophical Method and Biological Time," in Henri Bergson, *Creative Evolution*, trans. A. Mitchell (Lanham, Md.: University Press of America, 1983) (henceforth *CE*), xvii-li.

34. Julian Huxley, *Evolution: The Modern Synthesis* (New York: Harper and Brothers, 1943), 28.

35. Alexis Carrel, *Man, The Unknown* (New York: Harper and Brothers, 1935), 168; Pierre Lecomte du Noüy, *Biological Time* (London: Methuen, 1936), 180.

36. François Meyer, *L'Accéleration évolutive* (Paris: Librarie des Sciences et des Arts, 1947), 67; François Meyer, *La Surchauffe de la croissance* (Paris: Fayard, 1974), 140.

37. See Pete A. Y. Gunter, "Temps biologique et Développement biologique," *Cahiers de L'Association Lecomte du Noüy* 3 (1971), 16-22.

38. Karl Pribram, who also applies the concept of the holograph to problems of brain function, makes this suggestion; see in note 17 above, 170-72.

39. See Henri Bergson, *An Introduction to Metaphysics*, trans. T. E. Hulme (Indianapolis: Bobbs-Merrill, 1955), 62; or *The Creative Mind*, trans. M. L. Andison (New York: Philosophical Library, 1946), 159-200.

40. *CE*, 176,

41. Bertrand Russell, "The Philosophy of Bergson, " *Monist* 22/3 (July, 1912), 331.

42. Pete A. Y. Gunter, "Bergson and Jung," *Journal of the History of Ideas* 43/4 (1982), 635-52.

43. For a recent assessment of the behavior of the sphex, see Loren Eiseley, "The Coming of the Giant Wasps," in *All the Strange Hours* (New York: Scribner's, 1975), 243-54. Eiseley argues that Bergson's treatment of the solitary wasps touched on problems that have not yet been resolved. How the wasp can have innate ideas of its prey's nervous system is hard to explain through natural selection.

44. Henri Bergson, *The Two Sources of Morality and Religion*, trans. R. A. Audra and C. Brereton with W. H. Carter (New York: Henry Holt, 1935) (henceforth *TS*), 308.

45. Charles Hartshorne, "Bergson's Aesthetic Creationism Compared to Whitehead's," in *Bergson and Modern Thought*, ed. Papanicolaou and Gunter, 369-82, at 379.

46. *TS*, 109.

47. *TS*, 116.

48. *TS*, 121.

49. *TS*, 122.

50. *TS*, 124-25.

51. *TS*, 188-89.

52. *TS*, 189.

53. *TS*, 179.

54. *TS*, 199.

55. *TS*, 46.

56. *TS*, 51.

57. *TS*, 149.

58. See Dorothy Emmet, "The Concept of Freedom with Reference to Open and Closed Societies," in *The Concept of Freedom in Anthropology*, ed. D. Bidney (The Hague: Mouton, 1963), 91-105. This author describes three senses in which a society may be said to be open: (1) having freedom of entry (Max Weber), (2) being open-minded (Karl Popper), (3) being openhearted (Henri Bergson).

59. *TS*, 49.

60. Ibid.

61. Ibid.

62. *TS*, 67.

63. Ibid.

64. Ibid.

65. *TS*, 271.

66. Ibid.

67. *TS*, 203-04.

68. Pete A. Y. Gunter, "Bergson's Philosophical Method and its Application to the Sciences," *Southern Journal of Philosophy* 16/3 (1987), 167-81.

69. *TS*, 217.

70. *TS*, 220.

71. *TS*, 218.

72. *TS*, 209, 216.

73. *TS*, 214.

74. Karl Popper, *The Open Society and its Enemies* (New York: Harper and Row, 1962), 771.

75. *TS*, 287.

76. *TS*, 301.

77. *TS*, 280.

78. *TS*, 276.

79. *TS*, 301.

80. *TS*, 279.

81. *TS*, 271.

82. *TS*, 277.

83. *TS*, 291. This was no afterthought on Bergson's part. In an interview in 1913 (*Harper's Weekly*, March 8, p. 6), he argued that the then-current feminist movement was the most important event since the proclamation of the Christian ideal.

84. Pete A. Y. Gunter, "Creativity and Ecology," in *Creativity in Art, Religion, and Culture*, ed. Michael Mitias (Amsterdam: Rodopi, 1985), 107-16.

85. Pete A. Y. Gunter, "Process Philosophy: The Raw Cash Value of a Mere Metaphysical Speculation," in the proceedings of the 1988 Frontiers in American Philosophy conference (forthcoming).

4

ALFRED NORTH WHITEHEAD

John B. Cobb, Jr.

I. SPECULATIVE POSTMODERNISM

Although Whitehead (1861-1947) never used the term "postmodern," the way he spoke of the modern has a definite postmodern tone. Especially in his book *Science and the Modern World*, the modern is objectified and its salient characteristics are described. Whitehead is appreciative of the accomplishments of the modern world, but he clearly recognizes its limitations as well, and he points beyond it. He sees his own time as one of new beginnings as fundamental as those that constituted the shift from the medieval to the modern world.

   Whitehead explicitly identifies the new beginnings in two areas. The first is physics. Both relativity and quantum theory break with the assumptions of modern physics and call for fundamental reconstruction of the scientific program. Here Whitehead, himself a mathematical physicist, undertook to make a major contribution by developing his own relativity theory. While giving Einstein full credit for his discoveries, Whitehead was dissatisfied with the conceptual foundations and implications of Einstein's theory. From his alternative theory can be generated most, if not all, of the predictions that have been developed from the standard Einsteinian theory, but he avoids some of the paradoxes that have plagued efforts to understand Einsteinian relativity.[1]

The second area is philosophy. Whitehead identifies William James as the originator of a new type of philosophy. Whitehead's judgment that a new age, following the modern one, has already begun is nowhere more clearly expressed than in the passage from which the following quotation is taken.

The history of philosophy runs curiously parallel to that of science. In the case of both, the seventeenth century set the stage for its two successors. But with the twentieth century a new act commences. It is an exaggeration to attribute a general change in a climate of thought to any one piece of writing or to any one author. No doubt Descartes only expressed definitely and in decisive form what was already in the air of his period. Analogously, in attributing to William James the inauguration of a new stage in philosophy, we should be neglecting other influences of his time. But, admitting this, there still remains a certain fitness in contrasting his essay, *Does Consciousness Exist?*, published in 1904, with Descartes' *Discourse on Method*, published in 1637. James clears the stage of the old paraphernalia; or rather he entirely alters its lighting. . . .

The scientific materialism and the Cartesian Ego were both challenged at the same moment, one by science and the other by philosophy, as represented by William James with his psychological antecedents; and the double challenge marks the end of a period which lasted for about two hundred and fifty years.[2]

Whitehead believes that philosophical movements typically have two key moments. There is the genius who inaugurates the movement, and the systematizer who follows. He seems to depict himself in the latter role in relation to James. He accepts and adopts many of James' key insights, and then goes on to develop them in rich and rigorous detail.

Whitehead understands that this requires speculation, and he calls his *magnum opus* a work of speculative philosophy. Since the term "speculative" has been one of scorn for late modernist thinkers, it is important that we understand what Whitehead means by it. He certainly does not mean undisciplined thinking. Nevertheless, speculative philosophy is poles removed from a philosophy that limits itself to scientific method, to phenomenology, or to the analysis of language.

For Whitehead, "speculative philosophy is the endeavor to frame a coherent, logical, necessary system of ideas in terms of which every element of our experience can be interpreted."[3] This requires the search for first principles. Whitehead describes this as follows: "The true method of discovery is like the flight of an aeroplane. It starts from the ground of particular observation; it makes a flight in the thin air of imaginative generalization; and it again lands for renewed observation rendered acute by rational interpretation."[4]

Clearly, speculative philosophy is a rational enterprise. There is some dispute today as to whether this commitment to rationality binds one to modernity or separates one from it. We will not pursue the methodological issues determined by the commitment to rationality, but the next section will discuss how Whitehead himself views the relation of rationality to modernity. The remaining sections will take up some of Whitehead's basic postmodern speculative ideas, explaining them in such a way as to show their plausibility and illuminating power.

II. MODERNITY AND RATIONALITY

The modern period is often thought of as the age of reason. It is contrasted with the medieval period, which is seen as an age of faith or even superstition. From this perspective, the critique of reason initiated in philosophy by Hume and Kant provides the basis for a new, a postmodern, age.

Whitehead's study of the origins of modern thought led him to a quite different understanding. He came to the view that the origin of modernity was, most fundamentally, a shift from rational to historical thinking. Under the latter term he includes the empirical approach. In short, instead of seeking the ultimate reasons for things and events, the modern mind has sought to understand in more limited spheres, and it is satisfied with less ultimate answers. In particular, it seeks to understand the sources of things rather than their purposes or deepest natures. If we are to distinguish what is truly postmodern from what carries the modern through to its consistent outcome, this point is of utmost importance, and it is worthwhile to quote Whitehead at some length.

> The Reformation and the scientific movement were two aspects of the historical revolt which was the dominant intellectual movement of the later Renaissance. The appeal to the origins of Christianity, and Francis Bacon's appeal to efficient causes as against final causes, were two sides of one movement of thought. . . .
>
> It is a great mistake to conceive this historical revolt as an appeal to reason. On the contrary, it was through and through an anti-intellectualist movement. It was the return to the contemplation of brute fact; and it was based on a recoil from the inflexible rationality of medieval thought. In making this statement I am merely summarising what at the time the adherents of the old regime themselves asserted. For example, in the fourth book of Father Paul Sarpi's *History of the Council of Trent,* you will find that in the year 1551 the Papal Legates who presided over the Council ordered: "That the Divines ought to confirm their opinions with the holy Scripture, Traditions of the Apostles, sacred and approved Coun-

cils, and by the Constitutions and Authorities of the holy Fathers; that they ought to use brevity, and avoid superfluous and unprofitable questions, and perverse contentions. . . . This order did not please the Italian Divines; who said it was a novity, and a condemning of School-Divinity, which, in all difficulties, *useth reason*, and because it was not lawful [*i.e.*, by this decree] to treat as St. Thomas [Aquinas], St. Bonaventure, and other famous men did."[5]

Whitehead sees this shift from reason to attention to the particularities and sources of things as a gain. Without it, science could not have entered on its great age of progress. He celebrates the seventeenth century as the age of genius, and he notes that also in the following centuries there have been enormous advances in the sciences.

Nevertheless, Whitehead believes that something of value was lost in the abandonment of the quest for reasons. The ideas underlying modern science were not vigorously probed. They worked well, and their success sufficed to guarantee their adequacy. The task of philosophy was not to critique the basic ideas about the world presupposed by science but to justify them. When Hume interpreted causality in a way that could not support its role in the natural sciences, Kant reformulated philosophy so that not only causality but all the fundamental notions of the Newtonian worldview were preserved.

Finally, the antirationalism of modern thought displayed its limits in physics itself. Developments within physics demonstrated that the fundamental notions built into physics could not apply in the new levels of inquiry. There was, in the early part of this century, a considerable stirring of effort to rethink nature so as to take account of this new development. Whitehead saw himself as part of this, and thus was a participant in trying to shape a postmodern science.

But Whitehead evidently underestimated the power of the anti-intellectualism that he had identified as foundational to modern thought. While a few struggled to make sense of the non-Newtonian world that physics had brought to life, the majority turned their backs on this inquiry. They became more radically antirational.

Modernity in the seventeenth century had turned attention from ultimate questions to penultimate ones, believing that at that level an adequate, intellectually satisfying account of nature could be found. It did not press theoretical questions about its mechanistic model, but it did assume that this model was an adequate, and even accurate, replication of the most important features of the natural world. For the founders of modern science and philosophy, therefore, the world was rational in the twofold sense that it conformed to an intelligible pattern, and that thought about the world should be coherent. If the work of biologists could not yet be interpreted fully in the terms afforded by physics, this represented a gap that further research would fill. The goal was rational, *not* in the sense of probing the meanings of the key terms and seeking the ultimate reason for things, but in the sense of seeking a unified and accurate picture of the whole and of all the details of the natural world.

Whitehead evidently assumed that the commitment to rationality at this secondary level was such that the breakdown of the program would lead to a deeper rationality, that is, to raising again more ultimate questions about the reality that could no longer be pictured as a machine. But the majority response went the other way. It said: "If our mechanistic picture does not fit the world, we should give up trying to picture the world at all, or, at least, we should recognize that our pictures are only that. When we acknowledge that our pictures do not represent reality, then we can also give up the quest for a coherent system of thought to describe the world. If different models work for different purposes, that suffices. Their incoherence is unimportant."

Sometimes this radical abandonment of the effort to understand a reality other than ourselves is called *postmodern*. If modernity is defined in terms of its optimistic belief that it had attained to an accurate and adequate picture of how things truly are, then the abandonment of the optimism and of any and all programs for understanding nature can be called postmodern. Postmodernity then begins with Hume and Kant. This continues to be a widespread view, and it is increasingly celebrated as liberating in philosophical, literary, and religious circles. It is also factually embodied in the university, where little effort is made to examine the ideas on which the several disciplines are founded, or to bring their findings into any coherent relationship with one another.

If one understands modernity as Whitehead does, however, then a very different judgment follows. One discovers that the antirationalism at the inauguration of the modern age has become increasingly radical, that the role allowed to reason has been even more circumscribed. From this Whiteheadian point of view, Hume and Kant initiate a second phase of modern antirationalism. And Nietzsche, Heidegger, and Derrida can be seen as carrying this antirationalist mood to a still further extreme.

The antirationalism that appears from one point of view to be postmodern appears in this perspective to be carrying modernity to its logical conclusion. What appears from a Whiteheadian point of view to be truly postmodern is the emergence of new root metaphors or paradigms, radically thought through, and rigorously tested against the whole range of evidence.

Postmodernism in the Whiteheadian sense requires not only the reconstruction of individual disciplines but also the reconception of the organization of knowledge as a whole. Modernity began by dividing reality into the two worlds of mind and matter, freeing the latter from religious concern so that it could be explored by objectifying scientific methods. It then proceeded to separate the world into compartments, each of which could be studied in separation from the others. If the world truly were machinelike, this might work. The working of the individual parts of a machine are not greatly affected by their role in the whole. If one examines each part of a machine separately, it is possible to think of the whole as the joint working of the parts. With this model in mind, the university divides reality into segments, and it studies each as if it existed in separation from the others and could be understood in that separation. Little attention then needs to be given to distinctive characteristics of the whole.

A Whiteheadian postmodernism begins by insisting that such bifurcation and fragmentation falsifies reality, that all things are interconnected, and that this pattern of relationships is constitutive of the relata. What is said from this perspective cannot be contained within the organization of knowledge based on modern principles.

A Whiteheadian postmodernism recovers something of the rationalism rejected by modernity. This does not mean that it returns to the mode of thought that preceded modernity. But it does find contributions in that earlier period that have been obscured by the modern polemic against it. In order to determine what shifts of thinking are required to expand human understanding and to do justice to the whole range of questions we confront as a world, postmodern thought probes the fundamental assumptions of the ideas on the basis of which the vast gains of modernity were made. The following sections of this essay will explore some of Whitehead's shifts away from modern assumptions, explaining their speculative justification.

III. FROM SUBSTANCES WITH ATTRIBUTES TO EVENTS IN RELATION

Broadly speaking, there seem to be two types of things that can be taken as examples of what is actual by philosophical realists. We can call these substances and events. Initially, we should think of these nontechnically.

By "substances" I have in mind the objects that surround us all the time—tables and chairs, rocks and sticks, plants and animals, planets and stars. These objects remain the same through considerable periods of time, although in detail they change. When changing objects are analyzed philosophically, it can be said that there are changes in their attributes, but that what underlies the attributes, what the attributes are attributes *of*, remains strictly the same. The color of the table may fade, or the table may be repainted, but it is the same table.

Of course, there are limits to the endurance of a substance. The wood of the table may rot or be burned. At some point, what identified it as the same table or substance is destroyed. Hence, substances of this sort do come into being and disappear. There is generation and decay. However, the matter itself does not cease to be. The wood ceases to be wood, but when it is burned the atoms of which it is composed are not destroyed. Indeed, until recently it was supposed that these atoms were indestructible. They were long understood to be the ultimate substances, incapable of generation or decay or any other change except locomotion. The clearest and most consistent doctrine of substances and attributes was formulated in terms of unchanging atoms and their relative motions.

Unfortunately for this doctrine, it turned out that atoms were in fact not atoms in the sense of being indivisible. Scientists have now divided them. But this in itself would not count against a metaphysical substantialism. The real problem for this view is that the entities into which the atom is divided do not behave as substances are supposed to behave. Some of their properties are intelligible from a substantialist perspective, so that they can be called "particles," but others are not, so that for some purposes they must be viewed as "waves," but without having a substrate that can be understood to "wave."

A second problem for a realistic substantialism has been that it has difficulty accounting either for human thought or for the relation between human thought and the material substances. Descartes, of course, held that thinking was an attribute of mental substances, as extension was the fundamental attribute of material substances. But Descartes could not explain the relation between mental and material substances, and the modern epoch has been characterized by a series of unsatisfactory responses to this problem. Frustration with this problem is one of the reasons for the abandonment of the project of a realistic account of the world in the later modern development.

A few Western thinkers have pointed to the other option. Everyone knows that there are events as well as substances. There are meetings and games, accidents and healings, wars and conversations, births and deaths. No one would call these substances.

In general, however, events have been subordinated metaphysically to substances. It has been assumed that events can be explained finally in terms of the substances that participate in them, together with the locomotion of these substances. It is believed that, finally, a conversation can be analyzed into the movement of atomic constituents of the people and their environment that jointly make up the event. Of course, for practical purposes the event must be treated as such, but it is assumed that, metaphysically speaking, it has no existence in itself.

The deep-seated assumption that substances in relative motion are more real than events continues to characterize most thinking in our time. But, as indicated above, it does not fit with what we now know in physics. The analysis of the subatomic entities leads to quanta of energy that are much better described as energy-events than as substances. The apparently substantial things that so profoundly shape our sense of reality are more accurately described as stable patterns of activity than as substances.

When events are taken as the ultimate units of actuality, the difficulty of relating "mind" to "matter" is reduced. "Mind" is analyzed into mental events, "matter" into physical ones; and mental events and physical events need not be viewed as metaphysically different. Their common character as events can be described and their differences seen more as differences of degree than of metaphysical kind.

Just as substances such as chairs and tables can be analyzed into component substances such as atoms, so also events like wars and conversations can be analyzed into the component events that make them up. Because both of these examples are human events, the most salient units are human experiences. The conversation between two people includes as major components the flow of experience of these two people. The flow of experience of one of them, Ms. Smith, can in turn be analyzed into the momentary successive experiences that make it up. The analysis of Ms. Smith's experience during a conversation into the successive momentary experiences of which it was constituted corresponds in an event-metaphysics to the analysis of chairs into the atoms of which they are constituted in classical substantialist thought. These momentary experiences, too, may be called "atomic" in the philosophical sense, in that they cannot be divided into more basic units that have full actuality. (I will henceforth use "atomic" in this philosophical sense to mean "indivisible," whereas I will use "subatomic" in the scientific sense to refer to the constituents of what have been called "atoms" in modern science.)

But these atomic "occasions of experience," to use Whitehead's term, are very different from material atoms. First, they are four-dimensional, whereas material atoms are conceived to be three-dimensional. That is, the classical atom did not require any lapse of time in order to be what it is. It endured through time, but its locus and extent in time did not enter into its definition or affect it in any way. It was supposed to exist fully in an instant or in any infinitesimal period. The Whiteheadian atomic event, on the other hand, is necessarily located exactly where it is in space and time. Further, its extensiveness builds up temporal duration just as it provides the basis for spatial spread.

Second, the atomic occasions of experience are analyzable primarily not into attributes but into relations. Consider one occasion of experience of Ms. Smith. That experience is constituted very largely by a continuation of her experience a moment earlier. Perhaps in that moment she was hearing the beginning of a word spoken by Ms. Brown; now she is hearing the end of that word. The fact that she hears it as the end of that word indicates that the previous moment is still alive in the present. This is a very intimate relation indeed! To describe the present occasion of experience apart from this relation would be to falsify it drastically. It is not as though there were a present experience of hearing the end of the word that then, subsequently, relates itself to the previous one in which the beginning of the word was heard. On the contrary, the influ-ence of the previous occasion of experience is fundamentally constitutive of the present occasion. What Ms. Smith hears now is precisely the ending of the word, not a sound subsequently interpreted in that way by relating it to what was heard earlier. This immediate inflowing of the past into the occasion of experience is what Whitehead calls a "physical feeling," or "physical prehen-sion."

Still, Ms. Smith is in fact hearing a sound in this moment that she had not heard in the preceding moment. She hears the end of Ms. Brown's word. This sound is mediated to her through her body. Thus not only are her own past experiences flowing into her present, but also there is the inflowing or pre-hension of bodily events—in this case, events in the ears. Her present experi-ence is the integration of this new sound with the sounds she has heard before.

Obviously, this is still an extreme oversimplification. Ms. Smith is also having visual and tactile experiences. Further, her ability to understand what she hears as a word that is a part of a sentence entails relations to many other peo-ple and past experiences. The way she feels about what she is hearing—what Whitehead calls "the subjective form" of the prehension—is affected by her tiredness and the soreness of some of her muscles as well as by vague and half-conscious hopes and fears. The analysis goes on and on. The point is that this analysis is into physical feelings or prehensions—that is, into the internal relations of the event to other events, the way the other events participate in constituting the new one. The occasion of experience is a unification of its feelings or prehensions of the world out of which it arises.

For the most part, the emotional tone of its feeling conforms to the world that it feels. For example, if Ms. Smith is pleased by what she hears from Ms. Brown, that pleasurable feeling will tend to persist after Ms. Brown has stopped speaking and Ms. Smith has begun to reply. In more technical terms, the sub-jective form of the present prehension of the earlier occasions of experience tends to conform to the subjective form of those occasions.

That an occasion of human experience is a synthesis of prehensions is fairly clear to anyone who attempts to describe what is happening. But what about *nonhuman* atomic (unitary) events—for example, those at the subatomic level? Obviously, we cannot analyze them phenomenologically as we do our own experience. Nevertheless, Whitehead believes that these events, too, are what they are because of their pattern of relationships to other events. What is happening in one part of a field cannot be understood in abstraction from the field as a whole. Rather, it is better thought of as what that field is at that point. These subatomic events, too, can be better viewed as syntheses of prehensions of other events than as substances with attributes.

If both human occasions of experience and subatomic unitary events are best understood as syntheses of prehensions of other events, then their relation to one another is not as puzzling as has been supposed in the modern epoch. Instead, we may suppose that among the events to which an occasion of human experience is related are numerous subatomic occasions of experience. They, too, enter into the constitution of a moment of human experience. We may suppose also that among the internal relations or prehensions synthesized in the subatomic events are those to human occasions of experience. Hence, the effect of the physical world on the mental world is not the mystery that Descartes faced, but is to be expected, and similarly the effect of the mental on the physical world, assumed in all our actions, is what we should expect. I will explain the reasons for thinking of all atomic or indivisible events as "occasions of experience" in the next section.

IV. FROM SUBJECTS AND OBJECTS TO SUBJECT-OBJECTS

Even more fundamental to modern thought than substantialist metaphysics is the epistemological starting point. Descartes began with the analysis of immediate experience and how it provided evidence of a world beyond itself. This starting point has continued to characterize modern philosophy even when Descartes' realism is abandoned. This starting point almost inevitably divides the world into subjects and objects. The subjects are those whose experience is being examined. The objects are whatever is experienced.

This subject-object dualism is, in Descartes, much the same as the mind-matter dualism discussed above. But, in other philosophers, the metaphysical dualism may be abandoned without disturbing the epistemological dualism. The objects of experience might be simply phenomena or sense-data. What remains the same in this analysis is that the kinds of things that are subjects always remain subjects, and the kinds of things that are objects always remain objects.

Whitehead is among those who retain the distinction of subject and object while rejecting the accompanying epistemological and metaphysical dualisms. For him, all (actual) objects were once subjects, and all subjects become objects. (The term "actual" is inserted parenthetically, because there are also objects that are always objects—called "eternal objects" by Whitehead. These objects are not actualities but mere possibilities; they are discussed as such in section VII.) Subjects and objects are not two types of actual entities, but the same entities considered in different ways.

To understand this, return to Ms. Smith. Whitehead, no less than most modern philosophers, focuses attention on what is going on in Ms. Smith's experience. But whereas most modern philosophers have taken as their paradigm case Ms. Smith's visual experience of a physical object, Whitehead takes as the paradigm case the causal efficacy of Ms. Smith's immediately past occasion of experience in the present occasion, or Ms. Smith's present prehension of that past occasion. The present occasion of experience is the subject of this prehension. The immediately past occasion is the datum of this prehension. A datum is an object for the subject for which it is given. In this way the subject-object structure of experience is reaffirmed.

But notice that the *object* of the experience is itself an occasion of experience that had come into being as a subject of prehensions of other occasions. What is felt in the present occasion are the feelings of the past occasion. Those feelings or prehensions are its objects, but as feelings they have not lost their subjective forms. The difference is only that they are now completed and finished—in short, past. The world of (actual) objects is the world of past subjects.

This sweeping generalization from Ms. Smith's prehension of her past experience is based on the speculation that the relations that constitute all atomic events can also be understood as prehensions. That means that all such events are subjects appropriating from objects that are past subjects. This goes against the grain for those whose sense of reality has been shaped in the modern era.

Part of the problem is that the dualistic thinking that radically separates human beings from the physical world is deeply ingrained. Postmodern thinking must engage in a sustained effort to overcome this habit of mind. But part of the resistance comes from the real difference between ourselves and such objects as tables. Whereas we experience ourselves as subjects and do not find it difficult to attribute subjectivity to our pets, we are clear that tables and rocks are very different indeed. To say that they are subjects, like us and our pets, is profoundly counterintuitive. This natural resistance must be taken seriously.

The reason that tables seem so very different from cats is that the latter move about on their own and appear to be doing so purposefully. They seem to sense danger, to be attracted to food, and to react appropriately. In short, they display intelligent purposiveness. When they make certain sounds we hear them as cries of pain, and we notice that the circumstances in which they cry out are analogous to those in which we feel pain. To deny all subjectivity to cats, as Descartes did, is just as counterintuitive as to attribute such subjectivity to objects that have none of these characteristics.

The refusal to treat tables as subjects is, then, a sensible one. Tables are the sorts of things from which the idea of objective substances with attributes has arisen. For most practical purposes, this understanding makes good sense. The issue that was posed above was whether the exhaustive analysis of tables into subatomic entities yields tiny substances with attributes or, instead, events in relation. Whitehead is convinced that the latter conclusion fits the evidence much better. The issue now is whether these events in relation have a subjective aspect.

To answer this question requires rigorous reflection as to what is meant by "subjectivity," especially when it is contrasted with "objectivity." There are certainly some features of human subjectivity that cannot plausibly be attributed to subatomic events. For example, human subjectivity includes conscious thinking. Whitehead agrees that it is implausible to suppose that subatomic entities are conscious or that they think.

The word "subject" is ambiguous in its usage. Indeed, it seems to have two almost opposite uses. Sometimes, a subject is that on which power is exercised: a king exercises power over his "subjects"; some people are "subject" to occasional seizures. At other times, especially in its contrast with an object, a "subject" is an agent, one who is not merely acted on but acts, one who takes some responsibility for the course of events.

As Whitehead uses "subject," both meanings apply. To accent the receptive aspect he sometimes adds the word "superject."[6] An occasion of experience is a superject of its relations to past occasions. That means that the character of those prehended objects largely determines the character of the new subject. The "subject-superject" conforms to what it feels. It is largely the result of the unification of those objects.

But the subject is also agent. Among the possible ways of responding to, or taking account of, its world, it selects one. That is, it "decides." This decision is its act of becoming what it becomes rather than something else that it might have become. By becoming just that and not anything else, it also decides how it will influence the future. Every unified event is subject to the decisions of earlier events, therefore, and is a subject that decides just how to act upon subsequent events.

Does this mean that each atomic event has a subjective side? One might think of one object as affected by the motions of other objects without attributing any subjectivity to the affected object. Indeed, modernity thought in those terms until Hume showed that there is no basis in experience for positing causality of this sort. When we think of objects that are not subjects, we can speak only of a regular succession of events, not of one object's actually affecting another. If we want to find an instance of actual influence in experience, we must return to the way events in the body or in one's personal past affect the present experience. There we experience influence or causality. All other meanings of causality are derivative from this experience or else vacuous. Either the relation between successive events in the subatomic world is analogous to the relations we experience, or we have no way of thinking of them at all. Whitehead proposes that before we lapse into total silence we try out the hypothesis that there are analogies among all events.

The choice of the word "decision" highlights the hypothesis that there is an aspect of subjectivity in all atomic events. Yet the usual use of the word suggests the consciousness and thought that are not attributed by Whitehead to creatures without central nervous systems. To understand the continuity that underlies the many discontinuities among creatures, it will be useful to attend to what goes on in human decisions.

Usually we think of decisions only when they are major. One decides to go to one college rather than another or to take one job rather than another. One may spend days or even weeks in making such a decision. There is virtually no analogy between decisions of this sort and what Whitehead attributes to all occasions of experience.

But the use of "decision" in ordinary discourse is not limited to these protracted reflections. Consider a different example. When driving down the freeway, one observes that a speeding car is suddenly cutting in front. One sees also that it is cutting too close and that if one does not act immediately there will be an accident. To avoid this, one must either swerve or brake. But there is a car close behind and another in the lane into which one must swerve. If one is a skilled driver, one may yet be able to achieve just that combination of braking and swerving that will avoid an accident.

In this case everything depends on one's decision. But this decision cannot be reflective in the sense possible for the other examples. It must be virtually instantaneous. Does that mean that it is a "reflex" in which "decision" is absent? No. A reflex would have been established by repeated actions, and just this situation has never occurred before for the driver in question. The driver takes in the whole situation in a moment, processes the information immediately, and "decides" what to do. The action taken was not the only possible action, but only one among the possibilities.

Is this decision conscious? The driver is highly conscious at the time it is made, but the content of that consciousness is primarily the location and relative movements of the relevant cars. None of this is linguistically processed, and there is no reflection *about* the need to act. There is no consciousness *of* making the decision at the time it is made. It is only later that one is conscious of having made it.

Once we recognize that decisions, even complex ones, can be made almost instantaneously, we can also see that, in the examples given above, many, many decisions are made during the days or weeks of uncertainty about school or job selection. One decides with whom to talk and what to say in the conversations. One decides how to weigh the advantages and disadvantages. One decides which of these to think about more. On and on. Most of these decisions are not themselves the conscious outcome of consciously spelled-out procedures and arguments. The clearly conscious decisions are largely determined by many nonconscious decisions that govern the way one reflects about the issues.

It is such subtle, nonconscious decisions, usually quite minor, that Whitehead discerns in every occasion of human experience. In his view, no human experience is totally determined by the past it prehends. There is always some element of self-determination with respect to how it processes its data. And it is this element of self-determination, however slight it may be in many occasions of human experience, that he calls its decision.[7] It is this that provides the analogy to the "decision" involved in all elementary events. They, too, in much simpler ways, nonconsciously take account of their situation and constitute themselves in one of the ways that that situation allows.

The notion that there is a subjective aspect to all atomic events is so important that it will be worthwhile to clarify it in still another respect. The idea of an object that is not a subject is the idea of an object for some subject other than itself. That is, without a subject there cannot be an object. Because the only entities acknowledged to be subjects in the modern world have been human ones, objects have been understood to be objects of human experience. Indeed, to be an object has normally meant to be an object of human sensory experience, especially visual and tactile experience. The status of entities that cannot be data for human sense-experience has been tenuous at best.

This limitation of objects to what functions in human sense-experience has, for example, rendered the reality of God highly problematic, and, in late modernism, belief in the objective reality of God has been viewed as somewhat eccentric. The situation with respect to the entities discussed in the natural sciences has been more ambiguous. On the one side, physics commands respect and its language is taken as normative. On the other hand, the entities it talks about are not sensible. The "linguistic turn" has functioned as a resolution of this dilemma by ending reflection on the relation of language to a nonlinguistic world. But this view of language as self-contained poses many unresolved puzzles.

Unless one gives up realistic talk of the world altogether, the limitation of "objects" to "objects of human experience" leads to many strange conclusions. For example, human experience seems to have emerged through an evolutionary process. But prior to the emergence of human experience, what evolved, according to the modern view, were purely objective entities. Yet, as *objects*, they could have no existence apart from human experiences. The implausible conclusion is that the evolutionary past came into existence only as human beings learned about it! If we are to have any realistic view of what transpired before the appearance of human beings, it seems essential to acknowledge that things other than human beings are not merely objects of human experience, that they have some reality in themselves. To have such reality is to be not *mere* objects, but also subjects. Whitehead's hypothesis is that all atomic events are occasions of experience. In their moment of occurrence they are subjective, and as they complete themselves they become objective data for other events. A great deal that is otherwise extremely puzzling makes sense when this hypothesis is followed.

V. From the Primacy of Sensation to Physical Feelings

Modern philosophy consistently begins with epistemology, and the epistemology with which it begins is based on the primacy of sense-experience. In the preceding section we nodded toward epistemology on the way to ontology. For Whitehead, as for classical and medieval thought generally, ontology and cosmology are primary. Human perceiving and knowing are among the most important things to be understood. They are real; indeed, they are very remarkable features of reality. Any ontology that does not explain sensory perception and thinking is an inadequate ontology. But this is very different from supposing that we must begin with modern epistemology and only raise questions about the reality of the world after we have explained epistemologically how those questions can be answered.

This modern program has recently, and justifiably, been criticized from within the dominant philosophical tradition. That program was motivated by the desire to gain a completely secure foundation for philosophy; accordingly, it is called "foundationalism." The critics recognize that this program has never succeeded and cannot succeed. All discussion of epistemology has presuppositions. One cannot work out one's epistemology in a neutral way before proceeding to other topics.

Many draw from this fact the conclusion that philosophy must be still more restricted in its topics. For Whitehead, the implications are quite different. One should indeed give up any thought that certainty is accessible to human beings. But the recognition that human thought cannot attain any certain knowledge can liberate one to think freely and creatively over a wide range of questions that have often been taboo when one was supposed to limit thinking to areas in which certainty is possible.

For Whitehead, all thought has a hypothetical or speculative character. The best that human beings can ever do is to articulate the best theories they can invent, and then test them against a wide range of evidence. Theory informs the perception of the evidence to which it appeals; so there is always a circular element. Nevertheless, evidence cannot be entirely *controlled* by theory, and it does constitute a significant test. The task of thought is to build up a system of hypotheses that is consistent and coherent and that meets the tests of adequacy and applicability.[8] Epistemological theories also must be set in this context and tested in these ways.

Whitehead's speculations lead him to deconstruct ordinary sense-experience into two elements. He calls these "perception in the mode of presentational immediacy" and "perception in the mode of causal efficacy."[9] The former, he finds, has preoccupied philosophers and has often been taken to exhaust sense-experience. In the visual form, which has played the largest role in philosophy, perception in the mode of presentational immediacy is the awareness of patches of color spread out in space. Taken by itself, it not only gives no knowledge of an actual external world; it also is timeless in the sense that there is no reference to either past or future. Hence, when this is supposed to be the basis of all knowledge, that knowledge must be very restricted indeed!

But Whitehead points out that our ordinary language connects these sense-data with real things. We do not say that we see a patch of brown in a particular region of presented space. We say that we see a brown table. When challenged, we may have difficulty justifying what we have said, but at a deep level we remain convinced that we are seeing a real physical world and not simply colored shapes. This conviction arises, in Whitehead's view, because that real world impinges upon us. In his terms, when we are not grossly deceived, we are having physical feelings or prehensions of the events that took place in the immediate past in the region of space where the patches of color are located for us. It is these physical feelings that make us so sure that there is a real physical world, composed first of our own bodies and then of other physical entities that act upon us. This is perception in the mode of causal efficacy.

In ordinary sense-experience, these two modes are integrated into one feeling, the feeling of the brown table. This is "perception in the mode of symbolic reference." The brown patch given in presentational immediacy is referred to the physical entities that reflect the light that has acted on our eyes. This works well most of the time to orient us practically to our world.

But even in the best of circumstances there is a slight error. The events that affected the light that then affected our eyes are ever so slightly in the past, whereas the brown patch is in the present. When distances are great, this slight error becomes very important. The star is not now in the region where we see it. Complex calculations are required if we need to know where it now is. Further, the brown patch that we ordinarily locate in the external region because of events that happened in some external region may instead be located there because of chemical or electrical stimulation of certain parts of the brain. The patch is still there, but the symbolic reference to the events in that region is now delusive.

The error involved in symbolic reference is still greater. The patch of color that we project on a region of contemporary space is quite different from the events taking place in that or any other region. Except in delusive instances, it is derived from such events and in some important way continuous with them; but no event in any external region is entertaining the visual experience of that color! That color *as we see it* cannot, therefore, exist apart from being seen.

Perception in the mode of causal efficacy is not limited to that part of the external world that acts on our sensory organs. These organs magnify particular types of influence of the world upon us, and generally their data dominate our consciousness. But one's whole body is affected by its environment in complex ways. Further, there is no ontological necessity that all external events affecting human occasions of experience be mediated through bodily events. Each occasion of experience is affected by its entire past,[10] and some of these effects can be direct even when the occasions are not contiguous. To be more specific, the emotions of a person at some distance from us can affect our emotions even apart from sensory cues.[11] And there is considerable evidence that the ideas of one person can have effects on another that cannot be explained by ordinary physical mediation.

Whereas modernity found any action at a distance unacceptable, Whitehead's postmodern view of how the events in the world are interconnected renders evidence of this sort quite plausible. Perception in the mode of causal efficacy—that is, nonsensuous perception—is primary even in sense-experience. Nonsensuous perception is certainly not limited to the causal efficacy of the world on or through the sense organs. Hence, much of the causal efficacy of the past upon human experience is extrasensory. Whether physical feelings are only of contiguous occasions, with all other causal efficacy of the past mediated through these, or whether there are also physical prehensions of noncontiguous occasions, is a purely empirical question. Hence, evidence for action at a distance is to be examined in the same critical spirit as any other evidence.

VI. From Conceptual Relativism to Correspondence

Early modernism took for granted that its models of the world corresponded with the world as it is. It assumed that propositions corresponded, or failed to correspond, with the way things are. Its realism was poorly justified theoretically, especially in view of its epistemological starting point and its tendency to affirm the primacy of sensation. But it was too deeply immersed in common sense to question that there is a real world. Its antirationalism kept such questions at bay.

Nevertheless, the tensions between its sensationalism and its realism did become too obvious to deny. Especially in the work of Hume and Kant, the old commonsense approach was undercut. Both realized that while in practice we must assume a real world objective to us, the current epistemological theory provided no basis for this practice. Neither surrendered on that account the key focus on sensation that dominated the epistemological theory.

Late modernism (which sometimes calls itself postmodernism) has followed the implications of the sensationalist theory rather than the implications of Hume's and Kant's theories of practice. It has rejected commonsense views of the reality of an external world, holding that our thought and language cannot refer to such a world. The idea that our propositions correspond to some objective reality has been widely declared to be a naive error from which sophisticated reflection liberates us.

The result has been a focus of attention on the one who knows and the conditions of knowledge. This has indeed been remarkably illuminating and liberating. The early modern view of knowers as conditioned only by the known has given place to a far more insightful understanding of every act of knowledge as conditioned by the particular historical, cultural, economic, gender, and racial situation. Any claim to transcend these conditions and grasp a pure and objective truth is rightly viewed with utmost suspicion.

In late modernism, this profound recognition of the conditionedness or relativity of all thought has generally led to the avowal of some form of conceptual relativism. That is, all concepts are understood to make sense within a particular culture or linguistic system. *Within that context*, one can speak of some propositions as being truer, or at least better, than others. But this does not mean that they *correspond* more closely with a reality that is independent of the cultural-linguistic context.

Kant and his followers assumed that there *is* a human world, but that there is no access to any other world in which this human world is located. If there is another world, it is wholly unknowable. This is true for them almost by definition, because what is known is thereby introduced into the human world.

In late modernism, *the* human world has turned out to be *many* human worlds, often defined by cultural-linguistic communities, so that in fact there is no common appeal even to a shared human world. Among those who think in this way, some advocate efforts to overcome the barriers between diverse communities by such means as the "merging of horizons." But others, perhaps more consistently, question this possibility and encourage us to accept the relativity of thought to a particular context as final.

It is doubtful that any of the advocates of this extreme relativity are able to think and write consistently in these terms. It is apparent that the statement that there is a plurality of cultural-linguistic systems is intended by most of them as something more than a context-dependent statement. They believe that there really is a plurality of such systems, each of which provides the context for meaningful thought and discourse for some community. Hence, as part of the justification for claiming that all thought and language are meaningful only within a specified context, they make assertions that claim, at least implicitly, to correspond to the universal situation. Often they explain the history of thought and argument that has led to contextual relativism in ways that imply that their accounts correspond to important features of an actual tradition of thought.

From a Whiteheadian point of view, a position that can only be described and defended by the use of modes of reasoning that are not justified within that position is suspect. It may indeed contain a great deal of insight and wisdom, but it appears to deal with one part of the whole rather than with the totality, while claiming that the part *is* the totality. It seems to be only the deep-seated antirationalism of modernity that obscures this point.

The inconsistencies involved in the description and defense of conceptual relativism should open people to re-examination of the analyses that support it. At its foundation is the primacy of sensation with which the preceding section dealt. If all human experience arises from sensation, and if sensation is understood as what Whitehead calls "perception in the mode of presentational immediacy," then indeed each of us is shut in to her or his immediate experience. The fully consistent implication of sensationalism seems to be solipsism, the doctrine that each person's experience is self-enclosed and makes no reference to any wider context at all. Against that conclusion, we can be grateful for Kant's subordination of the individual to the human species or to Mind as such, and we can be grateful for the linguistic turn that locates reality in shared language. Nevertheless, these moves do not restore the reality of the physical world, which is so prominent in common sense. The rejection of the correspondence theory of truth, so widespread in late modernity, is primarily the denial that our thoughts or language could correspond to something physical, lying beyond our sensory experience.

The previous section described Whitehead's move from the primacy of sensation to physical feelings. Physical feelings are feelings of other actual occasions, and most of these occasions make up what we call the physical world. We are not shut off in our private experience, in the human world in general, or in particular cultural-linguistic systems. We live in the natural world as well.

From this it follows that one main reason for rejecting the correspondence theory of truth is overcome: we do directly experience actualities beyond our present moment of experience. But there is a second objection to this theory that must still be taken quite seriously. Supporters of the correspondence theory of truth often seem to claim that there is correspondence between verbal expressions, on the one side, and something nonlinguistic, on the other. This is inherently problematic. How can words correspond to people or natural objects? They are fundamentally different.

Usually the discussion of correspondence is in terms of propositions. The claim is that propositions correspond to states of affairs. When propositions are understood to be *linguistic entities* such as sentences, this leaves us with the puzzle referred to above. How can a linguistic entity correspond to a nonlinguistic entity?

Whitehead devotes great care and attention to this issue. His first step is to distinguish between propositions and linguistic entities such as sentences. A proposition is a possibility—the way some occasion of experience, or some group of such occasions, *may be*. The function of sentences and other linguistic entities is to evoke in the hearer attention to this possibility. For example, the sentence "Kant distinguished practical from theoretical reason" is intended to evoke attention to a great philosopher who flourished around the beginning of the nineteenth century and to connect with that philosopher a particular teaching. The relation between that philosopher and that teaching is the proposition. The sentences used to evoke attention to that proposition can vary.

When propositions are understood in this way, there is no mystery about their correspondence to states of affairs. They *are* possible states of affairs. They therefore may be embodied in actual states of affairs. It makes sense to discuss whether a proposition is actual or not—that is, whether that possibility has in fact been actualized.

Of course, there are complexities in this discussion. With regard to the above example, there can be no direct inspection of Kant's activity in making his distinction between practical and theoretical reason. We must instead examine certain writings attributed to Kant. The discussion might lead to the question of their authenticity. We might also need to ask whether the meanings of words as we are accustomed to interpreting them correspond closely with Kant's intended meanings. All of our reflection on these matters would depend on a wider context of experience. Thus our consideration would involve both other questions of correspondence and appeals to probability based on consistency and coherence as well.

To discuss at all requires that, at least for the most part, the participants are willing to try to avoid self-contradictions. But what we are aiming at is to be accurate about Kant, not to develop a system of consistent and coherent ideas about him. Consistency and coherence of thought are required in most instances if we are to achieve truth, but the *meaning* of "truth" is correspondence to actual states of affairs.[13]

There is still a problem with this formulation. If the argument in favor of the correspondence of an entertained *possibility* of a state of affairs to an *actual* state of affairs is entirely based on coherence and consistency, we seem to be left with the question as to what more is affirmed, when we claim correspondence, than that this is the most coherent and consistent belief to hold. If this is all that is intended by the claim, then the argument seems to be verbal only. The widespread opposition to the correspondence theory of truth has been the opposition to the idea that correspondence could be anything more than the most suitable tale, with suitability determined by the context in which it is told.

If we are to have a truly distinctive correspondence theory of truth, we must in some instances discover in our immediate experience a correspondence between propositions entertained and actual states of affairs. If we can do that in some instances then the *meaning* of correspondence can be decisively established independently of the usual ways of arriving at the belief that it occurs, and we can then generalize this meaning to all instances.

Consider a situation in which someone tells me that I am angry. Because my self-image is of one who is slow to wrath, my immediate tendency is to deny that I am, or recently have been, angry. But suppose that I am also a relatively honest person. Then the other's statement calls my attention to a possible relation between my immediately past occasions of experience and anger. I can ask whether the possible relation was actual. In this case, I do not approach matters through a complex process of reasoning. Instead I inspect directly. I compare those occasions as now prehended by me with the proposition that I also prehend. I may well find that the two correspond, that I *have* been angry, even if I do not like to admit this. Of course, I may also find that they do not correspond, that the proposition is false.

If I am told that I was angry two hours earlier, the situation is more complex. As the statement elicits attention to how I was feeling then, some element of immediate inspection may be possible. But here other types of evidence may become more important and reliable than my direct memory or prehension of that past. Those who saw me may tell me that my teeth were clenched or that I was red in the face or that I spoke in a peculiarly icy way. My general beliefs about how anger expresses itself in me and my degree of confidence in the veracity of these observers will introduce complex questions of consistency and coherence that will interact with such direct memories as I can elicit. If the statement is about someone else, and especially if I was not even present at the time, then coherence and consistency hold sway in my decision as to whether to believe the statement or not. But to believe the statement is to believe that the proposition it elicits corresponds with that person's feelings in the way that I immediately experienced in my own case. The *meaning* of correspondence and hence of truth is different from that of coherence and consistency.

So far my examples have come from the human world, and they all refer to elements of subjectivity in that world. The opponents of the correspondence theory, on the other hand, almost always take their examples from the inanimate world, which they take as purely objective. Some of them might allow that correspondence makes some sense within the world of human subjects, while continuing to deny its applicability to the inanimate, objective world.

For Whitehead this does not suffice. It assumes the dualism of subjects and objects that he opposes.[14] Human beings are part of nature, and our relation to the remainder of nature is continuous with our relations with one another. Every atomic entity is a subject in its moment of occurrence and passes into objectivity for subsequent occasions.

Nevertheless, to assert that language can evoke to someone's attention propositions or possibilities that correspond with physical states of affairs does require further reflection. First, it is possible only under the condition that dualism is rejected. Whitehead provides this condition through his doctrine that everything that is actual is an occasion of experience or a grouping of such occasions. Hence, a statement about an electronic occasion of experience can evoke propositions about such an occasion in much the way that a statement about human occasions can evoke propositions about human experiences. Thus the statement that electronic occasions take account of their past and influence their future can evoke propositions that may have some correspondence to physical states of affairs. Whitehead affirms this correspondence.[15]

There are, however, greater difficulties with what appear to be the simplest statements about the physical world, the ones most often taken as paradigmatic by those who deny correspondence. Consider "the stone is gray." "The stone" refers to a large grouping of molecular occasions rather than to any single occasion of experience. The grouping as such is not a subject, either in the present or in the past. The individual occasions that make up the grouping are subjects in the immediacy of their becoming, but they have had no visual experience of grayness. Hence, if "gray" means a particular datum of human visual experience, this cannot characterize either the individual stone molecules or the stone as a whole, except in its function as the object of visual experience. This means that the propositions most directly and properly evoked by the statement, "the stone is gray," are propositions about the visual experience of those persons who look in the direction of the stone under appropriate lighting. But that means that they are propositions about human experiences rather than about natural objects, which is just the point of much of the rejection of the correspondence theory of truth.

For Whitehead, it is not necessary to hold that there is any correspondence between propositions evoked by the statement that the stone is gray and the physical world in itself. What is crucial is that there are other statements that can be made about the physical world that evoke propositions that can correspond with it. It is primarily the world felt in perception in the mode of causal efficacy and not that felt in the mode of presentational immediacy to which humanly entertained propositions can correspond.

Nevertheless, Whitehead does not want to disconnect the two worlds. The world given in the mode of presentational immediacy derives from the world that flows into human experience in the mode of causal efficacy. That is, the difference in the gray and blue that I perceive in presentational immediacy ordinarily derives from a difference in the physical constitution of the physical objects that I perceive as gray and blue. Whitehead describes in some detail the transformations and transmutations that are involved in the process of human experience being affected by the physical events as transmitted through bodily ones. But he also believes that there are continuities as well as discontinuities. These are to be discerned in the subjective forms of the human feelings of gray and blue. These subjective forms are the emotional tones associated in a human experience with these colors. Whitehead believes that analogous emotional tones may be found in the molecules or cells in the physical world from which our color-experience is derived.[16] Hence, even in this most difficult case, often taken as paradigmatic by opponents of correspondence theory, Whitehead discerns the possibility of *some* correspondence .

VII. FROM THE SEGREGATION OF RELIGION TO ITS PERVASIVENESS

Modernity arose through a process of secularization. This was in part a continuation of the prophetic tradition within Christianity. In this tradition God is sharply distinguished from the world and the way things are. God's transcendence is emphasized. God judges the world. God's will calls for the transformation of the world. Thus the world as it is is not sacred. It is the creation of God but not itself divine. Human beings are free to explore it and to use it.

This note was present in medieval Christianity along with more sacramental views that connected the divine and the natural more closely. Early modernity rejected these sacramental views. God was the external creator of a machine whose workings reflected infinite knowledge and control. But the machine could be examined and adjusted without involving God in any way.

Although modernity from its origins was often anticlerical and extremely critical of Christian institutions and practices, the modern view was not antireligious in its origins. It encouraged the sense of divine greatness and even omnipotence, viewing worship as an eminently appropriate response. In the sphere of morality, it usually saw God as the giver of moral law and as the judge of how well individuals observed it. Rewards and punishments after death were widely affirmed. Religion had a place, but it was segregated from the natural sciences.

The fuller development of modernism involved the extension of secular thought further and further. Society and morality, like nature, came to be understood as separate from God and thus freed from religion. The area in which religion had an appropriate role became smaller and smaller, and, for an increasing number of people, it vanished altogether. Whereas in early modernism it was generally supposed that a rational religion of some form was needed to maintain social order, in late modernism religion in general is typically seen as an oppressive and distorting force from which the human spirit needs to be freed.

Constructive postmodern thought has reappraised this evaluation. It agrees about the oppressiveness of the early modern religion of radical transcendence that pictured God chiefly as lawgiver and judge. But it also sees that the role of religion in human life is multivalent. Religion cannot be identified with one ideology. It is by no means necessarily bound up with belief in a transcendent lawgiver and judge. Hence problems with that doctrine, while requiring fresh reflection for those for whom it is important, do not point to the end of religion. Even the Biblical religions, which have so often been understood in these terms, are not committed to them.

We can now see that the way in which secularism had won the day was by limiting the questions that people were allowed to ask. This is closely connected with the antirationalism so central to the modern spirit. If the barriers to deeper questioning are removed, then the religious issues reassert themselves. For example, to experience the world and ourselves within it as a matrix of interrelated events is religiously different from experiencing ourselves as mental substances set down in a world of material substances. To perceive the world of events as finally composed of present and past subjects rather than mere objects is also a change of religious importance. Quite different consequences follow for our relation to other animals and to the biosphere as a whole. One cannot separate the way we understand ourselves and our world from the meaning of that perception for our lives.

In his book on religion, Whitehead emphasizes that religion has to do with the ordering of our internal lives as subjects. He offers a variety of definitions of religion, all of which highlight this point. For example, "Religion is force of belief cleansing the inward parts."[17] Or again, "Religion is the art and theory of the internal life of man, so far as it depends on himself and on what is permanent in the nature of things."[18]

We are feeling beings, and how we feel is important. It shapes how we act and how we think, and these react upon how we feel. To understand the whole of things requires as much attention to this inwardness as to the evidence of how the world is constituted. Religion and science are, therefore, the two basic sources for reflection. The modern world has underestimated the wisdom about the inner life gained by human beings over the centuries and embodied in the religious traditions. On the other side, most of those who speak for religion have clung to ways of thought that do not fit our best knowledge about the objective world. As a result, religion has been in a long decline that will not end until those who give it leadership are as open to learning and transformation by new knowledge as are scientists at their best. In Whitehead's words, "Religion will not regain its old power until it can face change in the same spirit as does science." This requires an "unflinching determination to take the whole evidence into account."[19]

Whitehead's postmodern sensibility is thus highly critical of the dominant leadership of the traditional religions. In contrast to that of the late modern sensibility, however, this criticism is fueled by the conviction that religion is of utmost importance and that it needs to be liberated from the shackles in which it is now bound. One of these is the segregation of religion in narrow compartments in which it cannot perform its proper function. It needs once again to command the attention of the most reflective and sensitive people in order to give shape and discipline to the inner life appropriate to the best understanding of the whole that is available. Even this formulation understates its task, because its own evidence must participate in shaping the understanding that it appropriates and celebrates.

Whitehead himself contributes to this task. He reflects on the global history of religion, seeing in Buddhism and Christianity the most promising sources of fresh development. He believes that as these two traditions interact, each will be enriched and enabled to contribute to the needed deepening of religious thought and life.[20] He recognizes that his own cosmological vision has more affinities with East Asian modes of thought than with those that have been dominant in the West.[21] On the other hand, he finds in Plato (in thought) and in Jesus (in life) the deepest insight to which he himself is committed.[22]

The details of Whitehead's historical judgments about Buddhism and Christianity are not important here. The advance of research requires revisions even if some of his insights can still give guidance at the cutting edge of inquiry. What is more important is the re-emergence in his later thought of a kind of theism that has influenced the development of postmodern theology, especially in Christianity.

In conformity with Whitehead's view that science and religion should jointly contribute to the overarching vision that is needed, his understanding of God grows out of both. On the scientific side, his analysis of the world into partially self-determining events leads him to acknowledge the need for some principle of order and novelty that cannot simply be identified with the multiplicity of creatures themselves.[23] On the religious side, he sees the need for the belief that the values achieved in the world are not simply lost as they fade from human memory. The following paragraphs consider these two directions in turn, showing how at every point scientific and religious concerns interact and work together.

The simplest way of understanding Whitehead's systematic need for a principle of order and novelty is to reflect on the individual occasions of experience and how they come into being. The human example is the most accessible. Whitehead is convinced that Ms. Smith's experience in each moment is not simply the product of its prehensions of past events, important and determinative as these are. If it were, then finally Ms. Smith would indeed simply be a part of the world machine. Her life in every detail could be predicted by one who knew all the features of her world. There would be no alternative responses to her situation and hence no decision.

Many philosophers, on the one hand, operate explicitly in their theories with just those hypotheses. On the other hand, they seem in practice to treat their own choice of hypotheses as something more than simply the outcome of determined conditions. That is, they give arguments in favor of their views as if questions of better and worse, truth or falsehood, were relevant to the outcome—as if, in other words, rational decision were possible. For this reason, it is hard to take their announced deterministic hypotheses seriously as representing their deepest assumptions.

Probably the main reason for the widespread adoption of deterministic hypotheses is that most philosophers find it difficult to see how anything else is possible. If the explanation for what is happening now is not to be found in the past, where can it be found? To posit that something comes from nowhere is unacceptable. If the past is the only thing given to the present, then the present must come from there—exhaustively.

The other line of reflection, followed by Whitehead, is that, if there is something in the present that is not derivative from the past, then the given reality is not exhausted by the past. His hypothesis is that, in addition to the past actual world, there are also possibilities not realized by that world and yet relevant to the occasion of experience as it constitutes itself in the immediate present. In the examples discussed above, it is the fact that there are plural alternatives that leads to the necessity and the actuality of decision—that is, of cutting off all but one alternative. These alternatives are felt in a way that is somewhat analogous to the feelings or prehensions of past occasions.

Still there are differences. Whitehead calls the relations to past occasions "physical feelings," or "physical prehensions." The relations to relevant possibilities he calls "conceptual feelings," or "conceptual prehensions." They function differently. The physical feelings are determinative. They are decided by the past occasions for the present occasion. They can be called "causal feelings." But the conceptual feelings, especially as they are integrated with the physical feelings, are feelings of *alternative ways of responding*. They constitute much of the world as "lures for feeling," or what Whitehead also calls "propositions." Because of them, although we cannot but be affected by the past, just *how* we interpret it and value it and transmit it to the future is decided in the present moment. In this way, the effective presence of relevant possibilities is the principle of novelty by virtue of which decisions are real and genuinely free.

But if each occasion makes its own decision among possibilities, it would seem that chaos would ensue. And, of course, there are large amounts of chaos in the world. That there is not only chaos, that in fact extremely complex patterns of order have emerged and sustained themselves over eons, however, points to the fact that the possibilities are not ordered only in terms of immediate relevance but ordered also so that there are established limits that ensure some correlation among the many decisions that jointly make up the settled world. The principle of novelty is also a principle of order.

This argument is not independent of the deeply religious intuition that we are free and responsible beings, but, given the commitment to making sense of this, there are no further appeals to religion. Indeed, if the argument holds, then it is for religious people to adjust their understanding to this feature of reality. When they do so, the question arises as to how to identify, in religious language, the source of novelty and order that is philosophically understood as the realm of ordered possibility. Whitehead's judgment is that this realm is properly identified as that which is to be worshipped and supremely honored. For that reason it should be called "God." More specifically, Whitehead calls this the "primordial nature of God."[24]

The further development of the doctrine of God is jointly determined by philosophical and religious interests. Philosophically, it appears that this "principle" functions causally in the world, and that to be a cause is to be something actual.[25] Hence the principle of novelty and order should be understood to be an actual entity and, like all actual entities, to be subject as well as object. The view that God has a subjective aspect is supported by the religious traditions of the West and brings the principle of novelty and order into closer proximity to the main streams of Western religious experience. If the decision that establishes the order among possibilities makes possible the growth of value in the world, it seems to be for the benefit of the creatures, and hence to express love for them. Because it functions to free them from the necessity of sheer repetition of the past and to offer them alternative ways of constituting themselves, it is to be sharply contrasted with the coercive forces of the world.[26] Yet the alternatives among which decision is made are not all of equal promise, and they are presented so as to encourage the better choice. Hence Whitehead thinks in terms of divine persuasion. It is this insight that he associates especially with Plato and Jesus.

The final step in Whitehead's development of his doctrine of God is more directly shaped by religious intuitions. The ultimate evil, he believed, is that all achievements of value fade. If this is the last word, the religious impulse must be to withdraw energy from the shaping and reshaping of the course of events and to find an ahistorical fulfillment. But Whitehead saw "no reason, of any ultimate metaphysical generality, why this should be the whole story."[27] And indeed his own metaphysical ideas, developed for other purposes, provided him with another answer.

If God is an actual entity, then like all actual entities God should be dipolar; that is, God should have both conceptual and physical feelings. The former are entailed in the ordering of possibilities, and have already been affirmed and identified as God's primordial nature. But the latter have not been mentioned. These physical feelings are prehensions of all the creatures. Because they derive from the creatures, Whitehead speaks here of the "consequent nature of God."

Among creatures it is by means of their physical prehensions that the values of the past operate in the present. But in the creaturely world these values fade rapidly. The great majority of what has been felt in the past is no longer felt; most of it is not even remembered. This is because, in the course of time, events succeed one another and none are able to encompass more than a tiny fraction of what has been.

God is quite different from the creatures, even though God, like all occasions of experience, is an actual entity. Whereas the human soul, or personality, is a succession of occasions of experience, God is one everlasting process of integrating all that happens with all possibility. God is thus always feeling directly all the creaturely feelings that have ever been. Whereas for us to feel a few of these feelings vividly means to exclude many other feelings, for God such exclusions are not necessary. In contrast to the constant replacement of one set of attainments by another, which characterizes the temporal process, God feels all that has ever been in the fullness of its immediacy. Thus what is past in the world lives everlastingly in God. What is lost in the world is alive in God.

From the creaturely perspective, this establishes the real importance of all that we are and feel. What happens is not a moment of private feeling that occurs and then is forever lost. Instead, it is forever a contribution to the divine life. God suffers with us in our suffering and rejoices with us in our joy. When we inflict pain on an animal, we inflict pain forever on God. When we ease the thirst of a neighbor, God's thirst is forever eased as well. The primary understanding of God, then, is not as lawgiver and judge but as "the fellow sufferer who understands."[28]

Whitehead knows that this vision of God is different from that dominant in the tradition. Indeed, he is quite critical of the tradition.

> In the great formative period of theistic philosophy, which ended with the rise of Mahometanism, after a continuance coeval with civilization, three strains of thought emerge which, amid many variations in detail, respectively fashion God in the image of an imperial ruler, God in the image of a personification of moral energy, God in the image of an ultimate philosophical principle.[29]

Whitehead is deeply dissatisfied with these images, and adds:

> There is, however, in the Galilean origin of Christianity yet another suggestion which does not fit very well with any of the three main strands of thought. It does not emphasize the ruling Caesar, or the ruthless moralist, or the unmoved mover. It dwells upon the tender elements in the world, which slowly and in quietness operate by love; and it finds purpose in the present immediacy of a kingdom not of this world. Love neither rules, nor is it unmoved, also it is a little oblivious as to morals. It does not look to the future, for it finds its own reward in the immediate present.[30]

Whitehead sees his own vision of God as a more systematic articulation of this Galilean insight.

Although Whitehead is deeply interested in conceptual clarity and accuracy in thinking about the divine, the religious effects of this vision on the inner life are also of utmost importance. We will close by quoting one of the passages in which the meaning of these theological doctrines for Whitehead himself becomes most clear. The key term is "peace."

> The Peace that is here meant is not the negative conception of anaesthesia. It is a positive feeling which crowns the "life and motion" of the soul. . . . It is not a hope for the future, nor is it an interest in present details. It is a broadening of feeling due to the emergence of some deep metaphysical insight, unverbalized and yet momentous in its coordination of values. Its first effect is the removal of the stress of acquisitive feeling arising from the soul's preoccupation with itself. Thus Peace carries with it a surpassing of personality. . . .
>
> The experience of Peace is largely beyond the control of purpose. It comes as a gift. . . . Peace is the removal of inhibition and not its introduction. It results in a wider sweep of conscious interest. It enlarges the field of attention. Thus Peace is self-control at its widest,—at the width where the "self" has been lost, and interest has been transferred to coordinations wider than personality. . . .
>
> Amid the passing of so much beauty, so much heroism, so much daring, Peace is then the intuition of permanence. It keeps vivid the sensitiveness to the tragedy; and it sees the tragedy as a living agent persuading the world to aim at fineness beyond the faded level of surrounding fact. Each tragedy is the disclosure of an ideal:—What might have been, and was not: What can be. The tragedy was not in vain. This survival power in motive force by reason of appeal to reserves of Beauty, marks the difference between the tragic evil and the gross evil. The inner feeling belonging to this grasp of the service of tragedy is Peace—the purification of the emotions.[31]

NOTES

1. See A. N. Whitehead, *The Principle of Relativity* (Cambridge: Cambridge University Press, 1922). For the current state of the discussion about Whitehead's theory in comparison with Einstein's theory and the empirical data, see Robert J. Russell, "Whitehead, Einstein and the Newtonian Legacy," in *Newton and the New Direction in Science*, ed. G. V. Coyne, S. J. M. Heller, and J. Zycinski (The Vatican: Specola Vaticana, 1988), 175-92.

2. *Science and the Modern World* (1925; New York: Free Press, 1967), 143. Although the pagination of the (more accessible) Free Press edition is cited, the reading of the (more accurate) Macmillan edition of 1925 is followed (here and in n. 5).

3. *Process and Reality: An Essay in Cosmology* (orig. ed., 1929), corrected edition, ed. David Ray Griffin and Donald W. Sherburne (New York: Free Press, 1978), 3.

4. Ibid., 5.

5. *Science and the Modern World*, 8-9 (bracketed words added by Whitehead).

6. See, for example, *Process and Reality*, 29, 84, 222.

7. The centrality of decision for Whitehead's notion of actual entities is shown most clearly by his statement that "'decision' cannot be construed as a casual adjunct of an actual entity. It constitutes the very meaning of actuality. An actual entity arises from decisions *for* it, and by its very existence provides decisions *for* other actual entities which supersede it" (ibid., 43).

8. These four criteria are discussed at ibid., 3-6.

9. See ibid., 168-83.

10. "Each task of creation is a social effort, employing the whole universe" (ibid., 223). "The whole world conspires to produce a new creation" (*Religion in the Making* [New York: Macmillan, 1927], 109).

11. Whitehead discusses the possibility of influence at a distance in general, and of telepathic influence in particular, at *Process and Reality*, 307-08.

12. He says: "It is merely credulous to accept verbal phrases as adequate statements of propositions" (ibid., 11).

13. For Whitehead's affirmation of a correspondence theory of the truth of propositions (in distinction from a coherence theory of the correctness of judgments), see *Process and Reality*, 186-91.

14. Whitehead sees dualism as a chief stumbling block to the affirmation of truth as correspondence: "All metaphysical theories which admit a disjunction between the component elements of individual experience on the one hand, and on the other hand the component elements of the external world, must inevitably run into difficulties over the truth and falsehood of propositions, and over the grounds for judgment. The former difficulty is metaphysical, the latter epistemological. But all difficulties as to first principles are only camouflaged metaphysical difficulties. Thus also the epistemological difficulty is only solvable by an appeal to ontology" (ibid., 189). Whitehead's ontology is based on the denial that there is "any other meaning of 'togetherness'" besides "experiential togetherness"—or, more precisely, the denial that there is "any meaning not abstracted from the experiential meaning" (ibid.). Dualism, by contrast, creates an insuperable problem, because "there is no bridge between togetherness in experience, and togetherness of the non-experiential sort" (ibid., 190).

15. Of course, to say that a proposition *corresponds* to a physical state of affairs is not to say that it is *identical* with it. To be sure, in each the same actual occasions and the same possibilities are together. But there is lack of identity because the modes of

togetherness differ. In the state of affairs the possibilities are included in "the mode of realization," whereas in the true proposition the possibilities are together in "the mode of abstract possibility" (*Adventures of Ideas* [1933; New York: Free Press, 1967], 244).

16. See ibid., 250-51, 293-94.

17. *Religion in the Making*, 15.

18. Ibid., 16.

19. *Science and the Modern World*, 189, 187.

20. *Religion in the Making*, 140-41.

21. *Process and Reality*, 7.

22. *Adventures of Ideas*, 164-67.

23. Whitehead first expressed this view in *Science and the Modern World*, especially chapter 11, then developed it in *Religion in the Making* (esp. 143-54) and *Process and Reality*.

24. See *Process and Reality*, 32-34, 46, 343-44.

25. Whitehead's briefest formulation of his famous "ontological principle" is: "no actual entity, then no reason" (*Process and Reality*, 19). In a longer formulation in the same paragraph, he connects it with his basis for speaking of God, describing it as "the principle that the reasons for things are always to be found in the composite nature of definite actual entities—in the nature of God for reasons of the highest absoluteness, and in the nature of definite temporal actual entities for reasons which refer to a particular environment."

26. In Whitehead's view, the deep insight of Plato, alluded to earlier, was that "the divine element in the world is to be conceived as a persuasive agency and not as a coercive agency" (*Adventures of Ideas*, 166).

27. *Process and Reality*, 340.

28. Ibid., 351.

29. Ibid., 342-43.

30. Ibid., 343.

31. *Adventures of Ideas*, 285-86.

5

CHARLES HARTSHORNE

David Ray Griffin

Modern philosophy is self-destructing. This process of self-destruction has been going on for some time, but has become more obvious in recent times, especially through the discussions evoked by the writings of Richard Rorty, Jacques Derrida, and related thinkers. Philosophers are not only denying, as positivists long have, that philosophy has any capacity to discover truth beyond that learned through the natural sciences; they are even saying that philosophy cannot declare the results of science to be true, in the sense of corresponding to reality in some significant way. This relativism is sometimes called "postmodernism." These relativistic postmodern philosophers deny that philosophy has any unique role to play in the culture. Books have recently appeared with titles such as *After Philosophy* and *Ethics Without Philosophy*.[1]

From one point of view—a view that equates modern philosophy with philosophy itself—this development is surprising and disturbing. Surely, one thinks, it is neither conceivable nor desirable that we should no longer have professional philosophers. But from the point of view of the postmodern philosophy of Alfred North Whitehead and Charles Hartshorne (born 1897)—which is a *constructive* postmodernism, quite different from the deconstructive, relativistic form of postmodernism—this self-immolation of modern philosophy is neither surprising nor disturbing. It is not surprising because modern philosophy has from the beginning been based on faulty premises. It is not disturbing because the self-elimination of modern philosophy will create a void that may be filled by a postmodern philosophy that can perform the cultural tasks of philosophy in a more adequate way.

In this essay, I first explain what I take to be three basic theories of modern philosophy, and how these have led to its self-destruction. I then discuss the philosophic perspective shared by Alfred North Whitehead and Charles Hartshorne, which can be called "postmodern" because it rejects these basic theories of modern philosophy without returning to premodern modes of thought. Focusing then on Hartshorne's development of this postmodern perspective, I show how it overcomes several problems that have long plagued modern philosophy and that have recently led to its self-destruction. I conclude with a brief discussion of some of the practical implications of Hartshorne's position in his own eyes.

In this exposition, I deal to a great extent with ideas that Hartshorne shares with Whitehead, namely, panexperientialism, radical empiricism, and naturalistic theism. But I also point out several respects in which Hartshorne has strengthened their common position. He has done this by defending the position against rival doctrines, by emphasizing various features of the position that were implicit or present but not prominent in Whitehead's exposition, and, most importantly, by developing ideas that differ somewhat from Whitehead's but are arguably more consistent with the basic position and otherwise more adequate. I do not in this overview try to mention all or even most of Hartshorne's original ideas, especially his more technical contributions to philosophy and philosophical theology. I deal for the most part only with those central themes that challenge basic theories of modern thought.

I. Modern Philosophy

Because the term "modern philosophy" covers a very diverse set of systems, schools, and tendencies, any attempt to give a brief characterization of it must be very selective and formulated in extreme generalities that do not apply equally to all examples of modern philosophy. I focus on a set of features that I take to be fundamental to the main trajectory of modern philosophy, including that part of modern philosophy now called natural science.

Formally, modern philosophy has been characterized by various dualisms. Based on its substantive dualisms between matter and mind, and determinism and freedom, which I discuss shortly, modern philosophy has spawned a disciplinary dualism between facts and values, or between science, on the one hand, and theology, ethics, and aesthetics, on the other. As modern philosophy developed, this dualism became that between the objective and the merely subjective. The other great formal dualism is that not between the theories of different disciplines but between theory and practice—between scientific-philosophic theory, on the one hand, and the presuppositions of practice, on the other, whether that practice be scientific, philosophic, ethical, or simply everyday practice. For example, we presuppose in practice that our bodies and the world beyond them are real, and that they influence our experience; we presuppose that we are nevertheless partially free, and that our experiences or minds can influence our bodies and the world beyond them in turn. In other words, we presuppose the interaction of mind and matter, and the existence of both causality and freedom. We also presuppose the reality of values—that there is such a thing as truth, that some things are better than others, and that it is usually better to know the truth than to believe falsehood. Modern philosophical theory, however, has not been able to justify these presuppositions of practice.

These formal dualisms between objective facts and subjective values, and between theory and practice, have been supported by the *substantive* character of modern philosophy. Most of this substantive character can be derived from three basic theories: (i) a mechanistic, materialistic, nonanimistic doctrine of nature, (ii) a sensationist doctrine of perception, and (iii) a denial that divinity is naturally present in the world. The nonanimistic doctrine of nature says that the basic units of nature have neither experience nor the power of self-movement. The sensationist doctrine of perception says that all of our experience of the world beyond ourselves is through our physical senses and hence is limited to the types of things these senses are suited to perceive—namely, physical objects. The denial of natural divine presence in the world follows from the first two theories. If natural entities have nothing like mind or experience, a cosmic mind or experience cannot be present in them. If things can enter *our* minds or experiences only through our physical senses, then a cosmic mind or experience, if one exists, would also be barred from being present in *us*. Modern philosophers (including modern natural and social scientists) have sought to understand the world on the basis of the theory that its normal processes are fully intelligible in principle apart from any reference to divine presence.

These three theories largely account for modern philosophy's inability to explain the presuppositions of human practice. The nonanimistic doctrine of physical things such as atoms, molecules, and cells, according to which they have no experience and no capacity for self-motion or freedom, makes it impossible to understand how the human body can interact with its *anima* or soul. How can the experiencing and nonexperiencing interact? How can the free and the unfree interact? This latter question has led modern philosophy to deny that the human being as a whole has any freedom, most characteristically by asserting that the mind or soul is simply identical with the brain, which operates as deterministically as the rest of nature.

The sensationist doctrine of perception, which was originally designed to insist that we directly perceive nothing except physical objects, soon led to the conclusion that we do not even perceive *them*. David Hume showed that sense-perception as such provides nothing but sense-data. Sensationism hence implied that we have no direct knowledge of the existence of an actual world beyond our own experience. George Santayana pointed out that this doctrine leads not only to solipsism but to "solipsism of the present moment," because sense-data by themselves give us no knowledge of the existence of the past or a future. In not telling us of the existence of actual things beyond our present experience, sense-perception also fails to exhibit efficient causality, the causal influence of one actual thing on another. Santayana said that the reality of the world, the past, and causality must be accepted on the basis of "animal faith," just as Hume before him had said that we must presuppose them in "practice" even though philosophical theory cannot list them as items of knowledge.

The sensationist doctrine of perception has led to an even greater divorce between theory and practice in relation to values. The reason this divorce is greater is that sense-perception's inability to give us knowledge of those non-physical things we call values is even more obvious than its failure with regard to a real world and causality. While intellectuals in general have not been led by philosophers such as Hume and Santayana to deny that we have knowledge of an actual world, the past, and causality, they *have* been led to deny knowledge of values.

This development has led to self-contradictions. Modernity has, for example, relentlessly sought to replace primitive and medieval "falsehood" with modern "truth," while denying that we have any knowledge that truth is better than falsehood. The notion of "better than" has been taken as a purely subjective preference not capable of reflecting any relation inherent in the nature of things. Moral, aesthetic and religious assertions have been declared noncognitive—that is, incapable of being either true or false—so that arguments concerning them cannot in principle be rational. Modernity has held that the natural sciences give us truth about the physical world, but that ethics, aesthetics, and theology are incapable in principle of delivering truth, because sensory perception provides us with no knowledge of their alleged nonphysical objects. We can therefore have no objective basis for a rational discussion about those value-judgments we are constantly employing, at least implicitly—that some actions, attitudes, and ways of life are morally better than others, that some objects and actions are aesthetically more beautiful, fitting, or tasteful than others, and that our moral and aesthetic decisions are somehow really important because life has some ultimate meaning.

The recent call by relativistic postmodernism for an end to philosophy is closely related to this invidious distinction between science and the other realms of culture, especially the aesthetic-literary realm. The attack on philosophy is due in large part to modern philosophy's role in the authentication of natural science as the one source of truth, which gave it an overwhelmingly disproportionate role in determining the nature of modern culture. Relativistic postmodernism wants to bring science down to the same level as the other cultural pursuits by declaring it no more competent than they to discover truth.[2] It attempts to do this by attacking the notion of truth as such, in the sense of correspondence between idea and reality.[3]

Relativistic postmodernism's attack on the truth of the scientific worldview through an attack on truth itself simply carries the three substantive doctrines of modern philosophy through to their logical conclusions. (For this reason, this movement should be called *mostmodern* philosophy instead of postmodern.) Because sensory perception reveals no "given" reality which exists independently of our perception of it, we have no basis, they say, for speaking of correspondence between our ideas and independently existing objects. Because an idea can only correspond to an idea, furthermore, it is impossible for the scientist's ideas to correspond to material objects, which are incapable of having ideas. The idea that the history of science is the history of closer and closer approximations to *the* truth, finally, was only meaningful when people could believe in a divine, nonrelativistic perspective in which the truth was lodged. The sensationism, nonanimism, and atheism of modern philosophy, accordingly, provide three mutually supporting bases for rejecting the very notion of truth as correspondence. The willingness fully to realize this fact constitutes a large part of the self-destruction of modern philosophy.

This self-destruction, as I suggested earlier, is no surprise from the perspective of the postmodern vision of reality and philosophy shared by Alfred North Whitehead and Charles Hartshorne. From this perspective, as Hartshorne has emphasized, philosophy can be clear and consistent only insofar as it recognizes that the general principles by which we live our lives and interpret our experience are derived from a form of perception more basic than sensory perception, insofar as it affirms a postmodern animism, according to which all individuals experience and exercise self-determination, and insofar as it is explicitly theistic.[4] From this perspective, a sensationist, nonanimistic, atheistic philosophy was bound to self-destruct, and the fulfillment of this prediction provides some empirical evidence for the truth of the Whiteheadian-Hartshornean postmodern position.

In the remainder of this essay, I spell out this philosophy in terms of the three features that make it most clearly postmodern: its animism or panexperientialism, which differentiates it from the dualism, materialism, and phenomenalism among which modern thought has felt constrained to choose; its radical empiricism, in comparison with which modern sensationism is seen to be a very superficial form of empiricism; and its naturalistic theism, which differentiates it equally from the supernaturalism of early modernity and the atheism of late modernity. A philosophy based on animism, nonsensory perception, and theism will, of course, sound quaint, if not outrageous, to modern ears. But if we keep in mind the fact that modern philosophy, based on the denial of these three doctrines, is self-destructing, and that the modern world, which supports and is supported by the modern worldview, is wired to self-destruct, we may be able to suspend our modern prejudices sufficiently to consider the arguments for these doctrines.

II. PANEXPERIENTIALISM AND RADICAL EMPIRICISM

In contrast with modern philosophy, which assumed the basic units of nature to be enduring substances devoid of both experience and self-movement, White-head and Hartshorne begin with the hypothesis that nature is comprised of cre-ative, experiential events. The terms "events," "experiential," and "creative" indicate the three main aspects of this position. The term "events" indicates that the basic units of reality are not enduring things, or substances, but momentary events. Each enduring thing, such as an electron, an atom, a cell, or a psyche, is a temporal society, comprised of a series of momentary events, each of which incorporates the previous events of that enduring individual. The enduring self, understood as an enduring substance, is deconstructed.

The term "experiential" indicates that the basic unit-events of the world are not "vacuous actualities," devoid of experience. Whitehead called them "occasions of experience." This doctrine does not mean that all events have conscious thoughts and sensory perceptions. It means only that they have some-thing analogous to what we call feeling, memory, desire, and purpose in our-selves. To call this position "anthropomorphism," Hartshorne points out, is to presuppose that these experiential qualities belong uniquely to us: an animal caught in a trap does not have to become a human being in order to suffer.[5] One of the central features of Hartshorne's philosophy is the idea that the basic psychic qualities—such as feeling, memory, desire, and purpose—are "cos-mic variables," capable of *infinite* scope, both above and below their human forms. Memory, for example, could include the whole past, or it might extend back only a millionth of a second.[6] Desire and purpose might be equally vari-able in relation to the future. To say that all events are experiences is therefore not to say that they are very similar to human experiences; it is only to say that they are not absolutely different in kind.

The term "creative" gives special emphasis to one of these experiential variables. It says that, although all events are influenced by previous events, no event is fully determined by the past. Every event exercises at least some iota of self-determination or self-creation, and then some power to exert creative influ-ence on the future.

Although this position could be called "panpsychism," I prefer the term "panexperientialism."[7] The term "psyche" suggests a high-grade form of experience, and hence consciousness. That term also suggests that the basic units are enduring things. Also, many forms of panpsychism in which the basic units were enduring things, such as that of Leibniz, have been deterministic. By *panexperientialism* I mean the view that all the units of the actual world are experiencing, creative events.

Hartshorne has hailed this doctrine, which was first formulated with clarity by Whitehead, as one of the greatest philosophical discoveries of all time, and has spent much of his life explaining, developing, and defending it. He defends this doctrine both by bringing out its advantages and by responding to objections.

One advantage of panexperientialism, he says, is that it gives us some idea of what matter is in itself. Modern philosophy has left the nature of matter wholly mysterious,[8] saying that we cannot know what it is in itself, only how it appears to us. But, Hartshorne says, we should take advantage of the fact that in ourselves we have an individual piece of nature that we know from within as well as without.[9] If we are naturalists, and hence regard our own experience as fully natural, not as a supernatural something added to nature, should we not assume that all natural unities have two sides? The fact that it is only ourselves whose inside we know directly does not prevent us from assuming that other people have insides, that is, experiences. And most of us assume that other animals have experience of some sort. Why should we not assume that all natural entities, all the way down to subatomic events, have inside experience as well as outer behavior? We realize that a purely behavioristic approach is inadequate for human beings and other higher animals. By generalizing this insight to all levels of nature, we can have some slight intuition into what things are in themselves.[10] What we call matter is then the outer appearance of something that is, from within, analogous to our own experience.

Probably the most obvious advantage of panexperientialism is that it allows us to solve the notorious mind-body problem. By rejecting the dualistic assumption that lower individuals such as cells and molecules are absolutely different in kind, rather than merely different in degree, from our conscious experience, the problem is dissolved. In Hartshorne's words: "cells can influence our human experiences because they have feelings that we can feel. To deal with the influences of human experiences upon cells, one turns this around. *We* have feelings that *cells* can feel."[11]

By allowing us to understand our commonsense assumption that our experience is actual, that our bodies are actual, and that the two interact, panexperientialism proves itself superior to its alternatives. Materialism, by reducing mind to matter, forces us to deny that our own experience—the thing we know best in the universe—is really real and efficacious. Berkeleian idealism, by reducing matter to mind, denies that our body is actual and efficacious. Dualism says that mind and body are both actual but leaves us in the dark about how they interact, or at least seem to interact. Panexperientialism, which is nondualistic without being reductionistic, is the only doctrine that accounts for all the things we presuppose in practice: that our bodies are real and influence our experience, and that our experience is partly self-determining and influences our bodies in return.

A third advantage of panexperientialism is that it is, unlike materialism, truly nondualistic. This point, Hartshorne believes, will eventually lead science and science-oriented philosophy to embrace panexperientialism. The scientific mind, because of its drive to find universal explanatory principles, has a natural aversion to dualism.[12] The scientific community thus far, in overcoming the dualism with which modern thought began, has increasingly gravitated toward materialism. But this form of nondualism will not provide the conceptual unity science seeks, Hartshorne says, because it is really *dualism in disguise*. Because materialists cannot fail to believe that experiencing things exist, their assertion that nonexperiencing individuals exist means that the universe contains two fundamentally different types of individuals: experiencing and nonexperiencing.[13] This dualism is a "temporalized dualism": in its evolutionary account, it says that mere matter without a trace of experience first existed, and that then experience or mind "emerged."[14] Like other forms of dualism, this temporalized dualism has an unanswerable question. Its form of this question is: "How could mere matter produce life and minds?"[15] Panexperientialistic nondualism allows us to avoid this unanswerable question by speaking of "the emergence of species of mind, not of mind as such."[16]

If the case for panexperientialism is so strong—and there are still more advantages to come—why has it not been the most popular theory? The main reason, Hartshorne believes, is that much of the world as we perceive it does not give any evidence of animation, of having experiences and exercising self-determination. Rocks just stay where they are, unless moved by an external force. They show no sign of having feelings, desires, purposes, and the power for self-motion.[17] The difference between ourselves and a rock appears to be absolute, not merely a difference in degree. Hartshorne has a fourfold reply to this objection. The first part of the reply is the prior distinction between knowing something from within or only from without. The other three parts involve the indistinctness of sensory perception, the difference between aggregates and compound individuals, and the difference between high-grade and low-grade individuals. These four factors account for our idea of "matter" as inert, unfeeling stuff, which, Hartshorne says, we should now realize, thanks to modern science, to be an illusion.

Ordinary sensory perception, we now know, is indistinct.[18] Even the most precise of our senses, vision, does not give us the true individuals of which the world is comprised. We see a rock, not the billions of molecules of which it is comprised, let alone its atoms and subatomic particles; we see a plant, not the billions of cells of which it is comprised. If we could see individual cells, molecules, atoms, and electrons, we would not think of any of them as inert. The increased distinctness of perception made possible by modern science has in fact shown the inertness of the microscopic world to be an illusion.[19] Scientific experience has hence confirmed what Leibniz suspected, that the unities of sensory perception, such as rocks, plants, and stars, are pseudo-unities, produced by blurred perception. By penetrating these pseudo-unities, modern science has undercut the main basis for dualism and materialism.[20] We can think of all the true individuals of nature by analogy with ourselves.

Epistemological factors do not provide the only bases for assuming a dualism between active, experiencing things and inert, insentient things. Leibniz's most important but largely ignored contribution, Hartshorne says, was his distinction between two types of things that can be formed when multitudes of low-grade individuals are joined together: compound individuals and mere aggregates.[21] In a compound individual, such as an animal, there is a level of experience—a mind or soul (called by Leibniz a "dominant monad")—which turns the multiplicity into a true individual by giving it a unity of feeling and purpose, so that it can respond as a unified whole to its environment. In mere aggregates, such as a rock, by contrast, no such dominating experience exists. The highest centers of feeling and self-determination are the molecules comprising the rock. Without a dominating center, the various movements cancel out each other, so that the rock as a whole stays put unless pushed or pulled from without. The passivity of the rock is hence a statistical effect.[22] We can thereby understand how panexperiential animism is compatible with the mechanistic approach, which works so well for Galilean-Newtonian physics. Animism is true for individuals, while mechanism is true for aggregates of individuals.[23] Quantum physics supports this view, Hartshorne adds, by suggesting that the complete determinism implied by the mechanistic view of nature does not hold true for subatomic events.[24]

The fourth basis for the delusive idea of an absolute difference between mind and matter is that, whereas the human mind is a series of very high-grade experiences, with consciousness, self-consciousness, and hence very sophisticated purposes, the individuals constituting matter are very low-grade individuals, with feeling but no consciousness, let alone self-consciousness, and hence very short-range purposes.

The doctrine of the "compound individual" is one of Hartshorne's great contributions. Although Whitehead had suggested the Leibnizian distinction between aggregates and true individuals, it would be easy to miss it in his writings. Hartshorne has not only explained it time and time again but has also emphasized its importance. He says that, with this distinction, "Leibniz took the single greatest step in the second millennium of philosophy (in East and West) toward a rational analysis of the concept of physical reality."[25] Hartshorne did more, however, than simply draw attention to this distinction. Just as Whitehead improved on Leibniz's idea of the compound individual (by allowing real interaction between the dominant and subservient members of the society), so did Hartshorne improve upon Whitehead's formulation. Whitehead seemed to say that all occasions of experience are spatially tiny. This view made it difficult to understand how the dominant member of a society could directly influence all of its parts, and opened Whitehead to reductionistic interpretations. In Hartshorne's account, the dominant member of a society occupies the entire spatial region of the society, overlapping the regions of the lesser members.[26] Atomic occasions, for example, fill the entire region occupied by the atom, overlapping the regions of the subatomic events. The subatomic members hence live within the atomic experiences. The same principle applies to molecules, macromolecules, and cells. With regard to animals having a central nervous system, Hartshorne suggests that the mind or soul encompasses at least the region of the brain, perhaps that of the entire nervous system.

Another contribution by Hartshorne has been to make clearer than Whitehead did that there is a hierarchy of compound individuals. Although which identifiable things are to be designated compound individuals is an empirical question, Hartshorne suggests that at least the following are: atoms, molecules, macromolecules, cells, multicelled animals, and the universe as a whole. Each higher compound individual embodies lower ones, and contains the universal variables to a higher degree. Among these variables is power—the twofold power to determine oneself and to exert influence on others. Accordingly, power and breadth of experience rise proportionately.[27] Hartshorne thereby shows the relation between the human mind and its body to be simply one more form of a general principle characterizing the world. He thereby also paves the way for understanding God as the soul of the universe and thereby its supreme power.

Hartshorne's position provides, furthermore, an answer different from the two most dominant ones among modern philosophers on the relation between quantum indeterminacy and human freedom. One of these views is that quantum indeterminacy, even if interpreted realistically to mean genuine self-determination in subatomic events, is *irrelevant* for the question of freedom, because indeterminacy is cancelled out with large numbers of events; for example, a billiard ball's behavior is perfectly predictable even though that of its electrons is not. This argument assumes that a human being is structurally no different from a billiard ball. The other dominant position is that indeterminacy at the quantum level *accounts* for human freedom. This position assumes that a human being is nothing but a collection of subatomic particles and the relations among them, that we contain no self-determining individuals higher than electrons and protons.

Hartshorne's position is that the world contains a great number of types of genuine individuals more complex than electrons and having more power of self-determination. The discovery of quantum indeterminacy, by supporting the idea that true individuals even of the most primitive sort have some degree of freedom, is important for belief in human freedom primarily by analogy.[28]

Having given Hartshorne's response to the major objection against panexperientialism, I return now to his list of its advantages. The first three were that it gives us an idea what matter is in itself; it solves the mind-body problem; and it is truly nondualistic. A fourth advantage is that it makes both *time* and *natural law* intelligible. Both of these concepts have proved unintelligible for dualists and materialists, with their idea of dead matter, meaning matter that neither remembers nor anticipates. We can only conceive the unity of the past, present and future, Hartshorne points out, through memory and anticipation.[29] Panexperientialism says that nature is comprised exhaustively of experiencing events, each of which has memory, however minimal, of a settled past, and anticipation, however short-range, of a partly open future. If an electron, a photon, an atom, a molecule and a living cell are each a temporal society of such events, then time—with its distinctions among past, present, and future, and its irreversibility—is real for such entities. For dualism and materialism, by contrast, the objective temporal order is unintelligible.[30]

The same feature of panexperientialism renders natural law intelligible, solving the "problem of induction"—the problem of why we should believe the present laws of nature will hold true in the future. Materialists and dualists have assumed that the laws of physics will hold true throughout all time, while having no reason why they should hold true tomorrow. The Whiteheadian-Hartshornean position holds (in agreement with James and Peirce) that the so-called laws of nature are really its most long-lasting *habits*, the habits of those low-level societies with very little spontaneity with which to diverge from the patterns inherited from the past.[31] Thinking of the laws of nature as habits, and hence as sociological laws, implies that we should not consider them eternal; they have developed in time and can continue to evolve.[32] But we can reasonably believe that the habits of photons, electrons, atoms, molecules, and even macromolecules such as DNA will not change much within the short period of a few thousand years.

A fifth important advantage of panexperientialism is that the natural sciences have been increasingly supporting it, if unintentionally, and thereby increasingly undermining both materialism and dualism. Empirical science by itself cannot prove the true metaphysical position, Hartshorne says, but it can discredit false ones, especially insofar as they are based on an earlier, less precise science.[33] And empirical science can also provide positive support for the true metaphysical position. (In this very important sense, then—to anticipate a later discussion—Hartshorne is an empiricist.) Hartshorne says that, if it is true that the actual world is comprised exclusively of experiencing events, "science will tend more and more to reveal the fact."[34]

Hartshorne provides several examples. (1) He repeatedly cites that fact, mentioned earlier, that physics undermines the view, fundamental to dualism and materialism, that the basic units of nature are inert and fully determined. (2) He also points out that physics now shows nature to be most fundamentally a complex of events, not of enduring substances.[35] (3) By showing that space and time are inseparable, twentieth-century physics also supports the basic principle of Whiteheadian-Hartshornean process philosophy, that everything is related to time.[36] (4) Science has also increasingly confirmed the assertion of panexperientialism that the difference between lifeless matter and primitive life forms is merely a difference of degree.[37] (5) The idea that low-grade individuals, such as atoms and molecules, may have experience, even though they have no central nervous systems or specialized sensory organs, is also supported by science: physiology has revealed that paramecia can swim although they have neither motor nerves nor muscle cells, and that protozoa can digest without a stomach and can oxygenate without lungs. Accordingly, protozoa, and even molecules and atoms, may be able to feel, and even to perceive, in some lowly way. The fact that they do not have nervous systems only proves that they cannot feel and perceive to the same degree as can organisms with nervous systems. To say that it proves that they cannot feel and perceive at all, as Roger Sperry has, would be to presuppose that psychic variables, such as feeling, perceiving, and desiring, have a quite narrow range, which would be to beg the question.[38] Hartshorne's position is that the psychic variables have an infinite range. (I might add that Hartshorne's position, and his prediction that science will increasingly provide evidence for panexperientialism, have recently been supported by evidence that bacteria have memory and make decisions based on it.)[39]

As a way into the sixth benefit of panexperientialism—the one that Hartshorne seems to think should be the most important for those who understand the drive of science and philosophy for unification—I must discuss the epistemological side of panexperientialism, which I, following William James, call "radical empiricism."[40] The basic point, in contrast with the superficial empiricism of sensationism, is that sensory perception is not the basic form of perception. That this point follows from panexperientialism is obvious from the fact that individuals without sensory organs are said to perceive. Perception is, in fact, one of the universal variables, exemplified to some degree in all events. Hartshorne often uses Whitehead's term "prehension" to refer to this primordial, root form of perception, in which the present experience feels the feelings of previous experiences, thereby taking the previous events as objectified into itself. One meaning of "radical empiricism" is that this nonsensory prehension is at the root of sensory perception. For example, my visual perception of the paper before me presupposes that my soul (my mind, my series of dominant occasions of experience) prehends those brain cells that have received the visual data from the eye. My other sensory data likewise presuppose my direct prehensive relation to my body, as do my feelings of hunger, pain, and sexual excitement. All direct perception is prehensive.

The other clearest example of prehension is that relation we call *memory*, in which my present experience prehends some of my previous occasions of experience. This is an example of the perception of one actuality by another, given the hypothesis that my mind or soul is not a continuous "stream" of experience which is simply the same through time, but is instead a temporal "society" of discrete *occasions* of experience, each of which is a distinct actuality. The hypothesis that the actual world is made up exhaustively of events, in other words, implies that memory is an example of that primordial, nonsensory perception which we share with all other actual beings.

Memory and perception may seem to differ in that memory is prehension of antecedent events whereas perception is of simultaneous events. But— Hartshorne credits Whitehead with being the first clearly to see—perception also is always of antecedent events.[41] This fact is clearest when the perceived object is remote: we know, for example, that the sun that we see is the sun that was eight minutes ago. But even in the direct prehension of one's bodily parts, the events perceived are in the immediate past of the perceiving event, not absolutely simultaneous with it. Once this idea is accepted, perception and memory can be seen to share the same principle: direct prehension of antecedent events.[42] Looked at from the past to the present, memory and perception are both examples of the cause-effect relation, which is always a temporal relation, from past to present.[43] Given the idea that all unitary events are experiences, these causal relations all involve the sympathetic feelings by a present event of feelings of antecedent events. Through sympathy, the previous feelings are more or less repeated in the present experience, making it more or less similar to the prior ones.

The fact that memory and perception have all been explained in terms of a common principle brings us to Hartshorne's strongest basis for advocating panexperientialism to the scientific and philosophic communities. The drive of both science and philosophy, he holds, is toward conceptual integration.[44] *The goal is to explain as many phenomena as possible in terms of the fewest basic categories.* Through Whitehead's category of prehension—the nonsensory sympathetic perception of antecedent experiences—we are able to reduce several apparently very different types of relations to one fundamental type of relation. The category of prehension explains not only memory and perception, which seem different enough at first glance, but also temporality, space, causality, enduring individuality (or substance), the mind-body relation, the subject-object relation in general, and the God-world relation.[45]

I have already discussed the temporal relation, the mind-body relation, and enduring individuality (or self-identity) through time. The *spatial relation* is a complication of time; whereas time results from a single line of inheritance, space results from multiple lines of inheritance.[46] Given the notion that the actual world is made up exclusively of events that prehend and then are prehended, it is evident that *causality* in general is to be understood in the same way as the causal relations between body and mind, and between past and present events of the same mind. The *subject-object relation* in general is analogous to the relation between present and past in memory: a present event, which is a subject, sympathetically prehends an antecedent event, which is a subject-that-has-become-an-object. (In those subject-object relations that seem to be devoid of sympathy, or virtually so, as in the visual perception of the sun, the "object" is known only in a blurred and very indirect way. In all *direct* prehension by a subject of an object, the sympathetic feeling of feeling is evident.) Finally, the *God-world relation*, which is to be discussed later, can be understood in terms of God's prehension of the world and the prehension of God by the events comprising the world.

No fewer than *nine* relations, all apparently quite different from each other, have been reduced to *one!*[47] Hartshorne calls this result "the most powerful metaphysical generalization ever accomplished," and "a feat comparable to Einstein's."[48] While Hartshorne is speaking primarily of Whitehead here, calling him the "greatest single creator" of this generalization (while recognizing other contributors, such as Buddhists and Bergson),[49] it is Hartshorne who has called attention to this achievement. One could well read through Whitehead's writings several times without realizing that such a powerful generalization had been accomplished. It is also Hartshorne who has called attention to the similarity between this accomplishment and the type of unity that scientific thinking in general seeks. For these reasons, the achievement is one in which Hartshorne shares. Fully recognizing and naming an insight of genius can be as important as the insight itself.

Thus far, I have been explaining the advantages of panexperientialism in terms of philosophic theory, especially in relation to science. I come now to the relation of theory to practice. Can we have a scientific-philosophic theory that is adequate to the notions that are presupposed in the very practice of science and philosophy, and indeed in all human practice whatsoever? The capacity of postmodern panexperientialism to do just this is a seventh advantage. I summarize here eight examples of this capacity that have been given in the foregoing discussion. (1) Panexperientialism makes intelligible the mind-body interaction we all presuppose in practice. (2) Through the distinction between aggregates and true individuals, furthermore, we can understand how the behavior of billiard balls is fully determined by external forces while our own behavior is partly self-determined. (3) Through the idea of a hierarchy of compound individuals, we can understand how we have much *more* freedom than an electron, an amoeba, or even a chimpanzee. (4) The idea of the priority of nonsensory perception explains how we know that there is an actual world beyond our own experience, even though sensory perception as such provides only sense-data and hence appearances, not actuality. (5) The idea that each moment of human experience necessarily prehends the past as settled, hence as past, and anticipates the future as partly still to be determined, hence as future, explains our knowledge that there has been a past and that there will be a future. (6) The idea that all enduring individuals, including subatomic particles, are analogous to human minds in this respect provides a way of accounting for something else we presuppose; that time existed before the rise of human or even animal experience. (7) The idea that our basic way of apprehending reality is nonsensory makes it possible to explain our assumption that we have some knowledge of moral and aesthetic values. (8) The idea that the world given to human experience is comprised of things that embody the same stuff—feeling—that is embodied in human experience itself, including its ideas, explains how our ideas can correspond to things.

An eighth advantage of panexperientialism is that, besides unifying our basic theoretical categories and reconciling philosophical theory with the necessary presuppositions of human practice, it also effects a unification of our various forms of theory. In the first place, it overcomes the bifurcation between the natural and the social sciences. Human beings, on the one hand, are declared to be fully natural, exemplifying the same principles as the rest of nature. All natural things, on the other hand, are said to be social. Reality is, to use Hartshorne's term, "social process."[50] Even the endurance of an individual electron or atom is a social process, in which each event arises out of its social relations to prior events. The idea that the statistical regularities of nature are based on habits means, furthermore, that the basic laws of nature are sociological laws. They are different in degree, not in kind, from the statistical laws applying to human societies. Mechanistic, nonstatistical laws apply not to the fundamental processes of nature but only to the derivative processes between aggregates. We need not, therefore, have a dualism between the natural and the social sciences (perhaps calling the latter "hermeneutical" disciplines), or seek a unity of the sciences by reducing sociological to natural laws: *natural laws have already been elevated to sociological laws.*

Besides unifying the physical, biological, and social sciences, panexperientialism provides the basis for unifying epistemology and scientific cosmology with ethics, aesthetics, and philosophy of religion or natural theology.[51] One feature of this unification is that natural science is put on the same footing with these other cultural pursuits. Unlike relativistic postmodernism, however, panexperientialist postmodernism puts the natural sciences on the same cognitive level with ethics, aesthetics, and theology *not* by denying that science discovers truth, but by affirming that these other cultural pursuits are also pursuits of *truth*, that they also are *cognitive* enterprises.

Beyond putting our various cultural interests on the same level, panexperientialism allows for a real integration of them. Panexperientialism's key notion, that of sympathetic-creative value experience, most obviously suggests *aesthetic* experience, and Hartshorne indeed speaks of aesthetics as the fundamental discipline.[52] But sympathetic-creative value experience is for Hartshorne equally basic for understanding cosmology and epistemology, as we have seen, and ethics and theology, as we will see. Panexperientialism can thereby help us overcome the increasing intellectual fragmentation of modernity by moving toward a postmodern integration of our various cultural interests. The pluriversity could again become a university, in which courses in physics, biology, psychology, sociology, economics, ethics, and aesthetics would help students achieve an integrated view of themselves and the universe. Or, more radically, a postmodern university might no longer organize its approach to knowledge in terms of the modern disciplinary structure, a structure that presupposes absolute dichotomies between the supernatural and the natural, the animate and the inanimate, the sentient and the insentient, the social and the mechanistic, the human and the natural. Through this reorganization, along with the reunion of academic theory and the presuppositions of practice, the widespread custom of using the word "academic" as a pejorative term, as in "merely academic," might be overcome.

III. THEISM, PANEXPERIENTIALISM, AND DEEP EMPIRICISM

Hartshorne is probably best known and most discussed for his ideas about the divine nature and existence. Many of his most important contributions indeed come under this topic. It would be a mistake, however, to assume that his theism is separable from his panexperientialism. He says that most errors about God involve errors about the world, and vice versa.[53] His theism is, in fact, part and parcel of his panexperientialism, and his panexperientialism is part and parcel of his theism. Each implies the other.

To begin with panexperientialism, and then to see that it implies theism (of a nontraditional sort), was Whitehead's route. In Hartshorne's case, to the extent that any priority can be assigned—he says that one may proceed in either direction—the dominant order seems to be the reverse.[54] He characteristically portrays panexperientialism as an implication of theism, saying that "the idea of God contains implicitly the entire content of metaphysics."[55] He accordingly says: "Theism is not an adjunct to a world view; fully thought out, it is the most coherent of all explicit world views."[56] Hartshorne can even sound like the Vince Lombardi of theism, saying: "The theistic question . . . is not one more question, even the most important one. It is, on the fundamental level, and when all its implications are taken into account, the sole question."[57] Metaphysics can hence be called "the secular approach to theology."[58]

Fully thought out, Hartshorne maintains, theism implies panexperientialism, the philosophy of shared creative experience. If God is mind with infinite capacity, "then the zero of mind would be the zero of reality."[59] If God is infinite creative capacity, "the zero of this capacity which determinism posits must be the zero of the manifestation or presence of God" and hence "the zero of reality itself."[60] If God is infinite love, then "the zero case of love could only be the total absence of deity."[61]

"Theism," he maintains, sounding something like Luther and Barth, "should take its stand and not let itself be dictated to by bits of philosophy which had no origin in religious insight."[62] Regarded as implicitly atheistic are not only the ideas of determinism and insentient matter,[63] but also the idea of "self-identity as mere numerical oneness."[64] Besides making it difficult to understand how such individuals can be in God, this view takes self-identity as an irreducible, ultimate principle, not explainable in terms of spiritual categories.[65] Whitehead's idea that "society is more basic than 'substance,'" that the enduring individual is a temporal society of occasions of experience, each of which sympathizes with the feelings of earlier and later members, allows us to see how "the participation of experiences in other experiences, i.e., 'sympathy' or, in terms of its higher and happier forms, 'love,'" is truly the first principle of reality.[66]

Because (neoclassical) theism implies panexperientialism, Hartshorne can claim for theism all the virtues of panexperientialism recited earlier. The theistic insight that "love, as the relation of sympathy, . . . is the foundation of all other relations"[67] means that panexperientialism's reduction of nine categories to one is equally an achievement of theism. Hartshorne says that theism's insight into the centrality of sympathy and hence into the social structure of experience provides "the key to cosmology and epistemology, as well as ethics and religion."[68] Theism's ability to find "the key to facts and the key to values in a single idea," that of love or participation, Hartshorne hails as "an intellectual achievement than which none could be greater."[69]

Having indicated that for Hartshorne theism can be derived from panexperientialism, or panexperientialism from theism, and that for Hartshorne himself the latter direction may have been the dominant one, I return to the former order, from the world to God, showing how Hartshorne's panexperientialism supports and even implies his form of theism.

From Hartshorne's point of view, a philosophy cannot be consistent unless it is theistic.[70] Before this can be clearly seen, however, two major obstacles must be removed. The first of these obstacles is the fact that most people still equate theism with traditional or classical theism, which *cannot* be made credible. If one thinks of this traditional position as theism, then Hartshorne is an atheist. He fully agrees with the judgment of most modern philosophers that the arguments against the traditional idea of God are "as conclusive as philosophical arguments could well be."[71]

Hartshorne has, in fact, been one of the twentieth-century's major critics of traditional theism, pointing out many ways in which it makes an intelligible, consistent, and credible philosophy impossible. I mention six. (1) By asserting that God determines or at least knows the future, the traditional idea of God conflicts with our pressupositions about human freedom and responsibility. (2) By affirming an omnipotent goodness that can determine all details of the world, it conflicts with our presupposition about evil, that is, that not everything that happens is for the best. (3) By combining this idea of omnipotence with an anthropomorphic dualism, according to which only human beings have intrinsic value, supernaturalists developed a view of divine design that was disproved by the facts of evolution.[72] (4) By buttressing this doctrine of omnipotence with a doctrine of creation *ex nihilo*, supernaturalism affirmed the self-contradictory idea of a beginning of time. (5) Traditional theism attributed immutable consciousness to God, although we can think meaningfully of consciousness only as changing. (6) It spoke of God as an impassible being who could not be enriched or pained by anything happening in the world; it thereby contradicted its own injunction to serve God, and our presupposition that our lives have ultimate meaning. One reason that Hartshorne is distressed by this traditional idea of God is that it has led, by reaction, to complete atheism.

Modern philosophy became atheistic, however, not only because of problems inherent in traditional theism but also because the modern worldview rules out *any* significant idea of God. I mention four reasons. (1) A reductionism that would not allow the mind to influence the body would certainly not allow "downward causation" from God to the world, and would have no analogy for this. (2) The mechanistic view of nature allows for no divine influence in the world, because entities that interact only by mechanical impact make influence by a cosmic mind or soul unintelligible. According to the modern cosmology, it is impact, not love, that makes the world go round. (3) This mechanistic view also makes it impossible to understand how the world could be in God. (4) The sensationist theory of perception rules out any divine presence in human experience, and hence any direct awareness of God. Accordingly, portraying theism as a viable philosophy requires overcoming not only traditional theism but also the modern worldview.

The obstacles to theism created by both theistic supernaturalism and mechanistic naturalism are solved by Hartshorne's postmodern panexperientialism, to which theism is integral. The theism that is integral to this panexperientialism is a naturalistic, not a supernaturalistic, theism.[73] This means that a world of finite events exists necessarily, not through the arbitrary decision of the divine will. The existence of a plurality of finite experiences is as natural as God's own existence. The nature of the relations between God and the world is therefore a natural, necessary feature of reality. The Hartshornean position hence says not only that every event has creative power—the power to shape itself in part, and the power to influence future events. It also says that the fact that every event has this twofold creative power is not *simply* a "fact," that is, not simply a contingent feature of *our* world. It is a necessary, natural feature of reality, not an arbitrary decree of the divine will that could have been otherwise and that could be overridden from time to time.

The presence of evil in our world and of every possible world is thereby explained. Evil results from multiple finite freedom, and any world God could have created would have had multiple finite freedom.[74] The possibility of evil is necessary. No particular evils are necessary, but the possibility that evil can occur is necessary. We cannot accuse God of a deficiency in goodness for not interrupting the normal cause-effect relations to prevent particularly horrendous evils. Because the normal cause-effect relations are natural, necessary, given features of reality, they cannot be interrupted. God does influence every event, but divine influence is always persuasion. It could not be unilateral determination.

This position explains not only the possibility of evil in general, Hartshorne points out, but also the possibility of the extreme horrors that human beings have caused and suffered. Freedom and danger necessarily rise proportionately. Because human beings have more freedom than other creatures, they *necessarily* are more dangerous and more capable of suffering.[75]

Besides explaining evil, this position makes clear that belief in God in no way denies human freedom and human responsibility for the course of human history. We cannot declare that any status quo has been sanctioned by divine arrangement, or that God will step in to save us from our foolish ways, such as with nuclear weapons and other ecological threats.

Besides not determining the future, God does not even know the future, beyond those abstract features of the future that are already determined by the present. God's lack of knowledge of the details of the future betokens no divine imperfection. Because all events exercise some self-determining power, the future is simply not knowable, even by omniscience. The partial openness of the future, and our own partial freedom, which we all presuppose in practice, are hence not compromised by this naturalistic theism.

This position also simultaneously overcomes the charge that the idea of God's creation of the world is self-contradictory, and the conflict between creation and evolution. Because there never was a first moment of finite existence, the creation of our world involved a creation not out of nothing but "out of an earlier world and its potentialities for transformation." Divine creative causation, analogously to ours, always involves a transformation of a previous situation. No self-contradictory idea of a beginning of time is therefore implied.[76] Also, because finite events necessarily have their own creative power, divine creative transformation is always persuasion, never unilateral rearrangement. No feature of our world in its present state of evolution is simply a divine product. Darwinian evidence that every species shows signs of "descent with modification" from earlier species is therefore no evidence against a divine creator.

Whereas the ideas about God that I have already mentioned are ones that Hartshorne shares with Whitehead (albeit with different nuances), Hartshorne has gone considerably beyond Whitehead in developing a coherent and fully articulate doctrine of God that is consistent with the rest of the system. Whereas Whitehead had evidently thought of God as a single, everlasting actual entity, Hartshorne conceives of God by analogy with the human soul, and hence as a "living person"—that is, as a temporal society of occasions of experience. Whitehead had said that God should be the chief exemplification of metaphysical principles, not an exception to them.[77] In speaking of God as a single actual entity interacting with the world, he seemed to violate this ideal, because the denial that contemporary actual entities can interact seems to be a metaphysical principle. The idea of an actual entity that "remains numerically one amidst the changes of accidental relations and of accidental qualities" is clearly called a *metaphysical error* by Whitehead,[78] and yet that description seems to fit his idea of God. Hartshorne's reconception of God overcomes this problem of coherence. God is no longer an everlasting actual entity with changing relations, but an everlasting series of divine occasions of experience; and these divine occasions of experience prehend not contemporary occasions in the strict sense but only past ones. (Of course, God knows "the present" as ordinarily understood, in that "the past" includes events that occurred less than a billionth of a second ago.)

This reconception also involves a revision of the doctrine of divine dipolarity. Traditional theism was, to use Hartshorne's term, "monopolar." The idea that God was unchanging in some respects therefore meant that God was unchanging in *all* respects. This created the two problems mentioned earlier: how could an unchanging consciousness know a changing world, and how could a changing world, including our lives, contribute anything to changeless perfection? Some modern thought has been monopolar in the opposite way, saying that all is flux. At least some representatives of relativistic postmodern philosophy, which denies any unchanging principles to which all thought must conform to be adequate, portray it as a despiritualized version of Hegel's monopolar theology.[79]

Hartshorne credits Whitehead with being the first philosopher to suggest clearly that God has two natures or poles, the one changing, the other unchanging.[80] In Whitehead's version, this "dipolarity" of God is analogous to the dipolarity of an actual entity, that is, to its physical and mental poles. Followers of Whitehead disagree as to whether problems created by this analogy are intolerable. In any case, Hartshorne avoids these problems by making the two poles of God's reality analogous, respectively, to the abstract characteristics and the concrete states of a human soul. For example, God's *omniscience* is an abstract feature that belongs to every divine occasion of experience; it is the unchanging feature of knowing everything that is knowable at the time. God's *concrete knowing*, by contrast, changes in each moment, because there are always new things to be known. While the abstract pole or nature of God is absolutely unchanging, the concrete pole is constantly changing. A similar distinction can be made for other characteristics, such as love. God's love as the abstract characteristic of loving all creatures that have existed is unchanging, whereas God's concrete loving changes in each moment, because new creatures with new experiences are constantly arising. Thanks to this distinction between the two poles of God's experience, the incoherencies of traditional theism can be overcome. We can understand how God can know a changing world while having an unchanging nature. We can understand how God's *experience* can be enriched and therefore served by our lives even though God's *character* is beyond improvement.

Besides overcoming the many problems inherent in traditional theism, the panexperientialist position overcomes the distinctively modern reasons for believing divine presence in the world to be unintelligible and unnecessary. The doctrine of compound individuals, as I mentioned earlier, is generalized to the universe as a whole, with God as the soul of the universe. The general doctrine of compound individuals, in which causation runs downward as well as upward, makes downward causation from the soul of the universe to its various members an exemplification of general principles, not an exception to them. The idea that all individuals experience, and that all causation between individuals involves the sympathetic feeling of feelings, shows how God can influence, and thereby be in, the world, and how the world can influence, and thereby be in, God. The idea that human perception in particular is fundamentally nonsensory shows how we can have direct awareness of God's reality. The idea that power rises proportionately with breadth of experience and mentality makes it natural to think of the soul of the world as its most powerful member.[81]

Besides showing belief in God to be intelligible, panexperientialism shows it to be necessary. The idea that the actual world is comprised exhaustively of partially *free* experiences makes it clear that the order of the world can be made intelligible only through the idea of an all-inclusive soul, whose purposes order the world through becoming internalized by the creatures, somewhat as our purposes order our bodies through becoming internalized by our bodily members.[82]

The remainder of Hartshorne's arguments for the existence of God do not follow from his panexperientialism as such. These arguments do presuppose panexperientialism's demonstration that it is possible to formulate an idea of God that is self-consistent and consistent with our knowledge of ourselves and the world in general. But most of the other arguments (the ontological argument is here excluded) consist of showing that belief in God is implicit in our experience, in the sense of being "required for the interpretation of some fundamental aspect of life or experience."[83] These arguments are, therefore, in a sense, *empirical* arguments. Because this claim is controversial, I need to defend it before coming to these arguments.

Hartshorne is often considered to be a rationalist as opposed to an empiricist. And this characterization has considerable support in Hartshorne's writings. He makes a strong distinction between science, which must use the empirical method, and metaphysics, whose method should be nonempirical or *a priori*. Metaphysical or necessary truths, such as the existence of God, are to be discovered *a priori*, through an analysis of meanings.[84]

This distinction should not lead us to conclude, however, that for Hartshorne philosophy is not based on experience. In the first place, metaphysics is only one part of *philosophy as a whole*, which involves a synthesis of metaphysics and the special sciences.[85] In the second place, even the metaphysical part of his philosophy is based on experience. As we saw earlier, Hartshorne argues in many ways that recent science supports panexperientialism against dualism and materialism. He also says that he first came to hold panexperientialism through the recognition that nature as immediately given is essentially feeling.[86] He furthermore endorses "the whole drive of modern philosophy to relate concepts to perceptions" and endorses the empiricist principle that all meaningful ideas are derived from experience and refer to experience.[87] The empiricism he endorses is, of course, a *radical* empiricism, in which nonsensory perception is fundamental. So understood, "the principle of empiricism" is the "basis of intellectual integrity."[88] Unlike some empiricists, Hartshorne does not deny that direct perceptual experience can and must be transcended, but he insists that it should be transcended only by imaginative experience, and then only in accordance with principles given in perception.[89]

When Hartshorne calls metaphysics nonempirical, he is using "empirical" in a narrower sense. In this narrower sense, an "empirical fact" is a state of affairs that might not have been. Karl Popper's criterion is used: an empirical truth is one that could in principle be falsified by conflicting with a conceivable observation.[90] Metaphysics is not empirical in this sense because the truths it seeks are necessary truths. Because necessary or metaphysical truths must be illustrated by *every* experience, no conceivable observation could conflict with them. A different method must therefore be used to discover them. Having accepted the narrow, Popperian definition of "empirical," Hartshorne uses the term *"a priori"* for the method appropriate to metaphysics.

Whether or not it was wise to refer to metaphysics as *a priori* and nonempirical,[91] Hartshorne has clearly stated that metaphysics is not unrelated to experience. To call metaphysical concepts *a priori* means they are *prior not to all experience but only to particular, contingent aspects of experience*. They are based instead on the strictly general traits of experience.[92] Because they are illustrated in any experience whatsoever, they need not be sought through special experiments or in special places; they can in principle be derived by reflection upon any experience.[93] Hartshorne has stated that he, at the age of seventeen, decided to "trust reason to the end."[94] He could equally well say that his method involves the decision to trust experience to the end, or, better, in its depths. The basic task of philosophical theology, says Hartshorne, is to discover, through cooperation, "what the bottom layer of our common human thought really is."[95] Instead of *a priori* and nonempirical, this approach could well be called "deep empiricism," because it seeks those universal features at the depths of every experience, beneath the fleeting superficialities.

Hartshorne points out that the ingredients of this bottom layer can be compared with what John Locke called "innate ideas."[96] A crucial difference is that for Hartshorne these ideas are not the result of a supernatural implantation at the time of the soul's creation, as they were for some of Locke's contemporaries, but are directly perceived or intuited by the soul at each moment. By rejecting modernity's restriction of perception to sense-perception, Hartshorne's postmodern philosophy can give a naturalistic explanation of these universal ideas. Relativistic postmodernism, by contrast, which denies that there is any deep layer common to all people, follows from retaining early modernity's sensationism while rejecting its supernaturalism. Richard Rorty, for example, claims that all the "intuitions" we have are due to tradition and education, so that "there is nothing deep down inside us except what we have put there ourselves."[97] In other words, all of our apparently deep ideas are culturally conditioned. By affirming nonsensory perception as fundamental, Hartshorne's postmodern philosophy rejects supernaturalism without falling into relativism. Through our nonsensory apprehension we all share a common set of beliefs. These beliefs, in their preconceptual form, can be called knowledge, because they consist in direct apprehensions of those universal features of reality which are always present to experience.[98]

The task of metaphysics is, hence, simply to formulate explicitly, and thereby to make us more conscious of, what we all already know in an implicit, preconscious way.[99]

That everyone knows or believes in the universal truths becomes evident in their action, which is the ultimate expression of what we most deeply believe.[100] We can verbally espouse a doctrine that contradicts one of these deep truths, but we cannot live in terms of such a doctrine. For example, we all know, down deep, that the future is partly open, that it is only relatively, not absolutely, determined. Everyone, including the philosopher who professes to be a determinist, is "busily engaged in trying to decide what the future is to be as though it were *not* yet wholly fixed."[101] Even animals reveal by their behavior that they know merely relative determinism to be true.[102] With the pragmatists, Hartshorne says that, if a doctrine cannot be lived, it cannot be true, and no one *really* believes it.[103]

Hartshorne puts belief in God in the same class. If God as the all-inclusive soul of the universe exists, then God, being ubiquitous, must be "present in the experience of the most hardened skeptic or sinner."[104] The reality of God can therefore be denied only by contradicting consciously what is intended "in some underlying stratum of affirmation."[105] Hartshorne claims, for example, that all people know, "and at some point betray that they know, that the object of our total allegiance is God."[106] The difference between believers and unbelievers is, therefore, "nothing but a difference in self-consciousness and consistency in regard to what all believe 'at heart.'"[107] "The real argument for God," Hartshorne says, "is just that every view which tries to deny him also denies . . . some practically indispensable belief."[108]

Among these beliefs that are indispensable in practice are the beliefs in the reality of truth, the past, an inclusive ideal, and an ultimate meaning to our lives. Apart from an all-inclusive perspective, there is no locus for that complete truth whose existence is presupposed everytime we criticize an inadequate perspective on reality.[109] Apart from a cosmic memory, there is no conceivable locus for truths about the past, yet historians and the rest of us constantly presuppose that assertions about the past can be true or false.[110] Apart from belief in a cosmic ideal and evaluation, we cannot account for our common conviction that there is a standard of importance and value in terms of which to criticize inadequate human desires.[111] Without belief in a cosmic and permanent receiver of value-experiences, we cannot make sense of the idea, which we all presuppose at some level, that our experiences and decisions have an ultimate meaning.[112]

Hartshorne also states his basic argument in terms of the meanings implicit in our categorical terms. Good is that "which is good in the eyes of God."[113] Truth is "conformity to what is experienced by an omnipresent 'observer.'" The past is "what unlimited or cosmic memory can never forget." Reality is "that which God knows."[114] We find God "in our fundamental meanings," Hartshorne says. Theism is hence simply "the elucidation of the full bearings of unavoidable word uses, categorical meanings. . . ."[115]

We presuppose all these ideas, Hartshorne maintains, because God not only exists necessarily but is also necessarily present in our awareness, at some level.[116] Theism is, accordingly, implicitly present in our basic beliefs and meanings. A philosophy that denies theism necessarily denies at the explicit level various beliefs that it is implicitly presupposing. An atheistic philosophy, therefore, can never be consistent.

The continued association of the word "God" with the classical idea of God should not lead us to misunderstand Hartshorne's argument here. He is not saying that all people down deep believe in the God of Augustine, Thomas, or Calvin. He, in fact, is saying that the presuppositions of our practice show that *no one* really believes in this idea of God. No one can really live in terms of a doctrine of divine providence that says that all events are determined, or that everything that happens is for the best.[117] Our presupposition that what we creatures decide and experience makes some ultimate difference, furthermore, is contradicted by classical theism's doctrines of divine impassibility and immutable perfection, which say that our lives make no difference to God, the ultimate standard of truth and value. At the bottom layer of our experience, which is expressed willy-nilly in our actions, we do not believe in that God. Hartshorne means his own doctrine of God to be an explication of the God in which we all do at least implicitly believe.[118]

I conclude by looking briefly at some of Hartshorne's reasons for thinking that metaphysics, including metaphysical theology, has practical importance.

IV. THE PRACTICAL IMPORTANCE OF EXPLICIT METAPHYSICAL BELIEFS

It might be asked: If all people believe in God and the other metaphysical truths down deep, and if we all necessarily feel, think, and act in terms of this deep belief regardless of our conscious, explicit beliefs, what difference does it make what we consciously believe? Of what value is metaphysics, including philosophical theology?

We need metaphysics, in the first place, Hartshorne says, to attain integrity. We live in terms of two levels—in terms of our conscious, conceptualized beliefs as well as of our deep, preconceptual beliefs. As long as there is serious tension between these two levels, we will never attain consistency and sincerity.[119]

This integrity, besides being valuable for its own sake, is important for our behavior. If our conscious symbols are inadequate to our deep beliefs, Hartshorne says, our behavior will eventually deteriorate.[120] The affirmation of atheism, nihilism, absolute determinism, absolute relativism, or absolute selfishness is self-contradictory, and cannot therefore be fully meant and lived; but it can nevertheless be very destructive.[121] Contrary to Richard Rorty's hope, the conscious affirmation of such negative doctrines cannot remain "merely philosophical";[122] it will have an effect on our behavior.

To take the example of selfishness: Hartshorne believes that a "kind of 'altruism' is the universal principle," and that all people "'in their hearts' know that they are 'members one of another,' and do not live for themselves alone, or even essentially."[123] Absolute selfishness is therefore impossible. Absolute *un*selfishness is equally impossible for finite beings: it is given that we are all relatively selfish, necessarily caring more for ourselves and our intimates than for people in general and for all sentient beings. What is *not* given is the degree of our relative selfishness. The idea that a person is an enduring substance, which would mean that our relations to our own past and future would be absolutely different in kind from our relations to other people, makes it seem metaphysically impossible that we could in principle love our neighbors *as ourselves*. The substance-idea of identity has in fact promoted a self-interest doctrine of motivation, according to which we cannot really care at all about anyone except ourselves. If we accept this doctrine, our relative selfishness will tend to become as close to absolute selfishness as possible.

The insight that the enduring self is really a temporal society, comprised of a series of events, shows that our identification with our past is already an example of sympathy, and that our concern for our future welfare is already a form of altruism. It also shows that our relations to our own past and future are not different in kind from our relations to other people. This insight shows that we really can, in principle, love other people in the same way as we love ourselves.[124] This implication of panexperientialism is so important to Hartshorne that he says: "On this ground alone I would not give up the event doctrine without the most rigorous proofs of its erroneousness."[125]

With regard to belief in God, Hartshorne offers many ways in which conscious belief in the God of his metaphysics can have practical importance for our lives. I will mention four.

First, by explicitly recognizing that God's perfect power does not and cannot eliminate, control, or occasionally override the power of the creatures, we can retain faith in the basic goodness of life in the face of its inevitable tragedies.[126] Second, explicit belief in God will encourage us to imitate God— both God's sympathy for all feelings and desires, and God's creativity, in which the creation of new values is combined with respect for old ones.[127] The vision of God will also lead us to aspire to approximate that unity of love with knowledge and power that God alone embodies.[128] Third, theism "implies that love is the supreme good, not pleasure or knowledge or power, and those who think otherwise will be disappointed."[129] Fourth, explicit belief in God provides an answer to the final question of human life: What is its ultimate meaning, what should be our central aim? "Be the aim Nirvana, the Classless Society, the Welfare State, Self-realization," Hartshorne says, "the query is never silenced, what good is it, from the cosmic and everlasting perspective, that one or the other or all of these aims be attained for a time on this ball of rock?"[130] Belief in God, as the One in whom we all live and who cherishes all good things everlastingly, provides an infinite aim for life—to contribute to the divine life. And this infinite aim strengthens rather than weakens our commitment to finite aims. I close with a statement from Hartshorne in which he seems to state in these terms the central motivation of his own life, a life that has produced over twenty books and 450 articles. In a gloss on the idea that all of one's life should be a "reasonable, holy, and living sacrifice" to deity, Hartshorne says, "if I can inspire multitudes who will never see me in the flesh, then the incense I send up to God will continue to rise anew for many generations."[131]

NOTES

1. Kenneth Baynes, James Bohman, and Thomas McCarthy, eds., *After Philosophy: End or Transformation?* (Cambridge: MIT Press, 1987); James Edwards, *Ethics Without Philosophy* (Gainesville: University Press of Florida, 1985).

2. Richard Rorty, *Consequences of Pragmatism* (Minneapolis: University of Minnesota Press, 1982), 86-87, 165, 194.

3. Ibid., xvii, xxv, xxvi, 192.

4. Charles Hartshorne, *Beyond Humanism: Essays in the Philosophy of Nature* (1937; Lincoln: University of Nebraska Press, 1968), 86-87, 216, 226, 267-68; "Physics and Psychics: The Place of Mind in Nature," in *Mind in Nature: Essays on the Interface of Science and Philosophy*, ed. John B. Cobb, Jr., and David Ray Griffin (Washington, D.C.: University Press of America, 1977), 89-96.

5. *Beyond Humanism*, 120.

6. Ibid., 116-17.

7. Hartshorne at one time used the term "panpsychism," but later switched to "psychicalism" (cf. *Beyond Humanism*, passim, and "Physics and Psychics," 91). I have explained my reasons for eschewing both of those terms in favor of "panexperientialism" at greater length in Cobb and Griffin, eds., *Mind in Nature*, 97-98.

8. "Physics and Psychics," 90.

9. Ibid., 90; *The Logic of Perfection and Other Essays in Neoclassical Metaphysics* (Lasalle, Ill.: Open Court, 1962), 183-84.

10. *Beyond Humanism*, 202, 266; *Logic of Perfection*, 225; "Physics and Psychics," 90.

11. *Logic of Perfection*, 229.

12. "Physics and Psychics," 90; *Creative Synthesis and Philosophic Method* (London: SCM Press, 1970; Lanham, Md.: University Press of America, 1983), 9.

14. *Omnipotence and Other Theological Mistakes* (Albany: State University of New York, 1984), 83-84.

15. "Physics and Psychics," 92.

16. *Logic of Perfection*, 125.

17. "Physics and Psychics," 91; "Why Psychicalism? Comments on Keeling's and Shepherd's Criticisms," *Process Studies* 6/1 (Spring, 1976), 67-72, esp. 67.

18. *Beyond Humanism*, 199, 304, 314.

19. *Logic of Perfection*, xii; *Reality as Social Process: Studies in Metaphysics and Religion* (Glencoe, Ill.: The Free Press, 1953), 33.

20. *Beyond Humanism*, 199, 314.

21. *Creative Synthesis*, 90; *Logic of Perfection*, 213; "Physics and Psychics," 95.

22. *Man's Vision of God and the Logic of Theism* (1941; Hamden, Conn.: Archon Books, 1964), xvi.

23. *Beyond Humanism*, 70, 315.

24. *Logic of Perfection*, 224; *Creative Synthesis*, 203: *Beyond Humanism*, 143, 144.

25. "Physics and Psychics," 95; see also *Creative Synthesis*, 90.

26. For a reductionistic interpretation of Whitehead, see Ivor Leclerc, *The Nature of Physical Existence* (London: George Allen & Unwin, 1972), and "Some Main Philosophical Issues Involved in Contemporary Scientific Thought," in *Mind in Nature*, ed. Cobb and Griffin, 101-08. For a nonreductionistic interpretation, see David Ray Griffin, "Whitehead's Philosophy and Some General Notions of Physics and Biology," ibid., 122-34. For Hartshorne's view, see "The Compound Individual," in *Philosophical Essays for Alfred North Whitehead*, ed. Otis H. Lee (New York: Longmans, Green, 1936), 193-220. For a discussion of Leclerc's interpretation of Whitehead, and of Hartshorne's advance beyond Whitehead, see John B. Cobb, Jr., "Overcoming Reductionism," in *Existence and Actuality: Conversations with Charles Hartshorne*, ed. Cobb and Franklin I. Gamwell (Chicago: University of Chicago Press, 1984), 149-63.

27. *Beyond Humanism*, 208; *Omnipotence*, 60.

28. *Logic of Perfection*, 224; *Beyond Humanism*, 146.

29. *Beyond Humanism*, 174, 181-82, 234.

30. *Reality as Social Process*, 74; *Beyond Humanism*, 138, 174, 181-82, 202, 234.

31. In a lecture delivered in 1934, Whitehead referred to "the general physical laws of inorganic nature" as "those widespread habits of nature" which "exist as average,

regulative conditions because the majority of actualities are swaying each other to modes of interconnection exemplifying those laws" (*Modes of Thought* [1938; New York: The Free Press, 1968], 154-55). In 1937, Hartshorne (who evidently did not know this Whiteheadian passage) wrote: "But the 'laws of nature' are only the habits of the species of which nature is composed. Physics investigates the behavior of the most universally distributed species—electrons, photons, atoms, molecules, crystals. The laws of physics are the behavior patterns, the habits of these species, no more and no less" (*Beyond Humanism*, 139; see also 138, 163). Rupert Sheldrake has recently emphasized this idea ("The Laws of Nature as Habits: A Postmodern Basis for Science," *The Reenchantment of Science: Postmodern Proposals*, ed. David Ray Griffin [Albany: State University of New York Press, 1988], 79-86). Sheldrake correctly credits Charles Peirce with suggesting this idea a century ago (80). It is interesting to note that the only passages I found in which Hartshorne uses the language of "habits" for the laws of nature were in *Beyond Humanism*, which was published early in his career when the influence of Peirce on him was quite fresh, and which was in fact dedicated to Peirce. This side of Hartshorne's thought seems to be in some tension with his more well-known doctrine that laws of nature are imposed through divine persuasion, a doctrine which has led to the criticism that the divine persuasion in this case is really coercive imposition (Barry L. Whitney, "Process Theism: Does a Persuasive God Coerce?", *Southern Journal of Philosophy* 17 [1979], 133-43, esp. 137-39, and *Evil and the Process God* [New York and Toronto: Edwin Mellen Press, 1985], 100-11). Had Hartshorne continued to speak of the laws of nature as the habits of its various species, this criticism might have been avoided. These habits could be portrayed as the joint product of divine and creaturely causation, which seemed to be Whitehead's position (see his passage about habits, cited above, and his description in *Adventures of Ideas* (1933; New York: The Free Press, 1967) of his position on the laws of nature as intermediate between the doctrines of pure immanence and pure imposition [111-15, 129-30]). Sheldrake's idea of morphic causation provides a possible way of assigning a larger role to creaturely causation in explaining how the habits become so pervasive.

32. *Beyond Humanism*, 139.

33. Ibid., 142, 292, 293.

34. Ibid., 260.

35. *Logic of Perfection*, 218; *Creative Synthesis*, 187, 189.

36. *Beyond Humanism*, 257.

37. "Physics and Psychics," 92.

38. *Reality as Social Process*, 54; *Beyond Humanism*, 201; see Roger Sperry, *Science and Moral Priority: Merging Mind, Brain, and Human Values* (New York: Columbia University Press, 1983), 20-21, 70.

39. A. Goldbeter and D. E. Koshland, Jr., "Simple Molecular Model for Sensing and Adaptation Based on Receptor Modification with Application to Bacterial Chemo-

taxis," *Journal of Molecular Biology* 161/3 (1982), 395-416; Julius Adler and Wing-Wai Tse, "Decision-Making in Bacteria," *Science* 184 (June 21, 1974), 1292-94.

40. The term "radical empiricism" has various meanings, even within William James' own writings. Given some of those meanings, Hartshorne would emphatically *not* be a radical empiricist. I am using the term only in reference to the doctrine of the priority of nonsensory perception, which allows other actualities, causal relations, and values to be directly perceived.

41. *Creative Synthesis*, 92, 107; "Ideas and Theses of Process Philosophers," in *Two Process Philosophers: Hartshorne's Encounter with Whitehead*, ed. Lewis S. Ford (Tallahassee, Fl.: American Academy of Religion, 1973), 100-03, esp. 102.

42. *Creative Synthesis*, 91-92.

43. Ibid., 107.

44. Ibid., 9.

45. *Beyond Humanism*, 195; *Creative Synthesis*, 92, 107; *Reality as Social Process*, 74-75; *Logic of Perfection*, 129.

46. *Creative Synthesis*, 218-19.

47. *Beyond Humanism*, 192.

48. *Creative Synthesis*, 107, 92.

49. Ibid., 107.

50. See *Reality as Social Process*.

51. *Creative Synthesis*, xviii; "Physics and Psychics," 92.

52. *Creative Synthesis*, 303-21.

53. *Logic of Perfection*, xiii, 138-39, 144.

54. Besides *Creative Synthesis*, 40-41, see xvii, where Hartshorne says that the firmest residuum from his early pious if liberal Christian outlook "is summed up in the phrase *Deus est caritas*, together with the two 'Great Commandments': total love for God, and love for neighbour comparable to love for self. . . . If there are central intuitive convictions back of my acceptance or rejection of philosophical doctrines, these may be the ones." His "natural theology" should therefore probably be called "a Christian natural theology" in John Cobb's sense of this term as explained in the final chapter of *A Christian Natural Theology: Based on the Thought of Alfred North Whitehead* (Philadelphia: Westminster Press, 1965).

55. *Creative Synthesis*, 55; see also 44.

56. *Logic of Perfection*, 126.

57. Ibid., 131.

58. *Creative Synthesis*, 24, 28.

59. *Logic of Perfection*, 123.

60. Ibid., 126.

61. Ibid.

62. Ibid., 122.

63. *Logic of Perfection*, 122-23, 143; *Omnipotence*, 62-63.

64. Ibid., 120.

65. Ibid., 120-21.

66. *Creative Synthesis*, xvii-xviii.

67. *Beyond Humanism*, 26.

68. *Logic of Perfection*, xviii.

69. Ibid., 129.

70. *Beyond Humanism*, 86-87.

71. *Man's Vision of God*, 58.

72. *Logic of Perfection*, 205; "Physics and Psychics," 94. Given Hartshorne's distinction between metaphysical and empirical (in the narrow sense) issues, which is discussed later, one must be careful in saying that Hartshorne believes the traditional doctrine of God to have been disproved by the "facts" of evil and evolution. Hartshorne insists that contingent facts could not disprove a God-idea that was not already inherently incoherent, even apart from these facts (*Logic of Perfection*, 157; *Creative Synthesis*, 19-22, 292). What is inconsistent with traditional theism is not simply the great amount of evil in our world, and some of the details of the evolutionary process, but the very reality of processes not controllable by a supreme agent. The reality of creaturely creativity or freedom is not simply a contingent fact about our particular world but a necessary feature of any world. Particular evils and particular facts about the evolutionary process may be important in focusing our attention on the incompatibility of traditional theism and the nature of the world, but the proper lesson to be drawn, Hartshorne says, is that the traditional idea of God, including God's relation to the world, is an incoherent idea.

73. See *Logic of Perfection*, xiii: "a Neoclassical Theism belongs in a Neoclassical Metaphysics." Hartshorne had at one time used the term "naturalistic theism" (*Beyond Humanism*, 25, 56, 253, 263). But he later gave it up, conceding the term "naturalism" to the doctrine that all knowledge is empirically testable, in the narrow sense of "empirical" defined in the text below. In relation to naturalism thus understood, he has

said, "I am an unabashed supernaturalist" (ibid., viii, which is in the preface written for the 1968 edition). In terms of the meaning I am giving to the contrast between naturalistic and supernaturalistic theism, however, Hartshorne is unabashedly a naturalistic theist. As he points out, his theism is "about equally distinct from the old naturalism and the old supernaturalism" (*Reality as Social Process*, 23).

74. *Omnipotence*, 15, 21; *Logic of Perfection*, 209; *Creative Synthesis*, 237-38; *Man's Vision of God*, xvi, 14, 30-31, 36, 89.

75. *Creative Synthesis*, 13-14; *Reality as Social Process*, 107; *Logic of Perfection*, 13-14; *The Divine Relativity: A Social Conception of God* (1948; New Haven, Conn.: Yale University Press, 1964), 136; *Whitehead's Philosophy: Selected Essays, 1935-1970* (Lincoln: University of Nebraska Press, 1972), 93-94; *A Natural Theology for our Time* (Lasalle, Ill.: Open Court, 1967), 81-82.

76. *Man's Vision of God*, 230, 231, 233.

77. Alfred North Whitehead, *Process and Reality*, corrected edition, ed. David Ray Griffin and Donald W. Sherburne (New York: The Free Press, 1978), 343.

78. Ibid., 79.

79. Richard Rorty, "Postmodernist Bourgeois Liberalism," *Journal of Philosophy* 80 (1983), 583-89.

80. "Ideas and Theses of Process Philosophers," 102.

81. *Beyond Humanism*, 209, 308; *Logic of Perfection*, 120.

82. *Logic of Perfection*, 157, 285; *Creative Synthesis*, 284-85; *Beyond Humanism*, 285.

83. *Creative Synthesis*, 280. Hartshorne points out in this passage that the ontological argument does not share this feature of the remainder of his arguments. I do not deal with it in this essay, in spite of the fact that it has been extremely important to Hartshorne, partly because of this difference, partly because its discussion would require too much space, and partly because I have never found it convincing. (It seems to me to prove only that *something* exists necessarily, not also that this something has other divine attributes, such as perfect love, knowledge, and power.)

84. *Creative Synthesis*, 29-31, 85; *Logic of Perfection*, ix, 157; *Man's Vision of God*, 62.

85. *Man's Vision of God*, 72.

86. *Beyond Humanism*, 233; *Reality as Social Process*, 19; *Creative Synthesis*, 76; "Why Psychicalism?," 67; George Wolf, "The Place of the Brain in an Ocean of Feeling," in *Existence and Actuality*, ed. Cobb and Gamwell, 167-84, esp. 167.

87. *Beyond Humanism*, 229; *Man's Vision of God*, 79, 86; *Reality as Social Process*, 44; *Beyond Humanism*, 135.

88. *Beyond Humanism*, 321. On Hartshorne as a "radical empiricist," see note 40, above.

89. Ibid., 231, 229.

90. *Logic of Perfection*, 150, 208; *Creative Synthesis*, 215, 278.

91. It seems to me that Hartshorne's decision to refer to his method as "*a priori*" and "nonempirical" was unfortunate. No matter how many times he or his commentators may explain that these terms do not mean "prior to all experience" and/or "deductive," these connotations seem to be inevitably suggested. For example, most of Eric von der Luft's review of Donald Wayne Viney's *Charles Hartshorne and the Existence of God* (Albany: State University of New York, 1985) (*Process Studies* 15/3 [Fall, 1986], 207-212) is devoted to demonstrating that Hartshorne's arguments for God's existence are inductive arguments, from which it is concluded that they are not, in spite of claims of Viney and Hartshorne to the contrary, really *a priori* or nonempirical arguments. Neither Viney's discussion of what Hartshorne means by nonempirical, nor Hartshorne's statement in the foreword of his "preference for not giving the arguments a deductive form," could forestall the assumption that *a priori* and nonempirical *mean* deductive.

92. *Man's Vision of God*, 29, 63; *Beyond Humanism*, 263.

93. *Creative Synthesis*, 31, 93, 284-85.

94. *Logic of Perfection*, viii. In stressing that Hartshorne is a "deep empiricist," I am not denying that he is a rationalist. I am only pointing out that his rationalism is based on this deep empiricism, which seeks to bring to consciousness and to formulate all the elements comprising the bottom layer of experience which are always presupposed in practice. Hartshorne in fact describes his rationalism as one that has learned from empiricism (ibid., viii). Whitehead's view of rationalism, according to which it is the "search for the coherence of the presuppositions of civilized living," is endorsed by Hartshorne (ibid., viii; *Creative Synthesis*, xvi). Hartshorne makes the same point by characterizing philosophy at its best as "an agonizing struggle for balanced definiteness" (ibid., 93). Animals are said to have the deep truths in a balanced way, but vaguely, whereas any bright person will become definite about such truths, but in a one-sided way. The reason to have a philosophic profession is to struggle for "the sharp vision of the whole truth" (ibid.).

95. *Man's Vision of God*, 80.

96. *Creative Synthesis*, 31.

97. Richard Rorty, *Consequences of Pragmatism*, xxix, xxx, xlii.

98. *Beyond Humanism*, 274. Hartshorne distinguishes between our intuitions as such and the verbalization of them, stressing that the latter is an art and a very fallible one (*Creative Synthesis*, xvi, 31-32).

99. *Beyond Humanism*, 274; *Man's Vision of God*, 152.

100. *Man's Vision of God*, 79.

101. *Beyond Humanism*, 137; see also 157, and *Creative Synthesis*, 204.

102. *Creative Synthesis*, 93.

103. Ibid., xvi, 291.

104. *Man's Vision of God*, 79; see also *Beyond Humanism*, 86-87.

105. *Man's Vision of God*, 80.

106. *Beyond Humanism*, 37.

107. *Man's Vision of God*, 79.

108. *Beyond Humanism*, 164.

109. *Logic of Perfection*, 152; *Creative Synthesis*, 286-88.

110. *Logic of Perfection*, 152; *Omnipotence*, 33-34; *Creative Synthesis*, 287.

111. *Man's Vision of God*, 59; *Beyond Humanism*, 89, 103, 261; *Logic of Perfection*, 292; *Creative Synthesis*, 286-88.

112. *Beyond Humanism*, 13-16; *Omnipotence*, 15; *Logic of Perfection*, 286.

113. Ibid., 257.

114. Ibid., 153.

115. Ibid.

116. *Beyond Humanism*, 37, 86-87; *Man's Vision of God*, 80.

117. *Logic of Perfection*, 12; *Omnipotence*, 19, 25.

118. Hartshorne says that "each of the arguments points not simply to the theistic conclusion, but to the neoclassical form of the conclusion" (*Logic of Perfection*, 296).

119. *Man's Vision of God*, 80-81.

120. *Beyond Humanism*, 72.

121. *Logic of Perfection*, 12, 189.

122. Rorty, "Postmodernist Bourgeois Liberalism," 588-89.

123. *Logic of Perfection*, 18, 16.

124. Ibid., 16-18; *Creative Synthesis*, 191.

125. *Creative Synthesis*, 198.

126. *Logic of Perfection*, 11-14.

127. *Beyond Humanism*, 316; *Man's Vision of God*, 116, 229.

128. *Beyond Humanism*, 208-09.

129. Ibid., 256.

130. *Logic of Perfection*, 132.

131. Ibid., 257-58.

NOTES ON CONTRIBUTORS
AND CENTERS

JOHN B. COBB, JR., is author of *A Christian Natural Theology: Based on the Thought of Alfred North Whitehead*, *Process Theology as Political Theology* and *Beyond Dialogue: Toward a Mutual Transformation of Buddhism and Christianity*, and co-author of *The Liberation of Life: From the Cell to the Community* and *For the Common Good: Redirecting the Economy Toward Community, the Environment, and a Sustainable Future*. He is professor of theology at the School of Theology at Claremont, emeritus, professor of religion at Claremont Graduate School, and founding director of the Center for Process Studies, 1325 North College, Claremont, CA 91711.

MARCUS P. FORD is author of *William James's Philosophy: A New Perspective*, and editor of *A Process Theory of Medicine: Interdisciplinary Essays*. After serving as departmental chair at Eureka College, he has been taking time off from full-time teaching to work toward the founding of a postmodern college. He does some teaching in humanities and religious studies at Northern Arizona University, P.O.B. 6031, Flagstaff, AZ 86011.

DAVID RAY GRIFFIN, editor of the SUNY Series in Constructive Postmodern Thought, is author of *God, Power, and Evil* and *Evil Revisited*, co-author of *Process Theology* and *Primordial Truth and Postmodern Theology*, editor of *Physics and the Ultimate Significance of Time*, *The Reenchantment of Science: Postmodern Proposals*, and co-editor of the Corrected Edition of Whitehead's *Process and Reality*. He is professor of philosophy of religion at the School of Theology at Claremont and Claremont Graduate School, and executive director of the Center for Process Studies, 1325 North College, Claremont, CA 91711.

PETE A. Y. GUNTER is the author of *Henri Bergson: A Bibliography*, the editor of *Bergson and the Evolution of Physics*, and co-editor of *Process Philoso-*

phy: Basic Writings and *Bergson and Modern Thought: Towards a Unified Science*. He is professor of philosophy at the University of North Texas, Denton, Texas 76203.

PETER OCHS, who is currently completing a book on "The Pragmatics of Charles Peirce's Pragmatism," is editor of *Understanding the Rabbinic Mind: Essays on the Hermeneutic of Max Kadushin* and *The Return to Scripture in Judaism and Christianity: Essays in Postcritical Scriptural Interpretation*. He is Wallerstein Associate Professor of Jewish Studies at Drew University, Madison, New Jersey 07940.

This series is published under the auspices of the Center for a Postmodern World and the Center for Process Studies.

The Center for a Postmodern World is an independent nonprofit organization in Santa Barbara, California, founded by David Ray Griffin. It promotes the awareness and exploration of the postmodern worldview and encourages reflection about a postmodern world, from postmodern art, spirituality, and education to a postmodern world order, with all this implies for economics, ecology, and security. One of its major projects is to produce a collaborative study that marshals the numerous facts supportive of a postmodern worldview and provides a portrayal of a postmodern world order toward which we can realistically move. It is located at 6891 Del Playa, Isla Vista, California 93117.

The Center for Process Studies is a research organization affiliated with the School of Theology at Claremont and Claremont University Center and Graduate School. It was founded by John B. Cobb, Jr., Director, and David Ray Griffin, Executive Director; Mary Elizabeth Moore and Marjorie Suchocki are also Co-Directors. It encourages research and reflection upon the process philosophy of Alfred North Whitehead, Charles Hartshorne, and related thinkers, and upon the application and testing of this viewpoint in all areas of thought and practice. This center sponsors conferences, welcomes visiting scholars to use its library, and publishes a scholarly journal, *Process Studies*, and a quarterly *Newsletter*. It is located at 1325 North College, Claremont, California 91711.

Both centers gratefully accept (tax-deductible) contributions to support their work.

INDEX

DATE DUE

FEB 25 '01		
5/40/01		

Brodart Co.   Cat. # 55 137 001